CONSTANTINE

A GREAT CHRISTIAN MONARCH AND APOSTLE

CONSTANTINE

A GREAT CHRISTIAN MONARCH AND APOSTLE

by

PAUL KERESZTES

PROFESSOR OF CLASSICS AND HISTORY

J.C. GIEBEN, PUBLISHER

AMSTERDAM, 1981

CONTENTS

A FOREWORD

Ever since his death on May 22, Pentecost Sunday, 337 A.D., his memory has been maligned by ancient and modern writers. For turning to Christianity and bringing about the end of pagan Rome, he was branded by some of his bitter critics as a traitor. For joining and championing the Christian Church, he was accused by some modern writers of using the altars of the Church as a convenient footstool to the throne of the Roman Empire. Even when the sincerity of his conversion to Christianity is, though grudgingly, admitted, he is often described as one sunk in an abyss of superstition — since without an appreciation of simple and genuine faith, sincere religion often appears in the eyes of the beholder, even though he may be a student of history, as some dark superstition. As a result of this treatment by pagans and Christians, professed atheists, agnostics and believers, there emerges a series of pictures so utterly contradictory that most of them cannot, of course, be accepted as true representations of Constantine.

Most fortunately, however, we possess a very large number of documents relating to Constantine that illustrate his personal beliefs as well as his Imperial administration relating to the Christian Church. These documents include Imperial constitutions, edicts, letters by Church Councils and individual Churchmen, high and low Imperial officials, and, most importantly, by the Emperor Constantine himself.

Most of these documents are preserved in the works of contemporary and later writers, namely, in Lactantius' *On the Deaths of the Persecutors*; Eusebius' *Ecclesiastical History* and *Life of Constantine*; the great Athanasius' *Defence against the Arians* and other works; Saint Augustine's letters and tracts; the Bishop Optatus' rich collection of documents and historical notes; and the histories of Socrates, Sozomen, Theodoretus, and Gelasius. To these are to be added the collection of Imperial enactments, some important speeches of praise addressed to the Emperor, and, finally, some inscriptions and Imperial coins with messages from the Emperor. Zosimus, the violently anti-Constantinian historian, and some of his ancient confrères should not be forgotten either.

The purpose of this book is to study Constantine's relationship to Christianity, on the basis of these documents and reports and with a view to some modern expressions of opinion. Most of the relevant documents are presented here, in a translation, based on the originals, occasionally difficult due to problems of text and the often awkward style of the Emperor. A study of these documents and reports will show, not that Constantine was a perfect Christian in his life, and always well-informed in matters of doctrine, but that he was a sincere Christian, a truly great Christian Emperor and a genuine Apostle of the Christian Church.

On the 28th of October, 1977.   Paul Keresztes
University of Waterloo
Waterloo, Ontario, Canada

CONSTANTINE ARRIVES AT ROME: A MIRACLE?

Constantine appeared before the gates of Rome, but not as one making war against a persecutor of the Christian Church. The war between Constantine and Maxentius was not, it seems, a war of religion in the usual sense of the words.[1] Maxentius was, however, accused of taking away age-old privileges from the Romans and the praetorians,[2] and, thus, became unpopular. There is no reason to doubt the truth of the reports[3] that Maxentius was dissolute, adulterous, and cruel to the people; that he killed numerous senators; and that he resorted to abominable acts of magic and traditional superstition. But it was also admitted by ancient authors[4] that Maxentius ordered an end to the persecutions and granted the Christians freedom of worship in his territories.

On the other hand, as far as the Emperor Galerius and the other co-rulers of the Roman Empire (one of them Constantine) were concerned, Maxentius was a usurper of Imperial power, and ruled and held on to his territories in Italy, Africa, and Spain 'illegally'.[5] Simply put,[6] he was a "tyrant." Although it was said[7] that Constantine had liberated the Romans from the yoke of the tyrant, we do not know the immediate cause of the war between Constantine and Maxentius.

1. A. Piganiol, *L'Empereur Constantin* (Paris, 1932) 65; H. v. Schoene-beck, *Beiträge zur Religionspolitik des Maxentius und Constantin* (Leipzig, 1939) 6; J. Vogt, "Die Bedeutung des Jahres 312 f. die Religionspolitik Konstantins des Grossen," *Zsch. f. Kirchengesch.* 61 (1942) 171 ff.; J. Moreau, "Sur la vision de Constantin (312)," *Rev. des Etudes Anc.* 55 (1953) 307; H. Kraft, *Kaiser Konstantins religiöse Entwicklung* (Tübingen, 1955) 17; H. Dörries, *Constantine the Great* (New York, 1972) 29.
2. Lactantius, *De mort. pers.* 26.
3. Eusebius, *H.E.* VIII, xiv, 2-5; VIII, xiv, 17-18; etc.
4. *Ibid.* VIII, xiv, 1; Optatus, I, 18; *et al.*
5. Lactantius, *De mort. pers.* 26; *et al.*
6. Eusebius, *H.E.* VIII; xiv, 1; *etc.*
7. *Ibid.* IX, ix, 1; IX, ix, 11; *C.I.L.* vi, 1139; *etc.*

Constantine's campaign against Maxentius, and particularly, the final battle at the Milvian Bridge, was reported by many ancient authors,[8] but they are also reported and discussed by modern writers dealing with Roman History, and especially those writing on Constantine.[9] Whatever his motivation may have been, Constantine struck before Maxentius could or would have acted against him. Crossing the Alps by the Mont Cenis, and overcoming the stiff resistance of Maxentius' forces at Turin, Milan, Verona and other places with great victories, Constantine had the road to Rome open before him. The final battle[10] took place in the vicinity of the Milvian Bridge, on October 28, 312 A.D.[11]

Of all the ancient reports on Constantine's campaign against Maxentius, or at least on the final battle, there are three that stand out for the very special information they offer for an explanation of this most important event in the life of Constantine and the history of the Roman Empire and Europe. The first report, found in Eusebius' *Historia Ecclesiastica*,[12] is written in the Church historian's normal style and terminology, and offers for Constantine's victory nothing more and nothing less than the historian's usual Providential explanation: God helped Constantine against Maxentius in the same way He had helped the Israelites against the Pharaoh, and, at the same time, it was He who destroyed Maxentius just as completely as he had destroyed the Pharaoh:

8. *Paneg. Lat.* XII (IX), 16-19 in *Panegyrici Latini* ed. R.A.B. Mynors (Oxford U.P., 1964); Eusebius, *H.E.* IX, ix, 1-11; *Vita Const.* I, 26-40; Lactantius, *De mort. pers.* 44; Aur. Vict., *Caes.* 40, 23; *Epit. de Caes.* 40, 7; Libanius, *Or.* LIX, 20; Zosimus, II, 16; Jerome, *Chron. ad loc.*; Socrates, *H.E.* I, 2, 7; Orosius, VIII, 28, 16; Zonaras, XIII, 1.

9. E.g. A.H.M. Jones, *Constantine and the Conversion of Europe* (London, 1965) 74-78; Kraft, *op. cit.* 17-19; and many others.

10. Some ancient (e.g. Aur. Vict., *Caes.* 40, 23) and modern authors (e.g. H.M.Gwatkin,"Constantine and His City," *Cambridge Med. Hist.* (Cambridge U.P.) 1957, vol. i, 4) refer to it as having taken place at *Saxa Rubra*, incorrectly, as is demonstrated by J. Moreau, "Pont Milvius ou Saxa Rubra," *N. Clio* 4 (1952) 369-373.

11. Arguments of P. Bruun, "The Battle of the Milvian Bridge - The Date Reconsidered," *Hermes* 88 (1960) 361-370, are effectively refuted by Maria R. Alföldi, *Die constantinische Goldprägung* (Mainz, 1963) 32 and *idem* and Dietmar Kienast, "Zu P. Bruuns Datierung der Schlacht an der Milvischen Brücke," *Jb. f. Numismatik und Geldgeschichte* 11 (1961) 33-44.

12. IX, ix, 2-11.

Constantine, the senior Emperor both in dignity and rank and the first to take pity on those subjected to tyranny at Rome, calling in his prayers on the heavenly God and His Word, the Saviour of all, Jesus Christ Himself, as his ally, set out with all the army to secure for the Romans their ancient freedom. Maxentius, on the other hand, putting his trust in the arts of magic rather than in the goodwill of his subjects, did not dare even to go beyond the city gates, and with the help of an immensely large number of heavy-armed soldiers and many thousands of legionaries he enslaved every place and every region and every single city around Rome and in all Italy.

The emperor, sure in his alliance with God, battled with the tyrant's first, second and third armies and, gaining great victories over all of them, he advanced over a very large part of Italy, and was already very close to Rome itself. Then, in order that he might not be forced, on account of the tyrant, to fight against Romans, God Himself as if with some chains dragged the tyrant very far from the gates. And the stories of old concerning the punishment of the wicked, not believed by most as if they were fables from mythology, but believed by the believers because they are recorded in the Holy Books, are believed, when they actually happen before them, by all; in a word, by believers and non-believers, since they have seen the incredible happenings with their own eyes. Even as in the days of Moses himself and the once God-fearing race of the Hebrews He hurled into the sea Pharaoh's chariots and his host, his chosen horsemen and captains, and they were swallowed up in the Red Sea, and the sea covered them; in the same way Maxentius as well as the heavy-armed soldiers and the spearmen around him plunged into the deep like a stone when he turned his back before the power of God that was with Constantine and was crossing the river in his path, which he himself had properly bridged by joining boats, and thus constructed against himself an instrument of destruction. One might say about him: "He dug a pit, and made it deep, and will fall into the hole which he made. His work will return upon his own head, and his wickedness will descend upon the top of his head."

It was in a similar fashion that, when the bridge over the river broke up, the passage across collapsed, the boats with the men all at once went down into the deep. First, he himself, the most wicked of all men, but then also the shield-bearers around him, as the divine oracles foretold it, plunged into the violent water. So that fittingly, if not in words, at least in their actions, just like the followers of Moses, the great servant [of God], those who, by the grace of God, gained victory chanted and repeated the hymn directed against the wicked tyrant of old probably like this: "Let us sing to the Lord, for He is greatly glorified. He has hurled horse and rider into the sea. The Lord is my help and protector, he has become my salvation," and "Who is like you, Lord, among the gods, who is, like you, glorified among the Saints, marvellous in glorious deeds, performing wonders."

11

Singing, by his actions, these and other, similar and analogous, words to God the Supreme Ruler and Author of his victory, Constantine entered Rome with hymns of triumph, and all, as one body, accompanied by their children and wives, the members of the Senate and persons otherwise distinguished, together with all the people of Rome, received him, with joyous eyes and their very hearts, as a redeemer, saviour and benefactor, amidst songs of praise and insatiable joy.

But he, as one possessing a reverence towards God that was implanted in him, was not the least stirred by the shouts nor elated by the praises, for he was fully aware of the help that came from God. Therefore, he immediately ordered that the triumphal sign of the Saviour's passion be set up in the hand of his own statue. And when they were setting him up, in the most frequented place in Rome, holding in his right hand the sign of the Saviour, he ordered them to engrave this inscription with the following words in the language of the Romans: "By this sign of salvation, the true proof of courage, I saved and liberated your city from the yoke of the tyrant. Moreover, I freed and restored to their ancient distinction and splendour both the senate and the people of the Romans."

The second report, chronologically the last of the three, is found in Eusebius' *Vita Constantini.*[13] Basically it retains the story of the *H.E.*, but adds some more details to the earlier Providential explanation in that it relates how God miraculously manifested Himself from the very outset of campaign in the North, through extraordinary appearances on the sky and in Constantine's mind:

... Learning that the capital of the whole world, the royal city of the Roman Empire, was oppressed with tyranny and slavery, at first he left the task of its liberation to the rulers of the other divisions since they had seniority over him. But when not one of these was able to help, and, on the other hand, those who wished to hazard an attempt suffered a disgraceful outcome, he [Constantine] said that life for him was not worth living as long as he saw the royal city thus distressed, and he made preparations for the removal of the tyranny.

Being convinced, however, that, on account of the evil and magical enchant-ments zealously practiced by the tyrant, he needed aid more powerful than his army could give, he called on God for help, since he deemed the importance of the hoplites and masses of soldiers only secondary, but believed the help coming from God as invincible and unshakable. He considered, therefore, what God he should enlist in his help. But while he was searching,

13. I, 26-40.

the thought occurred to him that, of the many emperors before him, those who had put their hopes in a multitude of gods, and served them with libations, sacrifices and offerings, were in the first place deceived by pleasing oracles and divinations which promised them happiness, and met with an unhappy end, and not one of the gods stood by their right side to prevent them from being subjected to heaven-sent catastrophies. Only one, his own father, who followed an entirely opposite course and condemned their error, honoured the Supreme God of the universe all his life and was found to be the saviour and protector of his empire and the giver of everything good. He reflected on this, and considered the fact that they who had put their trust in the multitude of gods also fell victims to many forms of destruction, without leaving behind family, or offspring, or stock, or name, or even their memory among men. He also considered the fact that the God of his father had given many visible proofs of His power to his own father. He considered that those who had earlier marched against the tyrant and fought under the protection of a multitude of gods, met a disgraceful end. For one of them shamefully retreated without engaging in battle, and the other, slain in the midst of his troops, became an easy victim to death. Considering, then, all this in his mind, he judged it to be an act of folly to participate in the idle worship of those who were not gods, and to follow the wrong path even after receiving such great evidence. Therefore, he thought he had to honour his father's God alone.

Accordingly, he called on him in his prayers, begging and asking that he reveal to him who he was, and that he stretch out his right hand to help him in his current tasks. And while the Emperor was thus praying and supplicating with a fervent heart, a most wonderful sign appeared to him from heaven, and, had the story of this been related by any other person it would not be easy to accept. But since the victorious Emperor himself, long afterwards, reported and pledged the trustworthiness of the story to me at the time when I was writing this history and when I was deemed worthy of his acquaintance and company, who would hesitate to believe the report? Particularly because later events gave the story the proof of authenticity. He said that, at about the noon-tide sun, when the day was already on its downward slope, he saw with his own eyes the trophy of the cross, consisting of light, in the heavens and placed above the sun, and that next to it there was a writing which said: "By this, conquer"; moreover, he said that he was struck with amazement at the sight of the wonder, and so was the whole army, which was following him on the march and witnessed the marvel. Moreover, he said that he was being puzzled as to the meaning of the vision. And while he was pondering and thinking about it very much, night arrived and he fell asleep. Then in his sleep the Christ of God appeared to him with the sign that had appeared on the sky, and commanded him to make a likeness of the sign that had appeared on the sky and to use it as a protection in all encounters with his enemies.

At daybreak he woke up, and related the mysterious matter to his friends. And then, calling together all craftsmen in gold and precious stones, he sat down among them, and described to them the appearance of the sign, and ordered them to make a likeness of it in gold and precious stones. Once, the Emperor himself, by the favour of God, allowed me to see this.

Now, it was made in the following way. A long spear, covered with gold was made to have the form of a cross by a bar that transversed it. On the top of the whole there was a wreath put together of precious stones and gold, and within this the symbol of the Saviour's name, two letters indicating the name of Christ, the letter P having a X placed over it at its very center. The Emperor used to wear these letters on his helmet even though in later times. From the cross-bar of the spear there was a cloth hanging, a royal texture, covered with embroidery of brilliantly flashing precious stones and interlaced also with much gold, presenting the viewers an indescribable piece of beauty. This cloth fastened to the crossbar was of a square shape. The upright shaft, lifted up from the ground, had a lower section of great length, and bore a golden half-portrait of the pious emperor and of his children as well beneath the trophy of the cross and up to the very edge of the embroidered cloth. The Emperor made constant use of this sign of salvation as a protection against all adverse and hostile power, and ordered that copies of it be carried at the head of all his armies.

But these things belong to a slightly later time. At the above specified time, being amazed at the marvellous vision, and thinking it fit to worship no other god than Him who appeared to him, he summoned those who were initiated in His teachings, and enquired who that God was, and what was the meaning of the vision of the sign that appeared to him.

They said that He was God, the only-begotten Son of the one and only God; that the sign which appeared was the symbol of immortality; that it was the trophy of that victory over death which He had won when He came down to earth. They taught him the causes of His advent, and gave him a true account of His stay amongst men. He was instructed with these talks, and he was wondering about the Divine manifestation which had been presented before his own eyes, and, comparing the heavenly vision with the interpretation of his story, he was confirmed in his opinion, and was convinced, that the knowledge of these things came to him from God. Therefore, he decided to devote himself to the inspired writings of God. Furthermore, he made the priests of God his associates, and believed that he ought to honour the God who appeared to him with all devotion. Then, strengthened by great hopes concerning Him, he rushed to extinguish, from now on, the threatening fire of tyranny.

Having grabbed the Imperial city, he [Maxentius] was most daring in his acts of impiety and wickedness, so that he would not overlook any venture for

14

vile and impure actions. He would, for example, separate lawful wives from their husbands, and insulting them most shamefully he would send them back to their husbands. He practiced this drunken behaviour not toward common and obscure men, but to those who held the first places in the Roman Senate. Although he shamefully dishonoured a great number of free women, nevertheless he was unable to satisfy his intemperate and undisciplined spirit. But when he made attempts against Christian women, he was no longer able to contrive an easy way to adultery. For they would rather lose their lives than submit their bodies to him for corruption. There was a certain woman, wife of one of the senators who held the power of prefect, when she learnt that those who ministered to the tyrant in such matters stopped at her house. She was a Christian. She knew that her husband through fear ordered them to take her and lead her away. She asked for a short time that she might bedeck her body with the usual ornaments, and she entered her chamber. Being left alone, she put a sword into her breast. Dying immediately, she left her dead body to the procurers, but with her acts that spoke louder than any spoken word, she declared to all men, to both the present and future generations, that the chastity for which the Christians are famed is the only thing which is unconquerable and indestructible. This woman was seen to be such.

But all men, both the common and the leading people, famous and obscure alike, trembled through fear of the man who dared to commit such things, and were oppressed by his fearful tyranny. And even though they kept quiet and suffered the bitter slavery, there was still no deliverance from the bloody cruelty of the tyrant. Once, for example, on some trifling pretence, he let the people be slaughtered by his own body-guard, and countless multitudes of the Roman people were slain in the very middle of the city by the spears and weapons, not of the Scythians and barbarians, but of their own fellow-citizens. It is, besides, impossible to count how many senators were murdered with a view to the seizure of their own estates, for at different times multitudes were put to death on various fabricated charges.

The greatest of the tyrant's crimes was that he had recourse to sorcery, when, for purposes of magic, he, at times, ripped up women with child, but at other times he searched into the inward parts of new-born babies, and slew lions and was engaged in some abominable practices for evoking demons and averting the war. For he hoped that by these means he would gain victory. Thus it is impossible to list his acts by which during his tyranny at Rome he enslaved his subjects, so that by this time they were suffering from the scarcity and want of the necessary provisions. Our contemporaries do not remember that such scarcity ever before existed in Rome.

Constantine, however, moved to compassion by all this, got ready with all his preparations against the tyranny. Choosing, therefore, the supreme God as his protector, and calling on Christ as his helper, and setting His victorious trophy, the sign of salvation, in front of his soldiers and bodyguards, he led all his army in order to obtain for the Romans the freedom they had inherited from their ancestors. While Maxentius put his trust more in magical devices than in the good-will of his subjects, and he did not dare to go outside the gates of the city, but guarded every place and district and city which was subjected to him with countless multitudes of hoplites and a great number of bands of soldiers, the Emperor firmly relying on the help of God, went against the first, and the second, and the third lines of battle of the tyrant, overpowered them with great ease at the very first assault, and made his way into a very large part of Italy.

He was already very close to Rome. Then, that he might not have to make war against the Romans on account of the tyrant, God himself drew the tyrant, as if by fetters, a long way outside the gates. And the wonderful things recorded in the Holy Scriptures which were worked against the ungodly, not believed as mythological stories by most people, yet believed by the faithful, were made worthy of belief to all alike, believers and non-believers, when the very things happened before their own eyes. For just as in the time of Moses himself and the God-fearing race of the Hebrews, He cast the Pharaoh's chariots and his host into the sea, and He drowned his chosen horsemen in the Red Sea, in the same way Maxentius and his hoplites and bodyguards around him went down into the depths just like stone, when, turning to flight before the divinely helped army of Constantine, he was crossing the river which was in his path. Over this he had easily erected a bridge of boats and thus put together a tool for his own destruction, although he had hoped to capture by it him who was dear to God. For God stood by the right of this, while the other was putting together secret devices for his own destruction. About this, one might say, e.g.: "He dug a pit, he dug it up, and he will fall into the ditch which he made. His work will return to his own head, and his wickedness shall descend upon the top of his own head." Thus, in this case, by will of God, after the secret mechanism on the bridge fell apart before the appointed time, the bridge went down, and the boats crowded with men sank to the bottom. And first that wretched man himself, but then his attendants and body-guards, even as the Divine Scriptures had before said, sank just as lead into the mighty water. So that those who gained victory from God might, if not in their words then in their actions, sing and speak the same words as the people of His great servant Moses did against the impious tyrant of old: "Let us sing to the Lord, for He has been glorified exceedingly. The horse and his rider He has thrown into the sea. He has become my helper and my shelter unto salvation." And: "Who is like You, O Lord, among the gods? Who is like you, glorious in holiness, marvellous in praises, doing wonders?"

Having sung these and similar words to the Almighty and the Author of his victory, following the example of His great servant Moses, Constantine entered the Imperial city in triumph. In great crowds, the members of the

16

Senate, those otherwise famous and distinguished at this place, freed as it were from prisons, with all the Roman people, with eyes expressive of their feelings, they all received him with praises and overflowing joy. Men, women, children and countless masses of slaves greeted him, all together, as deliverer, saviour and benefactor, with unrestrained shouts. But he, having in his heart piety toward God, did not become arrogant on account of the shouts nor elated as a result of the praises, but being aware of the help he received from God, he immediately offered a prayer of thanksgiving to Him as the Author of his victory.

With loud proclamation and inscriptions he proclaimed the sign of salvation and erected a great trophy of victory over his enemies in the middle of the Imperial city, and had it engraved in indelible characters saying explicitly that this sign of salvation was the safeguard of Roman rule and the whole Empire. Therefore, he immediately ordered that they place a lofty spear in the form of a cross into the hand of a statue representing his own figure, in the most frequented place of Rome. He ordered that the following inscription be engraved on it in his words in the language of the Romans: "By this sign of salvation, the true proof of courage, I have saved and freed your city from the yoke of tyranny. By making them free, I have restored the Senate and the people of the Romans to their ancient distinction and splendour."

The third story, found in Lactantius' *De mortibus persecutorum*,[14] is deceptively similar to and usually identified with Eusebius' version in the *Vita Constantini*, and yet has most probably to do with another appearance of Christ to Constantine in the Emperor's sleep:

The civil was was already set in motion between them. Although Maxentius confined himself to Rome, because he had heard that an oracle said that he would perish if he left the gates of the city, the war was being nevertheless carried on by capable generals. Maxentius had greater forces at his disposal, because he had recovered his father's army from Severus and had recently withdrawn his own from the land of the Moors and Gaetulians.

The contest was begun, and the soldiers of Maxentius were prevailing until after Constantine, with renewed courage and readiness to conquer or die, moved all his forces closer to the city and settled in the region of the Milvian Bridge. The anniversary day of Maxentius' accession to Imperial power, *i.e.*, October 28, was approaching, and the celebrations for his fifth year of Imperial command were coming to an end. Constantine was warned during his sleep that he should mark the shields with the heavenly sign of God, and that, after doing this, he should engage in battle. He did as commanded, and

14. 44.

had "Christ" inscribed on the shields by crossing the [Greek] letter X [CH] with the letter I bent around at the top [Greek P = R]. Armed with this sign, the army went to battle. The enemy advanced without its commander, and crossed the bridge. The armies, drawn up in equal front-lines, clashed, and the battle was fought with the greatest violence on both sides: "Flight was unknown to either the one or the other side."

There was dissenssion in the city and the emperor was rebuked for abandoning the safety of the public. Whenever he was seen — for he was giving the public circus shows in honour of his anniversary — the people with one voice would suddenly cry out that Constantine could not be conquered. Perplexed by these cries, he hurried away and, calling together some senators, ordered that the Sibylline books be consulted. In them it was discovered that on that day an enemy of the Romans would perish. Seduced by this oracle into hopes of victory, he went out and engaged in battle. The bridge was destroyed behind him. When they saw this, the fighting became bloodier, and the hand of God appeared over the battlefield. The army of Maxentius was driven away by terror, and he himself, put to flight, hurried to the bridge which had been destroyed. Pushed along by the multitude of those in flight, he was plunged into the Tiber.

When this most bitter was was finally over, Constantine was received as emperor with great joy by the Senate and the people of Rome, and then, from the letters he seized and the statues and busts he discovered, he learned of the perfidy of Maximinus. The Senate, on account of his merits, decreed to Constantine the title of Senior Augustus, which Maximinus was claiming for himself. When the victory for the liberation of the city was reported to him, he viewed the matter as if he himself had been conquered. Then, when he learned of the decree of the Senate, his resentment so inflamed him that he publicly declared his hostility and uttered vicious and sarcastic statements against the Supreme Emperor.

The message of these three stories has become for 'modern' man a matter of serious controversy, a bone of contention, a rallying point for expressing ideological principles, and even, on occasions, for propaganda unworthy of students of history.

The point of this very serious controversy is not what are obviously historical facts in Constantine's campaign against Maxentius, such as the occasionally hotly debated dates or locales of certain battles, but something that may be regarded as touching on the supernatural, the "miraculous." What 'modern' man cannot accept and a student of history may not be at all competent to treat are the reported visions of the Emperor on his campaign against Maxentius.

The first attack against the historicity of these reports came from a not unexpected corner. Edward Gibbon[15] makes characteristic approach to the stories of Eusebius and Lactantius. From one who regarded the Middle Ages as the "triumph of barbarism and religion," and the Byzantine Empire as a medley of superstition and crime,[16] Constantine, Lactantius, and Eusebius could certainly not receive fair historical treatment. Indeed, Gibbon brands the stories as "one of those pious frauds of Constantine," a "Christian fable of Eusebius" which maintained an "honourable place in the legend of superstition" only until "the bold and sagacious spirit of criticism presumed to depreciate the triumph, and to arraign the truth, of the first Christian Emperor." Only a protestant and philosophical reader would, according to Gibbon, be inclined to believe that Constantine told Eusebius a wilful falsehood, and that, by his oath, he committed a solemn and deliberate perjury! A rationalist and therefore a non-believer in the supernatural, Gibbon denied the possibility of the 'miracles' of Constantine *a priori*, and declared the stories reporting them as fables, legends, and fraudulent concoctions.

Gibbon's confrère, Jacob Burckhardt, a rationalist of the following century, makes[17] essentially the same conclusions and essentially for the same reasons. Other more modern writers[18] are likewise thoroughly mistrustful of the stories, or simply reject them as being unworthy of belief by rational beings, while some[19] simply refuse even the idea of any supernatural happening and explain the 'miracle' as a 'halo' phenomenon and a product of Constantine's anxious and agitated mind.

One of the most persistent, most zealous, and most recent attacks on the credibility of these stories of Eusebius and Lactantius, in our era, was conducted by Henri Grégoire, a true partisan

15. *The History of the Decline and Fall of the Roman Empire*, ed. J.B. Bury (1896) ch. 20.

16. *Ibid.*, see chapters on the Byzantine empire and the Middle Ages.

17. Jacob Burckhardt, *The Age of Constantine the Great*, transl. Moses Hadas (New York, 1949).

18. Th. Zahn, "Konstantin d. G. u. die Kirche," *Skizzen aus dem Leben der alten Kirche* (Erlangen-Leipzig, 1894); E. Schwartz, *Kaiser Konstantin und die christliche Kirche* (Berlin, 1936) 63; 66; etc.; H. von Schoenebeck, *op. cit.*

19. H.M. Gwatkin, *op. cit.* 4-5.

of his own ideology and a prolific writer, much admired by his faithful followers. It is difficult to decide whether Grégoire's complete rejection of the stories was the result of a genuine distrust of their sources, or of his absolute rejection of the supernatural and refusal to accept the genuine conversion of Constantine to Christianity. His views are most comprehensively presented in his article on the Emperor's conversion, but they recur again and again in several other works.[20] His reasons for rejecting Eusebius' story in the *Vita Constantini* appear to be that it did not find its way into Eusebius' *Church History*; that it did not seem to have been used by such writers of the 4th century as Saint Gregory Nazianzen, or Saint John Chrysostom; that the *Vita* was not catalogued by Saint Jerome; and that Saint Cyril of Jerusalem failed to mention the 'miracle' of the *Vita.*[21] To this series of incredible arguments *ex silentio* Grégoire adds[22] that he discards the story of the *Vita*[23] because it was admitted to be not exactly contemporary, and because it obviously does not speak of the same event as Lactantius' story.[24] But perhaps the story of *Vita* is about a different event. Furthermore, Grégoire[25] regards Lactantius' story as a legend, but believes that it had its origins in Constantine's alleged vision of Apollo in 310 A.D.[26] It is strange that Grégoire is willing to admit the authenticity of a 'pagan vision', though not that of a Christian one. It should be quite apparent that Grégoire is willing to go to almost any length, including clearly to non-consequential and false arguments, to discredit the reports of Christian mysticism if only to help deny Constantine's conversion to Christianity and, particularly, its sincerity.

For reasons quite similar to those of Grégoire, J. Zeiller[27] re-

---

20. H. Grégoire, "La 'conversion' de Constantin," *Rev. de l'Univ. de Bruxelles* 36 (1930-31) 231-272; *passim*; see also *id.* "La statue de Constantin et le signe de croix," *L'Antiquité Classique* 1 (1932); and other works.
21. I, 28-30.
22. See note 20, *above.*
23. I, 28-30.
24. Grégoire, "La 'conversion' de Constantin," *op. cit.* 255.
25. *Ibid.* 256-257.
26. *Paneg. Lat.* VI (VII).
27. "Quelques remarques sur la vision de Constantin," *Byzantion* 14 (1939) 329-339.

jects the story of the *Vita Constantini*, but is willing to accept that of Lactantius! A true disciple of Grégoire, J. Moreau[28] rejects the stories of both Eusebius and Lactantius. Applying 'form criticism', Moreau even refuses the story of Lactantius, stating that it was a reply, on behalf of the Christian Constantine, to both the pagan vision in the Gallic sanctuary and Licinius' alleged vision of an angel! W. Seston[29] agrees with Grégoire's complete rejection of the stories concerning Constantine's visions and dreams.

Gibbon's and Burckhardt's more modern and more refined colleague, R. MacMullen,[30] would, professedly, reject Burckhardt's "anachronistic" rationalism, and would not, as they did, call Eusebius' and Lactantius' stories of the supernatural plain lies, nor see behind these stories any secular motivation such as the alleged use of Constantine of the holy altars of the Church as footstools for the Imperial throne. He might regard Lactantius' story of Constantine's dream the night before battle at the Milvian Bridge as something authentic, but he definitely rejects the story of the Vision of the Cross in Eusebius' *Vita Constantini*, because, after all, Cyril of Jerusalem, Ambrose and others "knew nothing of it," and because the miracle passed "unnoticed among real men." MacMullen places the vision of Constantine in the *Vita* into the milieu of what he calls 4th century supernaturalism, and an era in which "magic spells, incantations were thought to influence human life, and the most mundane occurrences were commonly explained in providential terms." He clearly believes that Constantine's vision of the Cross and also of Christ is a regular feature of "pagan and Christian mythology" of the 3rd and 4th centuries, just as in the cases where any other superhuman beings reveal themselves to their worshippers at times of crises. For him Constantine's story in the *Vita* represents the darkness of irrationality, where "superstition blacked out the clearer lights of religion ... ."

28. "Sur la vision etc.," *op. cit.* 307-333.
29. "L'Opinion païenne et la conversion de Constantin," *Rev. Phil. Hist. Phil. Rélig.* 16 (1936) 250-264; *id.,* "La vision païenne de 310 et les origines du chrisme constantinien," *Ann. de l'Inst. de Philol. et d'Hist. Orient. de Univ. libr. de Bruxelles* 4 (1936) 373 ff.
30. R. MacMullen, "Constantin and the Miraculous," *Greek and Roman and Byzantine Studies* 9 (1968) 81 ff.; *id., Constantine* (London, 1970) 66-77.

A. Piganiol,[31] strangely, follows Grégoire in arguing that only the 'pagan vision' of 310 A.D. was authentic, and that the vision of 312 A.D. was nothing but a legend and a Christian adaptation of the 'pagan vision'.[32] He, like many of his colleagues, shows confusion about the reports of Lactantius and Eusebius' *Vita Constantini* in trying to maintain the belief that they are conflicting reports of the one and same story about Christ's vision to Constantine.

While sceptical and believing that the genuineness of the vision depends for us only on the credibility we place in Constantine's word, H. Kraft[33] takes the story of the *Vita Constantini* as probably true and containing nothing unnatural, though he likes the "legend" of Lactantius better since it is shorter. Although it is not quite clear what Kraft accepts or rejects of the stories of Eusebius and Lactantius, it is quite clear that he believes that they represented a developing legend.

These so-called legends about Constantine's visions on and off the sky in dreams had varying degrees of support. Some[34] argue against Grégoire and for the acceptance of Eusebius' report of the visions. Others[35] argue that divine interventions before his decisive battles against Maxentius were, as far as Constantine was concerned, completely natural, and that his sincerity is not to be doubted. The false arguments *ex silentio* of Grégoire and others are pointed out as such.[36] Truly, the fact that Saint Cyril, for one, does not mention the miraculous vision of Constantine is not proof that Cyril did not know of it. Besides, Cyril may have found it opportune not to mention Constantine's vision in that context. Writing more objectively than most writers, K. Aland[37] has no doubt that Con-

31. *Op. cit.* 48-75.
32. *Ibid.* esp. 72-73.
33. *Op. cit.* 20 ff., with a good discussion of the problem of historicity.
34. As e.g. B. Stephanides, "Die Visionen Konstantins d. G.," *Zschr. f. Kirchengesch.* 59 (1940) 463-464.
35. E.g. H. Dörries, *op. cit.* 35-39.
36. E.g. by A. Brasseur, "Les deux visions de Constantin," *Latomus* (1946) 35-36; N.H. Baynes, "Constantine", *Cambridge Anc. Hist.* (Cambridge U.P., 1956) vol. 12, 683; F. Winkelmann, "Konstantins Religionspolitik und ihre Motive etc.," *Acta Antiqua Acad. Scient. Hungariae* 9 (1961) 246; *et al.*
37. "Die religiöse Haltung Kaiser Konstantins," *Studia Patrist.* 1 (1957) 587-588.

stantine related the vision of the *Vita* to Eusebius, and that Constantine sincerely believed his vision in the sky. But Aland, too, is unable to make the essential distinction between the story of the *Vita Constantini* and that of Lactantius concerning the vision of Christ. Castigating those who, in the name of "enlightenment" rejected the miracle of the sky in the *Vita Constantini*, A. Alföldi[38] appears to be the strongest defender of the stories surrounding Constantine's campaign against Maxentius. Alföldi[39] recognizes that the story in the *Vita* had in it the kernel of history. In fact, he insists[40] that the divine announcement "on the sky — 'In this sign thou shalt conquer' — is an historical fact ...." These admissions – or rather concessions? – are made despite the fact that Alföldi agrees with Grégoire, that the *Vita Constantini* is "a highly-coloured romance, marred by rehandling and later interpolation," and despite the fact that, being unable, like many others, to make the necessary distinction, he, regretfully, finds the *Vita* story[41] quite inconsistent with the information of Lactantius.[42] He finds, of course, the Lactantius story[43] to be the correct, or the better version.[44] However, Alföldi not only believes the historicity of the vision of the heavenly Cross and inscription promising Constantine victory, but he also denies, against Grégoire and his followers, that it was in imitation of the so-called 'pagan vision' of Apollo. Furthermore, with J. Bidez,[45] he regards "the vision of Apollo" as a mere literary fiction.[46] Although he accepts the historicity of Constantine's vision, Alföldi regards[47] Licinius' reported vision of

38. *The Conversion of Constantine and Pagan Rome* (Oxford U.P., 1969) 1.

39. *Ibid.* 17; *id.*, "Hoc signo victor eris," *Pisciculi* (1939) 1 ff.; *id.*, "The Helmet of Constantine with the Christian Monogram," *J. of Roman Stud.* 22 (1932) 9; *id.*, "The Initials of Christ on the Helmet of Constantine," *Studies in Roman Economic and Social History* (Princeton, 1951) 303 ff.

40. *The Conversion etc., op. cit.* 18.

41. I, 28-30.

42. Alföldi, "The Helmet etc.," *op. cit.*, 9.

43. *De mort. pers.* 44, 5.

44. "Hoc signo etc." *op. cit.* 1 ff.; *The Conversion etc., op. cit.* 18; etc.

45. "A propos d'une biographie nouvelle de l'empereur Constantin," *L'Antiquité Classique* 1 (1932) 1-7.

46. Alföldi, *The Conversion etc., op. cit.* 18.

47. *Ibid.* 19.

Christ as unhistorical, despite Lactantius' apparent belief in it.[48] He also probably rightly regards Licinius' reported Christianity as pretence and hypocrisy. At the same time we find Alföldi castigating and looking with scorn at Constantine's and others' deep and simple faith in the supernatural.[49] While rejecting Licinius' vision and accepting Constantine's, Alföldi believed they were both sunk in darkest superstition. Is it because the one appeared to pin his hopes on the gods and the other on Christ? Or is it because the historicity of Constantine's visions are *suggested* by such historically respectable documents as coins and other precious archeological 'proofs', which were simple manifestations of a sincere faith?

Correctly stating that nothing is proved by the silence of contemporary and later writers on the supernatural events reported in Eusebius' *Vita Constantini* in connection with Constantine's campaign against Maxentius, N.H. Baynes[50] argues that these supernatural phenomena should not be lightly dismissed or explained away but that they must ultimately be explained. Explained? If it is, at all, possible. Historians may, of course, in all honesty and quite legitimately, conclude their investigations of these most extraordinary events, or, rather, of the sources in which they are reported, with a judgement of *"non liquet"*.[51] A.H.M. Jones,[52] admitting that "there is no reason to doubt the *bona fides* of Eusebius or Constantine," objectively concludes that the incidents described in Eusebius' *Vita Constantini* bear the stamp of truth. But Jones probably goes beyond the limits that are set for historical enquiry when he says that Constantine's vision in the sky was "a rare, but well attested, form of the 'halo phenomenon'." Even if "a cross of light with the sun in the centre has been on several occasions scientifically observed," Jones, as a historian, uses methods that are *ultra vires* in making this assertion and in trying apparently to explain away the implication that the phenomena were supernatural. The approach taken by Baynes[53] with regard to these highly controversial phenomena of the *Vita Constantini*

48. *De mort. pers.* 46.
49. "Hoc signo etc.," *op. cit.*; *The Conversion etc. op. cit.*, 16-24.
50. "Constantine," *op. cit.* 683-685.
51. *Ibid.* 684.
52. *Op. cit.* 96-97; 102.
53. "Constantine the Great and the Christian Church," *Proceedings of the British Acad.* 15 (1929) 347.

is worthy of a historian. Indeed, the historian cannot as Baynes says decide whether the "appearance of the cross of light was only a subjective experience or whether it was an objective reality." In either case, it is diverging even further from the generally accepted notion of the historian's function to determine whether it was something entirely supernatural, a miracle produced by God Himself. According to Baynes, in this field, the historian, as historian, is perforce silent. "He is unable to affirm miracle, but most certainly cannot deny it."

Constantine's vision of the Cross and Christ Himself appear to be similar to many other naturally inexplicable phenomena reportedly occurring on the sky, or in the atmosphere, or even, strictly speaking, in the minds of individuals which to the persons involved have objective reality. What can a historian — strictly as a student of history — do with Saint Paul's reported vision of Christ on the road to Damascus?[54] In this vision Saint Paul saw "a light from heaven, surpassing the brightness of the sun," and heard Christ talking to him. Closer to our times, there is the case of Saint Joan of Arc and her frequent visions of angels, particularly of Saint Michael, and of Saints, in particular of Saint Catharine, and the "voices" she so often heard.[55] Would anyone, even a 'modern scientist', be reckless enough to presume to explain away Saint Joan's experiences by saying that they were the result of "hallucinations"?[56] Or, to come even closer to our own era, what can anyone, but in particular the student of history, or a scientist, say about the well publicized sun miracle of Fatima, Portugal, which took place in the presence of many thousand witnesses, 'believers and unbelievers', fervent Catholics, agnostics, and professed atheists?[57]

54. *Acts* 9, 1-9; 22, 5-11; 26, 10-18.

55. *Procès de condamnation et de réhabilitation de Jeanne d'Arc* (5 vols.), ed. J. Quicherat (1841-49); *Procès de condamnation de Jeanne d'Arc* 2 vols., ed. P. Champion (1920-21); *et al.*

56. F.E. Kenyon, M.D., Clinical Lecturer, University of Oxford, "The Life and Health of Joan of Arc. An Exercise in Pathography," *The Practitioner* 207 (1971) 835-842.

57. W.T. Walsh, *Our Lady of Fàtama* (Numerous editions by The Macmillan Company, 1947-); C.C. Martindale, "A propos de 'Fatima et la critique'," *Nouvelle Revue Théologique* 74 (1952) 580-606; *et al.*; see also book on related phenomena: F. Sanchez-Ventura Y Pascal, *The Apparitions of Garabandal* (Detroit, 1967); J.A. Pelletier, *God Speaks at Garabandal* (Wor-

Just as in the case of the visions of St. Paul and Saint Joan of Arc, the sun miracle of Fatima, and many other reports of the supernatural, so in the cases of Constantine's reported visions in the sky and in his dreams, the historian is left with his sources, the eye-witnesses and the reporters, and he must consider the value of their testimony. We are left with the simple fact – and it is needless to deny this fact – that Eusebius reported and assured us that Constantine, the eye-witness, affirmed, with a solemn oath, the fact of these visions ... But, as asserted above, no student of history can declare that these reports of Eusebius were *not* true, or that these events were *not* miraculous, supernatural, happenings since they, of course, are beyond the competence of any historian. I, for one, would hesitate to hand over, as Baynes suggested, these reports to 'theologians' and 'philosophers', for the result would, unsurprisingly, be the same as it has been with the visions of Saint Paul and Saint Joan of Arc, and some other reports of the supernatural: either a most definite denial, or most religious affirmation, or any one of the shades of belief and disbelief in between, expressing the 'theology', or the 'philosophy' of the particular individual.

Very important, however, are certain facts and events that followed immediately and for many years after Constantine's reported visions. For after, and, as a matter of fact, even before, his final victory over Maxentius at the Milvian Bridge on October 28, 312 A.D., Constantine behaved as if something extraordinary, such as those visions, had indeed appeared to him; or at least as if he really believed that such marvels had indeed happened to him; or, finally, as if he had become a Christian, or at least were behaving like Saint Paul, the greatest supporter and, indeed, the pillar of the Christian Church, by putting an end to all persecutions and giving this newly found faith everything he had.

cester, Massachusetts, 1970); *Our Lady Comes to Garabandal* (Worcester, Massachusetts, 1971); *et al.*

CONSTANTINE IN ROME: A CONFESSION OF FAITH

After his reported visions, Constantine was behaving as if really obeying instructions received by him in these visions. The visions of the *Vita Constantini*[1] came quite clearly BEFORE his campaign against Maxentius but quite obviously at a time when he was still in the process of preparing for it – this in spite of the fact that many writers identify or, rather, confuse this vision in the *Vita Constantini* with that reported by Lactantius[2] as taking place at the very gates of Rome and on the eve of the final battle between Constantine and Maxentius. In his heavenly vision[3] Constantine saw the trophy of a cross of light right above the sun with the inscription: "Conquer by this". In the vision during the night that followed Constantine was instructed by Christ himself, appearing with the same sign which he had seen on the sky, to make a likeness of this very sign and to use it as a safeguard in all his engagements with his enemies. Constantine complied with these instructions the very next morning.

But did he produce, as a result, the sign of the cross *or* the Christ monogram of the first two letters of Christ's name as the very sign he had seen on the sky and in the subsequent vision of Christ? Opinions here diverge. P. Batiffol[4] and H. Grégoire[5] deny that Eusebius' description of the heavenly sign had the same form as the monogram of Lactantius.[6] One would expect that Constantine had the simple sign of the Cross made out as a likeness of

1. I, 28-31.
2. *De mort. pers.* 44.
3. *Vita Const.* I, 28.
4. P. Batiffol, *La paix constantinienne et le catholicisme* (Paris, 1914) 213 ff.; *id., Bull. de la Soc. Nat. des Ant. de France* (1913) 211 ff.
5. "L'étymologie de 'labarum,'" *Byzantion* 4 (1927-28) 477-482.
6. N.H. Baynes, "Constantine the Great and the Christian Church," *Proceedings of the British Acad.* 15 (1929) 398; also, 398-403, on this "heavenly sign."

his vision of the heavenly sign. But in addition to the reproduction of the sign of the Cross, made of a long spear and a cross bar, we find[7] that Christ's monogram composed of the Greek letters 'P' and 'X', enclosed inside a golden wreath, was placed on the top of the sign of the Cross.[8] This is the so-called *labarum*.[9]

Did the Christ monogram originally belong to the *labarum* and, indeed, to the vision of the heavenly sign as reported in the *Vita Constantini*?[10] A. Alföldi,[11] generally very unhappy with the Eusebian version and clearly confusing the two versions of Constantine's visions of Christ, categorically states that it was not the cross that appeared in *the vision* but the monogram of Christ consisting of the letters Chi & Rho. He recognizes Lactantius' version of *the vision* as the more (if not the only) authentic version.[12]

At any rate, Constantine also obeyed the instructions he had received during his Lactantian vision during the night preceding the Battle at the Milvian Bridge by marking 'the heavenly sign of God' on the shields of his soldiers.[13] While there can be hardly any doubt about the use of this Christ monogram clearly visible even on coins,[14] its meaning and significance, despite A. Alföldi, is disputed by doubters. The form and composition of this Christ monogram has had numerous variations of Chi and Rho in attempts aimed at interpreting this not so obvious sign. Scholars are quite puzzled.[15] They cannot decide whether this, the combination of

7. *Vita Constantini* I, 31.

8. The portraits of the Emperor and his sons were added to this simple and original structure, obviously, according to Eusebius himself, as a later development.

9. And is, fancifully, regarded by J.J. Haat, "La vision de Constantin au sanctuaire de Grand et l'origine celtique du labarum," *Latomus* 9 (1950) 427 ff., as a Celtic symbol, the result of Constantine's so-called pagan "vision" and used, as Hatt assumes, without basis, to counter-act Maxentius' magic, but later Christianized.

10. I, 28.

11. *The Conversion of Constantine and Pagan Rome* (Oxford U.P., 1969) 17; *id.*, "Hoc signo victor eris," *Pisciculi* (1939) 2 ff.

12. *The Conversion etc., op. cit.* 18.

13. Lactantius, *De mort. pers.* 44.

14. Alföldi, *The Conversion etc., op. cit.* 18; etc.

15. E.g. A. Piganiol, *L'Empereur Constantin* (Paris, 1832) 66; A. Brasseur,

the Chi and Rho, was a pre-Christian symbol, 'used even before the 4th century for the abbreviation of words starting with Chi and Rho,[16] or it was from the beginning of his rule used only from Constantine on and existed only as an abbreviation of the name of Christ.[17] Others[18] agree that this monogram was never used before Constantine as an abbreviation of the name of Christ.[19] The most interesting interpretation of this 'heavenly sign' is perhaps by A. Alföldi,[20] who speculates that what Constantine saw on the sky was a combination of the Cross and the sun, like ⳨, not like ☧. This may indeed have been the sign transmitted in the form marked on the soldiers shields at dawn of the day of the final battle against Maxentius. For it is indeed most unreasonable and unwarranted to deny that the sign of the Cross was an *essential* feature in Constantine's heavenly vision. The Cross is clearly and unequivocally mentioned by Eusebius[21] and it had been a symbol for earlier Christians. The *vexillum crucis Christi* was truly a standard of true Christians.[22]

Coins should be very helpful in trying to establish the historicity of the stories concerning Constantine's visions, or at least to establish the fact that Constantine really believed them and wanted to propagate them, even if they are not necessarily a proof of their actual occurrence and of Constantine's Christianity. Alföldi[23] has no doubt that the Christ monogram appeared on coins and on Constantine's helmet very soon after his vision as

"Les deux visions de Constantin," *Latomus* (1946) 36; J. Moreau, "Sur la vision de Constantin (312)," *Rev. des Etudes Anc.* 55 (1953) 307-333; *et al.*

16. J. Zeiller, "Quelques remarques sur la vision de Constantin," *Byzantion* 14 (1939) 336; *et al.*

17. A. Piganiol, *op. cit.* 66.

18. E.g. W. Seston, "La vision païenne de 310 et les origines du chrisme constantinien," *Ann. de l'Inst. de Philol. et d'Hist. Orient. de Univ. libr. de Bruxelles* 4 (1936) 393.

19. See also P. Bruun, *Roman Imperial Coinage* vol. VII, 61-64: the combination of Chi and Rho was by no means unusual in pre-Constantine times; its occurrence with a clearly Christian significance was exceedingly rare.

20. "Hoc signo etc.," *op. cit.* 4 ff.; see also H. Kraft, *Kaiser Konstantins religiöse Entwicklung* (Tübingen, 1955) 21.

21. *Vita Const.* I, 28.

22. As e.g. in Origen, *In iudic. hom.* 9.

23. "The Helmet of Constantine with the Christian Monogram," *J. of Roman Stud.* 22 (1932) 1 ff.; *The Conversion etc., op. cit.* 17; 27; 40 f.

described by Eusebius in the *Vita Constantini*. It is believed[24] that the different coins, the bronze multiples and, especially, the better issues of the famous silver coins of Ticinum prove without doubt at least the truth of Lactantius' story of the visions, and that the Emperor Constantine "embraced the Christian cause with a suddenness that surprised all but his closest intimates."[25] This strong belief is, however, not shared by some,[26] who say that none of the claims of Alföldi is proved by coins, and that, in particular, the coins give no *positive* and *necessary* evidence of any conversion, but only of a gradually changing attitude towards the old gods, and that, briefly, Christian symbolism has no place on the coins of Constantine.[27] But Constantine *did* make a practice of showing his religious convictions from the very beginning of his rule, even when he was only a 'Caesar'.[28]

After his extraordinary victory over Maxentius, Constantine was finally free to march into Rome. Eusebius[29] likens his procession into Rome to a most joyous triumphal march, flanked by senators and all the Roman people greeting the victorious Constantine as a ransomer, saviour, and a benefactor, with lavish praises and exuberant joy. When this triumphal procession arrived at the *forum Romanum*, and ought, according to ancient customs, to have gone on to the Capitol to offer the sacrifice of thanksgiving in the temple of Jupiter, the Emperor Constantine stopped. The sacrifice was not offered to Jupiter. This must be the correct inference to draw from the conspicuous failure to mention this

---

24. Alföldi, esp. in *The Conversion etc., op. cit.* 1 f.; "The Helmet etc.," *op. cit.*; "Hoc signo etc.," *op. cit.* 1 ff.; K. Aland, "Die religiöse Haltung Kaiser Konstantins," *Studia Patristica* 1 (1957) 572; *et al.*

25. Alföldi, *The Conversion etc., op. cit.* 2; see also, "The Initials of Christ on the Helmet of Constantine," *Studies in Roman Economic and Social History* (Princeton, 1951) 303 ff.; K. Kraft, "Das Silbermedallion Constantins des Grossen mit d. Christusmonogram auf dem Helm," *Jb. f. Numismatik und Geldgeschichte* 5 and 6 (1954-55) 151-178.

26. E.g. P. Bruun, *The Roman Imperial Coinage, op. cit.* 61 ff.; *The Constantinian Coinage of Arelate* (Helsinki, 1953); "The Consecration Coins of Constantine the Great," *Arctos* 1 (1954) 19-31; *et al.*

27. See also H. Lietzmann, "Der Glaube Konstantins des Grossen," *Sb. Preuss. Akad. Wiss. Phil.-Hist. Klasse* (1937) 263-275.

28. P. Batiffol, "Les étapes de la conversion de Constantin," *Bull. d'anc. litt. et d'arch. chrét.* 3 (1913) 178 ff.

29. *H.E.* IX, ix, 9 ff.; *Vita Const.* I, 39.

most traditional ritual in the panegyric delivered at Trèves in about July 313 A.D. in the presence of Constantine himself.[30] The silence of the Panegyrist about this very significant point, which seems to indicate that the sacrifice to Jupiter was — fatefully — not offered, has occasioned a great variety of comments, but the best of all are those by J. Straub.[31] According to him the Panegyrist was silent on the sacrifice to Jupiter because there was none, and there was no sacrifice because it was deliberately omitted, and for a most important reason.

This panegyric of 313 A.D. describes, in great detail, the entry of Constantine into Rome. In fact, its writer describes every single aspect of this triumphant entry and every detail of the traditional and joyous festivities of the triumphal celebrations, such as the enthusiasm of the people, and the games on the following days. The Panegyrist even registers Constantine's visit to the Curia, and his participation in the senate meeting. But the Panegyrist is silent on the most important aspect of traditional triumphal marches: the sacrifice to the Capitoline Jupiter and the gods. The inevitable conclusion must be that Constantine did not offer the sacrifice, and thus became the first Roman Emperor to break this hallowed tradition of the *veterum instituta* of the Romans[32] for the rituals of triumphal marches.[33] Some historians[34] mistakenly disagree denying the obvious and, without argument, simply state that Constantine *would not* have committed any such insulting act — at least not yet. Others[35] admit the undeniable omission by the Emperor of the traditional sacrifice, and try to explain away this omission by saying that Constantine was not celebrating a triumph since he was a conqueror in a 'civil strife.' But it has been rightly pointed out[36] that all the other ideas of traditional triumphal

30. XII (IX) in *Panegyrici Latini*, ed. R.A.B. Mynors (Oxford U.P., 1964).
31. "Konstantins Verzicht auf dem Gang zum Kapitol," *Historia* 4 (1955) 296-313; *Vom Herrscherideal in der Spätantike* (Stuttgart, 1939) 99; 194.
32. Straub, "Konstantins Verzicht etc.," *op. cit.* 306-307.
33. See also J. Vogt, *Konstantin d. G. und sein Jahrhundert* (München, 1949) 119; etc.; A. Kaniuth, *Die Beisetzung Konstantins des Grossen* (Breslau, 1941) 50 ff.; K. Aland, *op. cit.* 589-90; H. Dörries, *Constantine the Great* (New York, 1972) 29-30; *et al.*
34. Alföldi, *The Conversion etc., op. cit.* 62, n. 2.
35. J. Moreau, "Sur la vision etc.," *op. cit.* 319; *et al.*
36. J. Straub, "Konstantins Verzicht etc.," *op. cit.* 299.

celebrations were still being observed on this occasion, and that the occasion, described by the Panegyrist, was regarded as a proper triumph.[37] Later on, Constantine was to omit the pagan sacrifices at the occasions of his *decennalia*[38] of 315 A.D., of the *vicennalia*,[39] and of the *tricennalia*.[40]

To explain all these glaring omissions of sacrifice, but especially that in Constantine's triumphal entry into Rome, the most obvious answer seems to be that Constantine was himself a Christian at heart, or that for some reason he wanted to conform with what was clearly required of those who professed Christianity.[41] For he seems to have been observing the principle expressed in so many Acts of Christian martyrs: that he who sacrifices to the idols is not a member of the Christian flock, and that he who refuses to sacrifice to the idols, renounces and separates himself from paganism.[42]

Some other pronouncements and the very language of this panegyric of 313 A.D. are just as momentous as the omission of the pagan sacrifice by the Emperor Constantine. In this panegyric, addressed to Constantine himself, who had come up from Rome and Milan to Trèves to inspect the Rhine frontier, the Gallic orator naturally devoted much of his attention to Constantine's recent victory over Maxentius: How could Constantine, the Panegyrist asks, presume to wage such a war without the help of his associates in the Empire,[43] against an enemy who had stood up against the great armies of Severus and Galerius?[44] It was even more incredible to the Panegyrist that Constantine had achieved his victory with barely one quarter of his troops against — according to the orator — 100,000 men, after he had left behind the rest of

37. See Dessau, *ILS* I 694; *arcus triumphalis insignis; XII Paneg. Lat., op. cit.* IV (X) 32, 1: *quis triumphus inlustrior ... quae pompa felicior.* The Panegyrist of 313 A.D. and Eusebius make no secret of the most joyous and triumphal aspect of Constantine's entry to Rome after his victory at the Milvian Bridge.
38. *Vita Const.* I 48.
39. *Ibid.*, III, 15.
40. *De laud. Const.* II, 5; see also Zosimus.
41. See J. Straub, "Konstantins Verzicht etc.," *op. cit.* 307.
42. *Ibid.*, 306; K. Aland, *op. cit.* 589 f.; *et al.*
43. *Op. cit.* 2, 3.
44. *Ibid.*, 3, 4.

his armies on the Rhine.[45] "What sort of God" urged Constantine to liberate Rome?[46] The orator had no doubt in his mind that Constantine's behaviour in marching against Maxentius could only be explained by Constantine's certainty of victory promised to him by this very God.[47]

And who was this God? Some[48] have no doubt that the pagan orator had in mind no other than the Christian God, whose name for one reason or other he chooses not to mention. This same conclusion could perhaps be drawn from the fact that the orator also avoids, for the same reason, the mention of any of the established gods of Rome! The likelihood of this conclusion should stand despite the riskiness of basing such conclusion on this or any other panegyrics of high rhetoric.

The conclusion is nevertheless fairly sound when we take into consideration the traditional characteristics of these panegyrics and when we compare this panegyric with some others. These panegyrics were[49] usually expressions of Imperial ideology and changing policy. Even though the orators did not necessarily or officially speak in the name of the Emperor, they at least used a language they supposed was not disagreeable to him. When we place the Trèves panegyric of 313 A.D. in the context of these others and find that the Panegyrist did not even mention the names of the established gods of Rome, we are forced to the conclusion that something momentous had happened in the thinking of Constantine! Instead, the Panegyrist talks of *deus* and *mens divina*! Some finding these expressions rather vague, do not interpret them as attempts by the Gallic orator to hide the holy name of the Christian God but rather as indications that Constantine, like his predecessors before him, still enjoyed the support of heaven![50] Or that the orator was simply monotheistic,[51] but not

45. *Ibid.*, 3, 3.
46. *Ibid.*, 2, 4.
47. *Ibid.*, 3, 3.
48. As e.g. A.H.M. Jones, *Constantine and the Conversion of Europe* (London, 1968) 91-92.
49. See e.g. P. Batiffol, "Les étapes etc.," *op. cit.* esp. 180-184.
50. E.g. W. Seston, "L'opinion païenne de la conversion de Constantin," *Rev. Hist. Phil. Relig.* 16 (1936) 253 f.; R. MacMullen, *Constantine* (London, 1970) 72; H. Grégoire, "La 'conversion' de Constantine," *Rev. de l'Univ. de Bruxelles* 36 (1930-31) 253; *et al.*
51. F. Winkelmann, "Konstantins Religionspolitik und ihre Motive etc.,"

that he was implying Christ as the God!

Constantine himself was probably — or perhaps unquestionably — convinced, after his vision in the sky assuring him of victory in the sign of the Cross, that indeed the God of the Christians had given him the victory. Nevertheless he must have allowed his panegyrists to express *his* conviction, as Baynes[52] would put it, through the medium of their own interpretation of the fact. Or,[53] since he was supposed to voice the views of the emperor, the Panegyrist would use some fairly neutral expression to satisfy both the emperor and his own personal beliefs. But it is even more likely and, in fact, it was almost inevitable that the panegyrists would use this language. Panegyrics composed after the publication of the Edict of Milan imitated the terminology of this edict,[54] both by meticulously avoiding the names of pagan deities and by using the somewhat vague expressions concerning the new tutelary Deity who had helped the Emperor Constantine to his great victory over Maxentius.

Almost contemporaneous with these recent events and of similar significance is the erection of the statue of Constantine, reportedly[55] set up in the great forum of Rome. Although it would be unreasonable to doubt Eusebius' story about the setting up of this statue, there is, nevertheless, some doubt concerning the meaning of its inscription. This inscription[56] had in it the phrase τούτῳ τῷ σωτηριώδει σημείῳ, *i.e.* 'in this salutary sign'; or 'in this saving sign', or 'standard.' Taken by themselves, these words, and especially the rest of the inscription referring to the liberation of Rome from tyranny, may not have any allusion to the Sign of the Saviour, or the Sign of Salvation, the sign Constantine saw on the sky together with the inscription "in this sign you shall conquer." However, Eusebius in his introduction to this inscription clearly states that it *was* the Sign of the Saviour's passion that Constantine placed in the statue's hand. As if this

Acta Antiqua Acad. Scient. Hungariae 9 (1961) 251.

52. N.H. Baynes, "Constantine," *Cambridge Anc. Hist.* vol. 12 (Cambridge U.P., 1956) 684 f.

53. Dörries, *Constantine the Great, op. cit.* 29 f.

54. M.V. Anastos, "The Edict of Milan 313. A Defence of its Traditional Authorship and Designation", *Rev. des Etudes Byzant.* 25 (1967) 39 f.

55. Eusebius, *H.E.* IX, ix, 10; *Vita Constant.* I, 40; *De laud. Const.* IX, 8.

56. Eusebius, *H.E.* IX, ix, 1; *Vita Constant.* I, 40.

were still not clear enough, the Church historian states[57] that that 'sign' was a "high spear in the shape of a cross."

Modern authors differ widely in interpreting the meaning of this 'sign.' Who, indeed is right? The most widely favoured opinion is that it was the traditional *vexillum*, the banner under which Constantine reached his final victory over Maxentius,[58] but that Eusebius gave 'this rather neutral symbol' a Christian meaning: the Cross of the Saviour. Others[59] insist that the sign of the vision at the outset of Constantine's campaign was the *labarum*.[60] But Eusebius was probably right in his interpretation when he said that the sign in the hand of the statue of Constantine was the Sign of Salvation, *i.e.* a simple and straight cross, the obvious "sign of the Saviour's Passion," the heavenly sign in the skies of Gaul, or just *perhaps* the *labarum*, a modification of the simple cross. Nevertheless, even disregarding the Eusebian interpretation of this sign, it would be utterly frivolous to assume, as many have done, that it was the straight traditional *vexillum* vaguely resembling (if you had the wish and will to see the resemblance) the holy Cross of the Saviour. Is it likely that Constantine, in the wake of his great and most unusual victory against overwhelming odds, so often said by him to have been obtained with the special aid of Christ and under His heavenly sign – is it at all likely, I ask again, that he would have erected a statue of himself with the commonplace *vexillum* rather than the true Sign of Salvation, the Cross, in his hand? Not at all.

The triumphal arch of Constantine[61] dedicated by the Roman Senate and the People to Constantine in 315 A.D., is in a position somewhat similar to that of Constantine's statue in the *forum*, or

57. *Vita Constant.* I, 40.

58. J. Vogt, "Die Bedeutung des Jahres 312 f. d. Religionspolitik Konstantins des Grossen," *Zschr. f. Kirchengesch.* 61 (1942) 171-190; H. Grégoire, "La Statue de Constantin et le signe de la croix," *L'Antiquité Classique* 1 (1932) 139-141; Baynes, "Constantine," *op. cit.* 685; Aland, *op. cit.* 588 f.

59. Alföldi, "Hoc signo etc.," *op. cit.*, 1 ff.; *et al.*

60. Also, Dörries, *Constantine the Great, op. cit.* 41 f.

61. G.B. de Rossi, "Una questione sull' Arco trionfale dedicato a Costantino," *Nuovo Bullettino di Archeologia Crist.* 19 (1913) 7-19; *id.* "L'inscrizione dell' Arco trionfale di Costantino," *ibid.* 21-28; S.B. Platner and T. Ashby, *A Topographical Dictionary of Ancient Rome* (Oxford U.P., 1929) 36-38; Dessau, *ILS* (Berlin, 1960) 694, Jones, *op. cit.* 91; *et al.*

the Panegyric of 313 A.D. at Trèves. Its inscription may appear to be just as elusive as that of the statue:

To the Emperor Flavius Constantine, the Greatest, the Pious, the Fortunate, Augustus, because through the inspiration of the Divinity and the greatness of his mind, he with his army avenged the commonwealth with righteous arms both on the tyrant and on all his faction at the same time, the Senate and the people of Rome dedicated this arch to glorify his triumphs. To the liberator of the city. To the establisher of peace.

The interpreters of this inscription claim that its supposedly ambiguous, neutral, and ambivalent words were meant to be so 'in order to express gratitude for the supernatural intervention' in Constantine's victory, without indicating a preference for either the Christian God or the pagan divinities.[62] It seems[63] that the same neutrality was expressed here as in the panegyric of Trèves in 313 A.D., and that both the inscription of the Arch and the Panegyrist were following the cautious references to the supreme divinity in the Edict of Milan, which document, of course preceded both of them. In this sense it would be more correct to say that the Senate, the builders of the Arch, and the Gallic Panegyrist of 313 A.D. were quite eager to express respect for Constantine's new divinity rather than to camouflage or even neutralize it with ambivalent phrases.[64] This must be regarded as true in the case of the Arch as well, especially because just as in the Panegyric of 313 A.D., no pagan divinities are mentioned, not even Constantine's previous tutelary god, the *sol invictus*, and it might, for both the Senate and the Gallic Panegyrist, have been just too much to spell out the name of Jesus Christ, a name that had been proscribed until very recently and for the confession of which name Rome had, for about three centuries, peeple put to death. The features of pagan divinities *are* among the sculptures of the Arch, even though they do not figure in its inscription at all. This sculptural presence of pagan divinities has been interpreted as expressing the belief that the Arch had to do with paganism and the sun god, and that Constantine gained his victory from them rather than from

62. Anastos, *op. cit.* 40; see also Dörries, *Constantine the Great, op. cit.* 31; Vogt, "Die Bedeutung des Jahres 312 etc.," *op. cit.*; *et al.*
63. Anastos, *op. cit.* 40.
64. Cf. e.g. A. Piganiol, "L'état actuel de la question constantinienne," *Historia* 1 (1950) 82-96.

Christ.[65] Even though the Arch is not expressly Christian, and is, perhaps, deliberately ambivalent by the will of the senate, its builders, and perhaps, in imitation of the Edict of Milan, it is nevertheless, not an expression of any pagan cult, not even that of the sun god. The Arch was not in any way connected with the solar cult, neoplatonized or otherwise. Pagan elements suggesting this or that divinity were taken, like most sculptures on the Arch, from other Imperial structures of various kinds.[66] In view of the events of 312 A.D. – a main turningpoint in Constantine's life and history – it would be a most serious mistake to interpret the Arch of Constantine as an expression, made directly or through the Senate still loyal to paganism, of any adherence, or attachment by Constantine to any pagan tradition. In view of the Edict of Milan and the 'African letters' of Constantine, all of which pre-date this monument of triumph, it is much safer to say that in the Arch it was the Senate who expressed, and in the Edict of Milan and the 'African letters' it was Constantine himself who confessed the new Imperial faith.

65. Grégoire, "La 'conversion' etc.," *op. cit.* 253; H.P. L'Orange, "Sol Invictus Imperator," *Symbolae Osloenses* 14 (1935) 107 ff.; MacMullen, *Constantine, op. cit.* 72; *et al.*
66. Anastos, *op. cit.* 41.

THE FERVOUR OF THE NOVICE:

THE AFRICAN LETTERS
THE EDICT OF MILAN
A WARNING TO A PERSECUTOR

If anyone still entertained any doubts about Constantine's relation to the Christian Church at the time of his entry to Rome, but particularly if anyone had any doubts about Constantine's own belief in the reported divine interventions prior to his campaign and immediately before his victory over Maxentius at the Milvian Bridge, the three African letters, that followed soon after these events, should dispel any lingering uncertainty. For the young Conqueror made clear his beliefs concerning both the Church and the miraculous interventions of Christ Himself in his life and in the destiny of the Roman Empire and of Europe.

Constantine wrote these three letters after his entry into Rome, one to Caecilian, the Bishop of Carthage, and the other two to Anullinus, the proconsul of Africa, the letter to the bishop being chronologically in the middle, all three being written probably during the winter of 312/313 A.D., and the first two, but perhaps all three, still from Rome.[1] The first[2] of this trio of African letters, addressed to the governor Anullinus runs like this:

> Greetings, our dearest Anullinus. It is the nature of our love of (doing) good that we wish that whatever belongs to others by right should not only not be fussed over but even returned, dearest Anullinus. We therefore will that whensoever you receive this letter you see to it that if any things (that) belonged to the Catholic Church of the Christians in all and every city and other places

---

1. N.H. Baynes, "Constantine the Great and the Christian Church," *Proceedings of the British Acad.* 15 (1929) 348, n. 40; A.H.M. Jones, *Constantine the Great and the Conversion of Europe* (London, 1968) 80-83.

2. Eusebius, *H.E.* X, v, 15-17.

and now are held in the possession of private citizens or of any other persons, they be immediately restored to the same churches. For we have indeed decided that whatever the same churches previously possessed be restored to their lawful possession. Since therefore your Devotion sees that the order of this our command is most manifest, see to it that all things, whether gardens or houses or whatsoever belonged to the rightful ownership of the same churches, be restored to them as quickly as possible, so that we may learn that you have rendered a most attentive obedience to this our command. Farewell, our dearest and most beloved Anullinus.

What Constantine is doing here is not entirely new. It had already been done by Gallienus when he returned Church property earlier confiscated by his father the Emperor Valerian to the Christian churches. Here Constantine, as he says, only wishes to undo the wrongs done to the Church by his predecessors during the 'Great Persecution'. Nothing else. Obviously, Galerius' edict of toleration of 311 A.D. did not provide for this.

The letter written to the Bishop Caecilian[3] does something entirely new for the Christian Church, and goes beyond what could be regarded by the Church as its right:

Constantine Augustus to Caecilian, bishop of Carthage. Since I have decided that in all the provinces, the Africas, the Numidias and the Mauretanias, some provision should be made for the expenses of certain specified ministers of the lawful and most holy Catholic religion, I have dispatched a letter to Ursus, the most eminent finance minister of Africa and instructed him to see to it that he pay to your reverence three thousand *folles*. You therefore at the time, when you secure the payment of the aforesaid sum of money, order that the money be distributed to all the above-mentioned (persons) in accordance with the list sent to you by Hosius. But if you learn that anything is lacking for the fulfillment of this my plan in this matter concerning all of them, you must ask without hesitation whatever you might find to be needed from Heraclides, the administrator of our estates. For I even gave him orders when he was in my presence that if your reverence should ask any money from him he should see to it that he pay it without any hesitation. And since I have learnt that certain persons of unstable disposition wish to pervert the people of the most holy and Catholic Church by some foul corruption, you must know that I have given such orders to Anullinus, the proconsul, and in truth also to Patricius, the vicar of the prefects, when they were in my presence, that among all the other matters they pay due attention especially

3. *Ibid.*, X, vi, 1-5.

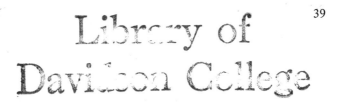

to this business, and not allow anything of the kind to be overlooked. Therefore, if you should observe any such men persisting in that madness of theirs, approach the above-mentioned judges without any hesitation and lay this matter before them, so that they turn their attention towards them as I ordered them when they were in my presence. May the divinity of the Great God preserve you for many years.

In this letter we learn that Constantine makes provision to cover the expenses of the *lawful and holy Catholic Church* in the provinces of the Africas, the Numidias, and the Mauretanias; that for this purpose his accountant in Africa will pay Caecilian 3000 *folles*; and that the Bishop was to ask the Emperor's administrator if any more money was needed. It is indeed almost incredible to read that an emperor of the Roman Empire is offering the Christian Church limitless financial help for its needs! First there is the cessation of persecution, and, now, the return of all wrongly confiscated Church property, and then this overflowing concern for the smooth and untroubled conduct of the Church's business. What could be the reason for all this? To compound this puzzle, Constantine insists that this financial aid should be given only to the *lawful and Catholic Church*; he shows awareness of certain "persons of unstable disposition" who wish to "pervert the people of the most holy Catholic Church", and promises action against these dissidents, obviously the Donatists, if they persist in their "madness". What is behind this apparently holy concern?

The last of these three letters, also written to the African Governor Anullinus,[4] is a further example of Constantine's fervour for the work of the Christian Church:

Greetings, our dearest Anullinus. Since from several circumstances it appears that the cessation of the worship in which the highest reverence of the most holy and heavenly power is maintained has brought great dangers upon public affairs, and that the lawful restoration and maintenance of the same worship has bestowed the greatest prosperity on the Roman name and an exceptional happiness on all the affairs of men, the divine beneficence granting this, it has been decided that those men who, with due holiness and the application of this law, bestow their ministrations on the performance of the divine worship shall receive the rewards of their labours, dearest Anullinus. Therefore I wish that those who within the province entrusted to you provide their

4. *Ibid.*, X, vii.

ministration to this holy religion in the Catholic Church over which Caecilian presides, whom it is customary to call clerics, shall be kept exempt from all public burdens whatsoever, so that they may not be drawn away by any sacrilegious digression or distraction from the service which is due to the Divinity, but may rather without any annoyance serve entirely their own law, since when they render the greatest service to the Divinity, the greatest benefit seems to be conferred on public affairs. Farewell, our dearest most beloved Anullinus.

In this letter Constantine relieves all the "clerics" of the Catholic Church under the authority of the Bishop Caecilian and within the entire province of Anullinus, of all free public services (*munera*) in order that they may dedicate themselves to the service of the Divinity and *thus confer the greatest possible benefit on the public at large.*[5]

The reason for this additional generosity to Catholic clerics is clearly stated by Constantine. The young Emperor confesses that he has found out that the worship in the Catholic Church is bestowing "the greatest prosperity upon the Roman name" and "exceptional happiness" on the public affairs in general; and that the cessation of the holy worship during the persecutions brought great dangers upon the Empire. Constantine now wanted to make sure that, as far as it depended upon him, this holy worship in the Catholic Church would be maintained and not interrupted by any diversions, including the rendering of the traditional free public service that might otherwise be placed upon the shoulders of the Catholic clerics. There can be little doubt that Constantine is referring, in this letter, *not* simply and generally to the good fortune and prosperity Rome, but much rather and even exclusively to the good fortune brought about by his own victory over the tyrant Maxentius. He was of course thinking especially about the extraordinary help he himself received in bringing about this good fortune from the God of the Christians. This is, in sober fact, the only interpretation, a religious one, that the letter will bear.[6] To discard this interpretation by dismissing Constantine's reported experience with the God of the Christians at the very outset of his campaign would be frivolous.

5. See also the constitutions of Constantine, addressed to provincial governors here and elsewhere, granting the same privilege to Catholic clergy, *Cod. Theod.* XVI, ii, 1 and 2.
6. H. Dörries, *Constantine the Great* (New York, 1972) 43 f.

41

This letter must of course have reached the governor Anullinus some (perhaps a considerable) time before April 15, 313 A.D., on which day Anullinus sent a report of great importance to Constantine.[7]

It was soon after Constantine's conquest of Maxentius on October 28, 312 A.D., and probably at about this time, *i.e.* in early 313 A.D.[8] that Constantine and Licinius met at Milan. At this meeting, arranged perhaps for the purpose of the marriage of the Emperor Licinius and Constantine's half-sister, Constantia, the two Augustuses discussed and undoubtedly agreed upon a common policy concerning the government of the Roman Empire. But there certainly was also an agreement concerning the legal status of the Christian Church and the Christians, for they officially received, as is clear from the document known as the Edict of Milan, complete and unreserved freedom of religion:[9]

Already a long time ago, being anxious that freedom of worship ought not to be denied, but that everyone should be given liberty in his mind and inclination to concern himself with divine matters, each according to his own preference, we bade the Christians to observe the faith of their own sect and worship. But since many and various conditions seemed to be clearly added in that rescript, in which such liberty was conceded to the same persons, it may have happened that some of them were shortly afterwards inhibited from such observance.

When both I, Constantine Augustus, and also I, Licinius Augustus, met under happy circumstances at Milan, and discussed all matters that concerned the public good and welfare we believed that this thing, among others, which we saw would be beneficial to many people, should be regulated first of all so that reverence for the divinity was preserved, namely to give both Christians and all men free choice to follow the religion which each one would; so that whatever Divinity there exists in the heavenly seat, might be appeased and propitious to us and to all those who are placed under our authority. Therefore, we believed that this policy was to be adopted on a salutary and most just basis, so that we decided that no one should be denied the opportunity of devoting himself either to the cult of the Christians or to whatever religion

7. Augustine, *Ep.* 88, 2; *Coll. Carth.* III, 216-220; probably in reply to this letter of Constantine to the governor; see Baynes, *op. cit.* 348 f., n. 40; also, Jones, *op. cit.* 83.

8. Perhaps, in February 313 A.D.; Baynes, *op. cit.* 349, n. 41; Jones, *op. cit.* 84.

9. Eusebius, *H.E.* X, v, 1-14; Lactantius, *De mort. pers.* 48.

he himself felt most suitable for himself, so that the highest Divinity, whose religion we obey with free minds, can exhibit to us in all things His customary favour and benevolence. Therefore it is fitting that your Excellency should know that we decided that all kinds of conditions contained in communications sent earlier to your office concerning the name of the Christians, having been completely removed, those things also which seemed to be directly injurious and foreign to our clemency should be removed, and that every one of those who have the same desire to observe the religion of the Christians is now freely and unconditionally to strive to do so, without any interference or molestation. We believed that this should be most fully explained to your Carefulness, that you might know that we gave to the same Christians an unimpeded and complete liberty to practice their religion. Since you see that this has been granted to the same by us, your Excellency understands that, for the sake of peace in our time, free and open liberty of religion or cult has been similarly granted to others, in order that every individual may have unrestrained opportunity to pursue what worship he chooses. We have done this that it may not appear that we have in any way diminished any cult or any religion.

In the case of the Christians, this is what we believed we had, in addition, to decree: if the places, in which they formerly had the custom to assemble, and concerning which also in letters previously sent to your office a certain plan was also expressed, appear to have been purchased at an earlier time by any people either from our treasury or by any other person, they shall restore the same places to the Christians without any payment and any demand of recompensation, and putting aside all delay and equivocation. Those also who received the same places as gifts, shall likewise return them to the same Christians as quickly as possible. Moreover, if those who purchased these same places or those who received them as gifts request anything of our benevolence, let them apply to the vicar, so that provision may also be made for them through our indulgence. All these things will have to be handed over to the corporation of the Christians by your mediation immediately and without delay.

And because the same Christians are known to have possessed not only those places in which they were accustomed to assemble, but also others which belonged not to the authority of individual people but to that of their corporation, that is, the churches, you will order that all these, in accordance with the law stated above, be restored to the same Christians, that is, corporation and congregations, without any equivocation or dispute of any sort, the above-mentioned method being clearly maintained, so that, since they restore the same properties, as we have said, without price, they should expect indemnity from our kindness. In all this you will have to exhibit your most efficient mediation in the interest of the above-mentioned corporation of the Christians, so that our command may be fulfilled as quickly as

43

possible, that in this matter also care may, through our kindness, be taken for the public peace. Only in this way will it come about, as has been explained above, that the Divine favour towards us, which we have experienced in such great matters, will continue for all time to be beneficent to our successive acts, bringing with it public happiness. But that an outline of this decree of our kindness may come to the knowledge of all, it will be your duty to publish everywhere these ordinances, set out in an edict of yours, and to bring them to the knowledge of all, in order that the decreeing of this our kindness may not possibly escape the notice of anyone.

This most precious document, as already stated, spelled out, in detail, a complete religious freedom for the Christian Church, and granted the Christians the same religious privileges as were enjoyed by the official pagan religion; in fact the document granted freedom to all religions.

Consequently, all restrictions and impediments previously placed and left upon the Christians were lifted. It was of course very important that all Christian Church properties confiscated during the persecutions were to be immediately restored to the Christian churches, but the pagans, or whoever else were thus deprived of confiscated Church property, were to be financially compensated by the state for their losses. It is interesting that nothing whatsoever was said about restitutions to private members of the Christian Church.[10]

It has been argued[11] that the Edict of Milan was the first Imperial constitution formally to recognise the Christian Church as a legal corporation authorized to 'receive, hold, and administer property'. Some scholars[12] admit the possibility that this document did indeed have this distinction, and argue that Constantine's order to Anullinus[13] was limited in scope, which it was, and that "the grant of these rights" in the document written to Anullinus was not connected with freedom of worship, which is true, but

10. Concerning measures by Constantine to identify these individuals, see *Vita Constantini* I, 41, 3; II, 20, 2; A. Ehrhardt, "Constantin der Grosse, Religionspolitik und Gesetzgebung," *Zschr. Savigny-Stiftung f. Rechtsgeschichte 72* (1955) 154-190.

11. E.g. by E. Chénon, "Les conséquences juridiques de l'Edit de Milan," *N. Revue historique de droit français et étranger 38 (1914-15) 255-263.*

12. M.V. Anastos, "The Edict of Milan 313," *Rev. Etudes Byzant.* 25 (1967) 19; *et al.*

13. Eusebius, *H.E.* X, v, 4.

there obviously was no need of such connection.[14] It is, however, very likely that Gallienus' constitutions, issued in and after 260 A.D. to undo the damage done to the Church by his father's persecutions, were as significant and just as generous as the Edict of Milan with regard to corporate owenership of property and the restoration of confiscated corporate property to the Church.[15] Furthermore, these constitutions of Gallienus were like the Edict of Milan, a guarantee of freedom of worship, for indeed Gallienus could, though many moden scholars cannot, see the nonsense of returning a church building to the Church without a guarantee of freedom of worship.

It is surmised[16] and quite plausible that it was Constantine who championed the cause of the Christians and Licinius that of the pagans at least by insisting on "strict impartiality". These attitudes appear to be quite probable, especially when one thinks of what Constantine had by this time already done for the Christians and when, looking into the future, one realizes that at least subsequent events poved that Licinius' sympathies were not at all pro-Christian but rather old Roman.

Though, perhaps due to the restraining influence of Licinius, the Edict of Milan is not exactly Constanine's confession of faith that it might otherwise have turned out to be, the same confession of faith that is shining through his many letters. But the Edict of Milan is truly what Eusebius called it:[17] "a most perfect law on behalf of the Christians."

The Edict has come down to us in two versions: one is Eusebius' Greek translation[18] from a Latin text; the other, preserved in Lactantius,[19] is probably the Latin text that was published in the East. Both the Eusebian and the Lactantian versions,[20] however, equally claim to be based upon the conference Constantine and Licinius had held in Milan.

14. Cf. Ehrhardt, *op. cit.*

15. Paul Keresztes, "The Peace of Gallienus: 260-303 A.D.," *Wiener Studien* 9 (1975) 174-185.

16. Jones, *op. cit.* 88 f.

17. *H.E.* IX, ix, 12.

18. *H.E.* X, v, 1-14.

19. *De mort. pers.* 48.

20. *H.E.* X, 5, 4; *De mort. pers.* 48, 2.

The Lactantian, or Licinian, version was published at least as early as June 13, 313 A.D. in Nicomedia. Licinius, presumably and logically, took the text of the Edict with him when he left Milan to return to his empire. No doubt impressed by Constantine's recent blitzkrieg and victory over Maxentius, and perhaps only too eager to please the senior Augustus of the Empire, he published the Edict of Milan with essentially and almost literally the same text as is found in the Eusebian version.

The Eusebian version, on the other hand, has been regarded[21] as a Greek translation of the original text of the Edict of Milan, but this, clearly, cannot be proved,[21a] since there is no document that can be identified as the original Edict of Milan. It is a curious fact that the Edict and some other Constantinian documents that should be placed immediately after Eusebius' reference to the "most perfect law,"[22] were, by some 'accident' in the transmission of the original manuscripts, shifted to where they are presently[23] found. Although the displacement of these documents is most puzzling, it should not in any way cast any shadow of doubt over the authenticity of the texts of these documents.[24]

The text of the Edict should be regarded as well authenticated on the basis of the versions transmitted by Eusebius and Lactantius. Although the versions are identical in essence, nevertheless there are understandably some very minor discrepancies between them. The existence of these discrepancies is not only understandable but also unavoidable because -- apart from the fact that Eusebius' version is a translation, even if from the original Latin text -- transcription and revision, especially of documents as lengthy as the Edict of Milan, almost invariably result, due to the involvement of

21. E.g. by V. Sesan, "Die Religionspolitik der Christlich-röm. Kaiser von Konstantin d. Gr. bis Theodosius d. Gr. (313-380)," *Kirche und Staat im römisch-byzantinischen Reiche seit Konstantin d. Gr. bis zum Falle Konstantinopels* (Czernowitz, 1911).
21a. Anastos, *op. cit.* 27.
22. *H.E.* IX, ix, 12.
23. *H.E.* X, v-X, vii.
24. Anastos, *op. cit.* 25 f. In fact, some MSS completely omit these displaced passages (*H.E.* X, v-X, vii). Despite H. Grégoire, *Byzantion* 7 (1932) 649; J. Moreau, "Les 'Litterae Licinii'," *Scripta Minora*, ed. W. Schmitthenner (Heidelberg, 1964) 102 f.; *et al.*, the authenticity of the edict itself should not be lessened by this omission in these MSS.

fallible human nature, in at best some innocent and insubstantial discrepancies.[25]

The dates of the conference and the Edict of Milan are uncertain. The date of the conference has been discussed in great detail.[26] It has been believed that Constantine both may[27] and may not[28] have been in Rome in January 313 A.D. even up to the 18th of the month, for some official function there. Constantine and Licinius certainly met in Milan, probably early in 313 A.D.,[29] to celebrate the marriage of Constantia and Licinius, and they eventually agreed on the common text of the Edict of Milan to give Christianity and all other religions full religious freedom. The conference was then suddenly broken up by the news that Maximinus Daia had crossed over the Bosporus into Licinius' empire. This may account for the relatively late date June 13, 313 A.D. of the publication of the edict in Nicomedia.

This date is, however, not the date of the Edict of Milan, but only of a publication of the Licinian copy in this Emperor's sphere of authority. Presuming, of course, that it was also published in Constantine's empire, many scholars have made attempts to establish its date of publication or publications in the West. Dates as early as early 312 or the summer of the same year have been suggested.[30] Late 312 A.D. has also often been favoured.[31] Even

25. To explain the discrepancies, Sesan, op. cit. and J. Wittig, "Das Toleranzreskript von Mailand 313,"Konstantin d. Gr. und seine Zeit, ed. F.J. Dölger (Freiburg, 1913) 40-63, suggest that the discrepancies are due to the fact that Eusebius translated the original edict into Greek, and that Lactantius gave the text of the later Nicomedian document, itself depending on the original. H. Hülle, Toleranzerlasse römischer Kaiser für das Christentum bis zum J. 313 (Berlin, 1895) 80-106, claims that both the Eusebian and the Lactantian versions went back to the text Licinius had sent to the governor of Bithynia.

26. S. Calderone, Costantino e il cattolicesimo (Florence, 1962) 158 ff.

27. O. Seeck, Regesten der Kaiser und Päpste f. die Jahre 311 bis 476 n. Chr. (Stuttgart, 1919) 35 ff.; 50.

28. Anastos, op. cit. 26.

29. In late 312 A.D., or January 313 A.D., with sessions extending up to March: Anastos, op. cit. 26 f.; Baynes, op. cit. 349; and Jones, op. cit. 84, favour February 313 A.D. , as the start of the conference.

30. Th. Keim, "Die römische Toleranzedikte f. d. Christentum (311-313) etc.,"Theol. Jbücher 11 (1852) 218 ff.

31. H. Valesius, Eusebii Caesar. H.E. (Paris, 1659) = Migne, P.G. XX, 823; 881; 883 f. Calderone, op. cit. 157 ff.; Sesan op. cit. 216 ff.

M.V. Anastos prefers a date[32] in late 312 A.D. to one shortly after the Milan conference, although it should of course be admitted with Anastos[33] that neither a date late in 312 A.D. nor one shortly after the conference is capable of being proved.

The date of publication of the Edict in Constantine's part of the Empire may well be related to the date of Constantine's letter to Anullinus,[34] the document which orders the governor of Africa to see to it that all confiscated Church properties be restored to the Christian churches. To avoid sheer speculation, it seems legitimate to surmise that the writing of this letter would have been entirely superfluous if the far more generous decisions of the Edict of Milan had been promulgated. There can really be very little doubt that the Edict of Milan must logically have followed this letter to Anullinus. The letter, on the other hand, was published not earlier than very late 312 A.D., but probably early 313 A.D. That the Constantinian Edict of Milan was published during the conference is not likely since this conference is referred to in the Edict as if it were in the past. Thus it is probable that it was published in Constantine's area only after the conference had broken up and the two Augustuses had gone their separate ways.

Since 1891 it has been quite fashionable to deny not only the existence of a *Constantinian* edict of Milan but even that of *any* Edict of Milan, and it became customary to refer to what used to be called the Edict of Milan as the "so-called" edict of Milan, or to put the "edict of Milan" in quotation marks. In this year, Otto Seeck[35] denied that Constantine was an author of the Edict of Milan or that he had issued it in his own empire. After Seeck there came a regiment of those who with Seeck denied that there was any Constantinian authorship of the document and that Constantine ever published it.[36]

32. Anastos, *op. cit.* 21.
33. *Ibid.*
34. Eusebius, *H.E.* X, v, 15-17.
35. "Das sogenannte Edikt von Mailand", *Zschr. f. Kirchengesch.* 12 (1891) 381 ff.
36. K. Bihlmeyer, "Das angebliche Toleranzedikt Konstantins von 312," *Theolog. Quartalschr.* 96 (1914) 65-100; 198-224; J.R. Knipfing, "Das angebliche 'Mailänder Edikt' v. 313 im Lichte der neueren Forschung," *Zschr. f. Kirchengesch.* 40 (1922) 206-218; H. Nesselhauf, "Das Toleranzgesetz des Licinius," *Hist. Zschr.* 74 (1954) 44-61; J. Vogt, *Konstantin d. Gr. und sein Jahrhundert* (München, 1949) 168 ff.; *et al.*

The Seeckian idea has been taken up and 'developed' by Henri Grégoire, the *advocatus diaboli* wherever Constantine's "sincere" Christianity, his service to the Church, and the supernatural are concerned. He regards the Edict as a part of the 'Constantinian legend'.[37] A champion of the case of Licinius as the real hero in the cause of the Christian Church, Grégoire declares that Licinius, not Galerius,[38] was the true author of the edict of toleration of 311 A.D.; that the first Christian victory was not Constantine's over Maxentius, but Licinius' on the *campus Serenus*[39] over Maximinus Daia; and finally that the Edict of Milan was the work of Licinius alone, and never promulgated by Constantine, but only by Licinius.[40] It is needless to say that J. Moreau,[41] a faithful disciple of Grégoire, follows in the master's footsteps. The idea that the Edict of Milan was not an edict but rather an Imperial rescript of Licinius, and, at best, only an edict of the governor of Bithynia, has been advanced by many.

But the cause of Constantine has also had its promoters and champions. Although the ideas of Seeck and his followers are incapable of being proved, many scholars, not content with declaring them to be mere speculations, have made strenuous efforts to prove them wrong. Indeed, the idea that Licinius was the sole author of the Edict of Milan appears to be completely absurd.[42] Scholars opposed to Seeck *et alii* agree that, technically speaking, the Edict of Milan is perhaps not an Imperial edict, and some prefer to call it an edict of the governor of Bithynia, or a rescript or even a *mandatum*, but most of them argue, on the basis of course of the testimony of Eusebius and Lactantius, that Constantine was an author of the Edict of Milan — even the main

---

37. *Byzantion* 10 (1935) 617.
38. "About Licinius' Fiscal and Religious Policy," *Byzantion* 13 (1938) 559.
39. *Byzantion* 10 (1935) 618.
40. In March, not in June: "La 'coversion' de Constantin," *Rev. de l'Univ. Bruxelles* 36 (1930-31) 263; *Byzantion* 7 (1932) 648 f.; *ibid.* 10 (1935) 616-619; "La statue de Constantin et le signe de la croix," *L'Antiquité Class.* 1 (1932) 135 ff.; *etc.*
41. "Zur Religionspolitik Konstantins des Grossen," *Ann. Univ. Sarav.* 1 (1952) 160-168; "Les 'Litterae Licinii'," *op. cit.* 99-105; etc.
42. L. Salvatorelli, "La politica religiosa e la religiosità di Costantino," *Ricerche relig.* 4 (1928) 312.

promoter of it – and that Licinius simply accepted it.[43]

The latest and best promoter of at least co-authorship by Constantine of the Edict of Milan, and of its publication not only by Licinius but also by Constantine, is M.V. Anastos.[44] The main basis of his arguments is naturally Eusebius, whom he defends against high-handed abuse by scholars of high repute.[45] On the basis of Eusebius and, in particular, of the Edict of Milan itself, there can be no sound reason for denying that Constantine was an author of the Edict and that he published it in his own part of the Empire.[46] Indeed, Constantine had to publish and address the Edict of Milan to the people or the officials of his own empire, because the copy or version published in June 313 A.D. in Nicomedia was of course valid only in Licinius' own territory, and had no force in Constantine's.[47] It may 'logically be assumed[48] that Constantine must have issued his version of the Edict in Rome', and though the date when this happened must still remain uncertain, it probably preceded the known date of publication of Licinius' version.

Thus Constantine's version of the Edict of Milan became "the perfect law issued on behalf of the Christians"[49] that guaranteed them full religious freedom and unhindered religious worship, coupled with the restoration of confiscated Church property.[50]

43. F. Görres, "Eine Bestreitung des Edicts von Mailand durch O. Seeck," *Zschr. f. Wiss. Theol.* 35 (1892) 285-95; Bihlmeyer, *op. cit.* 68; Wittig, *op. cit.* 47 ff.; J.R. Palanque, "A propos du prétendu édit de Milan," *Byzantion* 10 (1935) 607; N.H. Baynes, "Constantine", *Cambridge Anc. Hist.* v. 12 (Cambridge U.P., 1956) 686; R. MacMullen, *Constantine* (London, 1970) 93; Jones, *op. cit.* 84 ff.

44. *Op. cit.* 13 ff.

45. *Ibid.* 15; see also the important defence of Eusebius in F. Winkelmann, *Die Vita Constantini des Eusebius etc.* (Halle, 1959).

46. Anastos, *op. cit.* 17-20.

47. *Ibid.* 20.

48. *Ibid.* 21.

49. Eusebius, *H.E.* IX, ix, 12.

50. Although there is much disagreement on the identity of this "most perfect law" mentioned by Eusebius, it was certainly not Galerius' edict of toleration; see Anastos, *op. cit.* 23-25, against Grégoire, *Byzantion* 7 (1932) 649; and J. Moreau, "Les 'Litterae Licinii'," *op. cit.* 102 f. Eusebius' report (*H.E.* VIII, xiv, 1) concerning Maxentius' order to his people to cease persecuting the Christians is not clear and probably does not mean anything like

Anastos also vindicates the traditional title of the Edict of Milan,[51] and maintains that this traditional title "is not inappropriate if by it is understood the joint Imperial edict of toleration which, as a consequence of the understanding reached in Milan by Constantine and Licinius, became effective throughout the Empire upon promulgation by each of the emperors separately in his own realm." It was effectively an Imperial edict of Milan.[52] It is understood and implied that each of the emperors took a copy of mutually agreed text home and there published it in whatever way was convenient, but published it directly or indirectly to the whole area concerned. We happen to have one copy of the Edict preserved by Lactantius,[53] and another one by Eusebius.[54] Though they are essentially the same, the Eusebian copy may very well be based on a copy published by Constantine himself. It should add considerable weight to what has already been said, *i.e.* that the Emperors Constantine and Licinius use the technical term *quare ... placuisse nobis,*[55] a truly significant expression, in indicating the nature and introducing the matter of their legislation. The fact that Licinius published the Edict of Milan through the office of the provincial governor of Bithynia, and that Constantine published it, *if not directly*, then at least indirectly, through his Imperial offices, should be regarded as rather insignificant with respect to the nature of this legislation, and it should not put into question the fact that this document was an effective Imperial edict drafted and decided upon by the two Augustuses in the city of Milan.

Constantine, at least, was not forgetful of the fact that, in some

the truly perfect law, the Edict of Milan. Furthermore, though Gallienus actively and explicitly ended persecution and restored confiscated Church property (Paul Keresztes, "The Peace of Gallienus, etc.", *Wiener Studien, op. cit.*), his edict and rescripts were probably much less explicit and farreaching than the Edict of Milan.

51. *Op. cit.* 27 ff.

52. Concerning suggestions that our Edict of Milan was not an edict but a rescript, a *mandatum*, etc., see Anastos' rebuttal of these fastidious and archaizing efforts, *op. cit.* 28 ff.

53. *De mort. pers.* 48.

54. *H.E.* X, v, 1-14.

55. ἀρέσκειν ἡμῖν; Lactantius, *De mort. pers.* 48, 4 and Eusebius, *H.E.* X, v, 6.

areas of the Roman Empire, Christians, were still being persecuted. Whether or not Maxentius was[56] an ally of Maximinus Daia, a secret treaty of this nature would not have remained a secret for Constantine. It is, on the other hand, completely believable[57] that Constantine's first message after marching into Rome would be to have Maximinus Daia stop all persecutions in his territories. This is what Eusebius[58] says about this effort of Constantine:

And after this Constantine himself, and with him the Emperor Licinius, whose mind at that time did not yet turn towards the madness into which it later fell, having propitiated God, the cause of all their blessings, both with one will and thought established a most perfect law on behalf of the Christians, and to Maximinus, who was still ruling the people of the East and pretending friendship towards them, they sent a report of the marvellous events accomplished by God in their favour, as well as of the victory over the tyrant, and the law itself. He, being a tyrant, was much chagrined by what he learnt, but, not wishing to seem to be making concessions to the others, nor on the other hand to suppress the order on account of his fear of those who enjoined it, as if out of his own motion, he, compelled, wrote this first letter on behalf of the Christians to the governors under him.

What is intriguing about this information by Eusebius is the date of the intervention, its nature, and particularly, the identity of the "most perfect law" which Constantine (and Licinius!) drew up on behalf of the Christians and sent over to Maximinus Daia, and, finally, the date of this "most perfect law" itself if this "law" was something entirely separate and different from the initial intervention.

This intervention was Constantine's first measure, and it was an order by him the *Senior Augustus*[59] of the Roman Empire. Thus this intervention had to be made very promptly. Also, since Constantine himself most sincerely and zealously believed in the miracle of the sky and that his victory over Maxentius was due to

56. As Lactantius, *De mort. pers.* 44, 10, quite believably reports.
57. As Eusebius, *H.E.* IX, ix, 12; esp. IX, ixa, 12, and significantly, Lactantius, *De mort. pers.* 37, 1, suggest and as modern scholars, e.g. A. Piganiol, *L'Empereur Constantin* (Paris, 1932) 86-91, argue.
58. *H.E.* IX, ix, 12.
59. Lactantius, *De mort. pers.* 24; 44; together with Eusebius *H.E.* IX, ix, 12; see N.H. Baynes, "Constantine the Great and the Christian Church," *op. cit.* 86-91; J. Maurice, "La véracité historique de Lactance," *Comptes rendus, Acad. des Inscr. et Belles Lettres* (1908) 146-159; *et al.*

52

the Divine help of the God of the Christians, it should be understandable that Constantine did not delay in issuing his order to Maximinus Daia to cease the persecutions. This order went across the unusually calm Adriatic sea and all the way to Nicomedia and it reached the hands of Maximinus Daia not later than November 312 A.D.[60]

Was *this* "most perfect law" drawn up by Constantine and Licinius the Edict of Milan? It could hardly be anything else. That this "law" was the order itself to stop the persecution is possible but not very likely.[61] For 'the order' would not warrant the use of Eusebius' beautiful and rhetorical expressions describing this "law". That this "law" was the Edict of Milan itself[62] is quite possible and even very likely. For it is more likely that Eusebius was confused about the chronology of events but it is not necessary to assume this since he did not say that the initial communications of Constantine with Maximinus Daia[63] and the sending of this "most perfect law" on behalf of the Christians took place at the same time. This "most perfect law" could be sent to Maximinus Daia a few months after the initial warning and thus it could, indeed, be easily identical with the Edict of Milan.

Maximinus Daia's reaction was a letter[64] to Sabinus, his official, in which he grudgingly relaxed the persecution that was apparently still going on:

I am convinced that it is evident both to your Firmness and to all men that our masters Diocletian and Maximianus, our fathers, when they noticed that almost all men, having abandoned the worship of the gods, joined the people of the Christians, rightly ordered that all men who withdrew from the worship of the same gods, the immortal gods, should be recalled to the worship of the gods by public chastisement and vengeance. But when under happy circumstances I came for the first time to the East, and learnt that very many

60. On the controversy about this and other dates of Maximinus Daia's last two ordinances granting Christians first a grudging and then a complete freedom, see N.H. Baynes, "Two Notes on the Great Persecution," *Class. Quart.* (1924) 193 f.; H.J. Lawlor, *Eusebiana* (Oxford U.P., 1912) 211-234; "The Chronology of Eusebius' *Martyrs of Palestine*," *Hermathena* 15 (1908) 94-100; Palanque, *op. cit.* 612; *et al.*

61. Baynes, see n. 60, *above.*

62. Lawlor, *Eusebiana*, see n. 60, *above.*

63. See also Lactantius, *De mort. pers.* 37, 1.

64. Eusebius, *H.E.* IX, ixA, 1-9.

people who were capable of doing public service, were being banished to some places by the judges for the above-mentioned reason, I gave orders to each of the judges that none of them was in the future to deal cruelly with the provincials, but that they should rather call them back to the worship of the gods with flattery and exhortations. At this time, then, when, in conformity with my order, my commands were observed by the judges, it came to pass that none in the provinces of the East was banished or treated with insult, but rather they were recalled to the worship of the gods, because nothing violent happened to them. But after this, when last year under happy circumstances I went to Nicomedia and was staying there, citizens of the same city came to me with the statues of the gods, fervently requesting that in no way should such a people be allowed to dwell in their country. But when I learnt that very many people of the same religion were dwelling in those regions, I gave them the answer that I was glad and grateful for their petition, but that I perceived that this request was not made by all; if, then, any persevered in the same superstition, let each of them follow his own wish according to his own personal preference, and if they so wished, let them recognize the cult of the gods. Nevertheless to the people of the same city of Nicomedia and the rest of the cities, which also very earnestly addressed to me the same request on the same subject, namely, that none of the Christians should dwell in their cities, I was obliged to answer in a friendly manner, because all the former Emperors observed the same thing carefully and because to the gods themselves, by whom all men and the very administration of public affairs are maintained, it was pleasing that I should confirm such a petition as they were making on behalf of the worship of their deity.

Therefore, although letters were sent very specially to your Devotion before the present time, and it was similarly commanded by ordinances that nothing harsh should be done against provincials who desired to preserve such custom, but that people should deal with them with indulgence and moderation, nevertheless that they may not suffer insolence or extortions at the hands of the *beneficiarii* or any others at all, I have accordingly decided by this letter also to remind your Firmness that you should bring the provincials to the recognition of the worship of the gods rather by flattery and exhortations. Consequently, if any one should of his own accord decide that he had to recognize the worship of the gods, it is proper to welcome such people; but if any should wish to follow their own worship, you should leave it to their own choice. For this reason your Devotion must observe what has been commanded to you, and no person should have the authority to distress our provincials with insults and extortions, since, as we have written above, it is proper to recall our provincials to the worship of the gods rather with exhortations and flatteries. In order that this our order may come to the knowledge of all our provincials, you must publish my command in an ordinance made public by yourself.

54

The date of this letter to Sabinus is naturally uncertain, and it would be uncertain even without the doubts cast upon the identity of the "most perfect law". It can nevertheless be safely attributed to the winter of 312 and 313 A.D.,[65] or more likely to the early months of 313 A.D. All these communications between Constantine and Licinius on the one hand, and Maximinus Daia on the other, must of course, have taken place before Maximinus Daia's incursion into Licinius' territory.[66]

Still in the spirit of Galerius' edict of 311 A.D., this rescript to Sabinus grants a very grudging relaxation of the persecution and freedom of worship. Just like Galerius, too, Maximinus Daia is justifying earlier persecutions of those who had 'deserted the worship of their gods.' The facts that this rescript goes beyond simply granting freedom of worship for the Christians and that it guarantees it for all others as well[67] may very well echo a similar guarantee in the Edict of Milan.

It is clear, however, that Maximinus Daia issued this guarantee because he was forced to do so by Constantine's order, and his unwillingness is evident in the ambivalent character of the rescript. Christians must have remembered how, about a year earlier, they had been deceived by another rescript issued by Maximinus Daia through the same Sabinus.[68] Eusebius duly recalls this,[69] and adds that Christians were this time not deceived and dared not assemble for worship, despite the guarantee of this latest rescript.

That Maximinus Daia was not sincere and only playing for time became clear when he invaded Licinius' territory by crossing the straits. Eusebius,[70] and especially Lactantius,[71] give detailed descriptions of the aggression (taking place while Licinius was still at Milan with Constantine); of Maximinus Daia's subsequent defeat on April 30, 313 A.D. at the *Campus Serenus*;[72] then, of the flight of Maximinus Daia to the Taurus; of his death, which was, however, preceded both by his confession of Christ and his publication

65. Jones, *op. cit.* 87.
66. See e.g. Wittig, *op. cit.* 34.
67. Eusebius, *H.E.* IX, ixA, 6; ixA, 8.
68. *Ibid.* IX, i, 1-6.
69. *Ibid.* IX, ixA, 10-12.
70. *Ibid.* IX, x, 2-15.
71. *De mort. pers.* 45, 2-49, 7.
72. Or, *Ergenus?*

of an edict giving complete and unreserved freedom of religion and restoring confiscated property to the Church in the spirit of the Edict of Milan:[73]

We trust that no one is unaware, but also that every man when he recalls the events will fully realise that we by every means and continually take thought for the good of our provincials and wish to grant them such things as can best accomplish what are expedient for all, all things that are profitable and advantageous to their community, and such as are in harmony with the interest of the public and in accord with the opinions of every one of them. When, therefore, before the present time, it became manifest to our knowledge that, under the pretext that the most divine Diocletian and Maximian, our fathers, had ordered that the assemblies of the Christians be abolished, many extortions and robberies were committed by the officials, and that this, as time went on, was increasingly practiced against the provincials – and we most eagerly desire that proper care should be taken of them – while their personal properties were being destroyed, last year we addressed letters to the governors of all the provinces and laid down the law that if anyone wished to follow such custom or the same observance of worship, he should persist unimpeded in his purpose, and that he should not be hindered or prevented by anyone, and that they should have ample opportunity to do, without any fear and suspicion, as they please. But even now it could not escape our notice that some of the judges wrongly interpreted our orders, and were instrumental in that our people had doubts concerning our commands, and caused them to go rather hesitantly to those religious observances which were pleasing to them.

In order, therefore, that for the future all suspicion or uncertainty arising from their fear should be removed, we have decreed that this ordinance be published, so that it may be manifest to all that those who wish to follow this sect and worship are permitted, by virtue of this our bounty, as each of them wishes or finds it to his liking, to join the worship which they choose to make their religious observance. Permission has also been given that they build the Lord's houses. Moreover that our bounty may be even greater, we have also decided to decree that if any houses and lands, which formerly happened to belong by right to the Christians, became, by the order of our fathers, the lawful property of the treasury or were seized by any city, we have given orders that all these things, even though they may have been sold or given away as gifts, be restored to the Christians by their former right, so that in this also all may take notice of our faithfulness and solicitude.

73. Eusebius, *H.E.* IX, x, 7-11.

That the battle was between the enemies and protagonists of Christianity is made amply clear by Lactantius[74] when he attributes Maximinus Daia a vow to Jupiter for the eradication of Christianity if he helped him to victory, and relates that an angel gave Licinius the following prayer to be recited by his soldiers before the battle itself:[75]

Highest God, we pray Thee. Holy God, we pray Thee. We command all justice to Thee. We command our safety to Thee. We command our empire to Thee. It is through Thee that we live. It is through Thee that we become victorious and happy. Highest God, Holy God, hear our prayers. We stretch out our arms towards Thee. Hear us, Holy God, Highest God.

The publication by Maximinus Daia of his edict on behalf of the Christians, not quite a year after his campaign against them climaxed some time in June 312 A.D.,[76] may be confidently dated to May 313 A.D., *i.e.* a date prior to Licinius' own publication of his version of the Edict of Milan on June 13, 313 A.D.[77]

Thus after the description of the elimination of Maximinus Daia, Eusebius could confidently declare that Constantine and Licinius had an undisputed control of the Roman Empire.[78]

The peace of the Christians appeared to be assured enough.

74. *De mort. pers.* 46, 2-10.
75. *Ibid.* 46, 6.
76. See Eusebius, *H.E.* IX, x, 12.
77. Lactantius, *De mort. pers.* 48.
78. *H.E.* IX, xi, 8 (the end).

THE DONATIST SCHISM AND CONSTANTINE: HIS ZEAL FOR THE HOUSE OF THE LORD

Constantine could hear early enough the rumblings of what soon became known as the Donatist Schism, for in a letter[1] concerning his grant of almost unlimited sums to the Church he was warning Caecilian, the Bishop of Carthage, against certain people of unstable character who were trying to lead people away from the holy Catholic Church, and was also telling the Bishop to go to the Governor Anullinus for proper action should these turbulent people persist in their "insane designs." In another letter,[2] the Emperor informs the governor himself of his freeing the Catholic clergy of all free public services, and warns him to extend this privilege only to the clergy of the Catholic Church under the Bishop Caecilian.

"Donatist" reaction to being excluded from these Imperial benefices and power was swift. The Emperor soon received from the Governor Anullinus the following letters,[3] dated April 15, in the year 313 A.D.:

> After I received and communicated your majesty's ordinances to Caecilian and those who serve under him and are called clerics, my devotion had them entered among the records of my humility and, since they appeared to be completely freed by your majesty's indulgence from all public duties, I urged them that, with unity restored by common consent, and the sanctity of Catholic law safeguarded, they devote themselves with due reverence to divine service. But after a few days certain persons showed up with a multitude of people united with them, who thought that they had to speak against Caecilian and offered to "my reverence" a sealed packet (of documents) and an unsealed petition and strongly requested that I send them straight to the one sacred and venerable court of your divinity. My humility has seen to it

1. Eusebius, *H.E.* X, vi, 1-5.
2. *Ibid.* X, vii, 1-2.
3. Augustine, *Ep.* 88, 2.

58

that these were forwarded to you, so that your majesty may examine everything, with Caecilian remaining in his position and the minutes of the hearing(s)
recorded. Forwarded are two documents, one sealed in a leather pouch with
the title: "petition of the catholic church concerning the charges against
Caecilian, handed in by the party of Majorinus," and the other without seal,
attached to the same leather pouch. Given on the fifteenth of April at
Carthage during the third consulship of Constantine Augustus.

The "petition" mentioned in and attached to this letter ran like
this:[4]

We pray you, most excellent emperor, since you are of a righteous stock, and
your father did not with the other emperors follow the policy of persecution,
and Gaul is immune from this crime; whereas there are disputes between us
and the other bishops of Africa, we pray that your piety may order judges to
be given to us from Gaul. Given by Lucianus, Dignus, Nasutius, Capito,
Fidentius and the rest of the bishops of the party of Donatus.

Clearly, the Emperor was being kept informed, and, as has been
seen, was fully aware of the schism even at this very early stage of
splitting the so-called Donatists away from the orthodox Catholics
of the Christian Church in Africa.

The origin of this schism, historically speaking, goes back to the
Great Persecution.[5] Diocletian's, or rather the First Tetrarchy's
so-called first edict of persecution was issued in Nicomedia on
February 23, 303 A.D. and some time later it arrived and was also
published in Carthage and Numidia as well as in other parts of the
Roman Empire. It required the Christians to surrender their
Sacred Scriptures and it probably prescribed, among others, the
destruction of Christian places of assembly. Documents show that
many Christians, mainly clergy, became *traditores*, persons who
had surrendered Sacred Scriptures or other sacred objects; also
that others resisted the edict's order at the cost of much suffering
and even of their lives; and that there were also those who followed

4. Optatus, I, 22. The genuineness of this document is denied by O. Seeck,
"Quellen und Urkunden über die Anfänge des Donatismus," *Zschr. f. Kirchen-
gesch.* 10 (1889) 505-568; esp. 550 f.; "Urkundenfälschungen des 4. Jhun-
derts," *Zschr. f. Kirchengesch.* 30 (1909) 214 ff.; but see H. Kraft, *Kaiser
Konstantins religiöse Entwicklung* (Tübingen, 1955) 33 ff.
5. For a short and clear historical summary of the antecedents see A.H.M.
Jones, *Constantine and the Conversion of Europe* (London, 1968) 104-107;
W.H.C. Frend, *The Donatist Church* (Oxford U.P., 1952) 1-24.

a course between these two by going into hiding, and, perchance, offering heretical or even secular literature to the authorities for destruction.

Mensurius, the Bishop of Carthage and the Metropolitan of all the Africa, took the evasive course of going into hiding, taking the Sacred Scriptures with him and leaving behind texts other than sacred to satisfy, if necessary, the secular authorities carrying out the first edict's prescriptions. Secundus the Bishop of Tigisis and the Metropolitan of Numidia did not follow this middle course but, as he later claimed, refused to comply with the edict's commands.

In the meantime Bishop Mensurius died and when, during the rule of Maxentius, it was made possible, it was decided to elect a successor to him. A supporter and an arch-deacon of the late Mensurius, Caecilian became the chief candidate to be the successor of the dead bishop of Carthage. But, to complicate matters, Caecilian had many enemies and one of these was Lucilla, a rich woman, whom Caecilian had tactlessly and unwisely offended. Furthermore, the Numidian bishops, led by Secundus, for one reason or another – but apparently for his being a loyal supporter of Mensurius – did not support Caecilian.

Nevertheless, Caecilian was elected by a few bishops of the neighbourhood, and then accepted by the clergy and the people, but this election had an apparent flaw: it took place before the Numidian bishops arrived. Nevertheless Caecilian was then consecrated bishop by Felix, the bishop of a small place called Aptunga.

Caecilian's personal character being impeccable, the Numidian bishops, indignant that they had been left out of the process of election, refused upon arrival to acknowledge Caecilian's consecration, claiming that he had been consecrated by a *traditor*, one who had surrendered Sacred Scripture for destruction. At this point, Caecilian, unnecessarily and foolishly, offered the Numidian bishops to be re-consecrated by them, which they, naturally but inconsistently, refused to do for Caecilian. Declaring Caecilian's consecration to be invalid, they then elected one of Lucilla's favourites, one called Majorinus. Lucilla's great wealth is reported to have influenced this election.

After this the African Church was divided into two camps, one acknowledging the Bishop Caecilian, the other the Bishop

Majorinus. The first enjoyed the recognition of Rome but the second did not. The schismatics, however, did not care for the recognition of Rome. Their real interests seemed to be elsewhere.

Constantine's unbridled munificence and exclusive support of the Holy and Catholic Church, as has been seen, had the effect of making the schismatics to want the recognition of the most generous emperor, and this is how Constantine happened to receive the April 15, 313 A.D. letter and other communications from the governor of Africa. Angry[6] or not, Constantine agreed to humour the schismatics, but rejected their spirit of separation from the Bishop of Rome. He appointed three Gallic bishops, but it was the Bishop of Rome whom he asked to be the judge, with the assistance of the three Gallic bishops. Some modern scholars[7] wax emotional by pointing out 'the great historical moment' when Christian Church appeals to the Emperor to make decisions in spiritual matters. This shows either a pitiful misunderstanding or a partisan 'shortsightedness' on the part of these scholars, since they 'forget' that it was the schismatics who ran to the secular authority. It is equally unjust to say[8] that the Emperor was always pushing himself forward as a negotiator. Quite the contrary is true, for, very correctly, the Emperor Constantine, we have seen already, left the matter to the Bishop of Rome to decide. This is what he wrote to Pope Miltiades:[9]

Constantine Augustus to Miltiades, bishop of the Romans, and to Marcus. Since the several attached documents have been sent to me by his Excellency Anullinus, proconsul of Africa, in which it is implied that Caecilian, the bishop of the city of Carthage, is being accused on many matters by some of his colleagues in Africa; and since it seems to me to be an exceedingly serious matter that in these provinces, which the Divine Providence has voluntarily handed over to my Devotion together with their great multitude of people, the population should be found continually engaged in as it were forming divisions over trivial matters, I have decided that Caecilian himself, with ten bishops who appear to accuse him and ten others whom he himself

6. As suggested by Optatus, I, 23.
7. Jones, *op. cit.* 103; Frend, *op. cit.* 147; R. MacMullen, *Constantine* (London, 1970) 105; *et al.*
8. As A. Alföldi, *The Conversion of Constantine and Pagan Rome* (Oxford U.P., 1960) 50, does.
9. Eusebius, *H.E.* X, v, 18-20.

may pick as necessary for his own cause, should sail to Rome, in order that he may there be heard, as you may find fitting to the most sacred law, in the presence of yourselves and also of Recticius and Maternus and Marinus, your colleagues, whom I have ordered to hasten to Rome for this purpose. In order, however, that you may be able to have the fullest knowledge of all these matters, I have attached to my letter copies of the documents sent to me by Anullinus, and have dispatched them to your above-mentioned colleagues. On receiving them your Reverence will decide by what method the aforesaid case must be most carefully examined and justly terminated, since it does not escape your Diligence that I pay such great respect to the lawful Catholic Church that I wish that you leave behind no schism or division at all in any place. May the Divinity of the Great God preserve you for many years, dearest sir.

Perhaps unexpectedly, the Pope Miltiades went far beyond Constantine's suggestions, for he turned the affair into a much wider Church Council[10] by adding fifteen Italian bishops to the three Gallic bishops, and convened them on October 2, 313 A.D. in the Lateran house of Fausta.

Since Majorinus, the rival of Caecilian, had died in the meantime, another rival bishop, Donatus, was elected, who then gave his name to the schism and the movement which continued its separate existence for a very long time. In fact, Bishop Donatus appears to have been present with his party at this Council of Rome. This Council of nineteen bishops, then examined the case of Donatus and Caecilian, and then gave judgement in favour of the Bishop Caecilian. The following judgement was passed against Donatus by each of the bishops: that he confessed that he had rebaptized and laid his hands on fallen bishops, a thing foreign to the Church. The witnesses brought forward by Donatus admitted that they had nothing to say against Caecilian. Thus Caecilian was confirmed in his position as Bishop of Carthage by the Pope and the other eighteen bishops.

From a letter Constantine sent to Chrestus, the Bishop of Syracuse, we learn that the Donatists did not accept the decision of the Pope and the Council of Rome, and that they *appealed to the Emperor Constantine himself*, complaining that only a few persons had expressed their opinions and decisions, and that

10. N.H. Baynes, "Constantine the Great and the Christian Church," *Proceedings of the British Academy* 15 (1929) 349, notes 44; 45; *et al.*

these had not examined all the matters accurately and had been hasty in pronouncing their judgment. In this letter to the Bishop of Syracuse, the Emperor tells the Bishop that he has called a much larger council of bishops that was to take place in Arles, and that he should be there by August 1, (314 A.D.). The full text of the letter is as follows:[11]

Constantine Augustus to Chrestus, bishop of the Syracusans. Already on an earlier occasion, when some in a frivolous and perverted manner began to separate themselves in the matter of the worship of the holy and heavenly Power and the Catholic religion, I, wishing to cut short such discussions on their part, had given order to the effect that, after certain bishops were sent from Gaul, and also those of the opposing parties, who stubbornly and constantly spoke in public against each other, were summoned from Africa, in order that in the presence of the bishop of Rome the question which appeared to be the object of dispute might through their presence receive a correct solution as a result of a complete and careful examination of the matter. But since, as it happens, some forgetful both of their own salvation and the reverence that is due to the most holy religion, even now do not cease to prolong their personal hatreds, being unwilling to conform to the judgement already passed, and declaring that it was only a few persons who expressed their opinions and decisions, or that in addition these, without first having accurately examined all these matters that ought to have been looked into, hastened to pronounce their judgement too speedily and precipitately, with the result of all this that it has come to pass that even those very persons, who ought to have among them brotherly and unanimous harmony, are separated from each other in a shameful, or rather in an abominable fashion, and give to those people whose dispositions are unfavourable to this most holy worship a pretext for scoffing, therefore it has become my obligation to see to it that this affair which ought to have ceased through a voluntary agreement, after the judgement already pronounced, may finally now come to an end in the presence of many. Therefore we have ordered very many bishops from various and very numerous places to come together in the city of Arles by the first day of August, and I judged it good to write to you that you take a public vehicle from Latronianus, the most illustrious corrector of Sicily, take to yourself any two persons of the second rank, whom you yourself may decide good to choose, take also with you three servants able to serve you on the road, and present yourself at the above-mentioned place by that same day, so that both by your Reverence and the unanimous and general agreement of the rest of the bishops assembled,

11. Eusebius, *H.E.* X, v, 21-24.

this quarrel also, which has due to shameful rivalries miserably persisted up till now, when all has been heard that will have to be said by people presently separated from each other, whom we likewise ordered to be present, may, even though tardily, be restored to proper worship and faith and brotherly harmony. May the Almighty God preserve you in good health for many years.

Constantine also sent a letter to an 'Aelafius',[12] the apparently Christian Deputy-Prefect of Africa, in which the Emperor instructed him to make careful arrangements for the transportation of the Bishop Caecilian, his party, and their opponents as well, all the way to Arles. The letter:[13]

Constantine Augustus to Aelafius. Indeed, already before this time, when it was brought to my knowledge that several persons in our Africa, with mad fury and amidst groundless accusations against each other concerning the observance of the most Holy Catholic law, began to have divisions, I decreed that, in order to put an end to this sort of dissension, both Caecilian the Bishop of Carthage, against whom in particular the greatest possible number of people petitioned me, and also some of those, who believed that certain things were to be charged against him, should present themselves in the city of Rome. I also ordered certain bishops from the Gauls to go to our above-mentioned city of Rome, so that, by the soundness of their lives and their praiseworthy habits, they as well as the seven bishops of the same communion and that of the city of Rome, and their assessors, might bring the matter that seems to have been stirred up, to its due end. Now they brought to my knowledge, by their written records, everything that had been done in their presence, affirming in addition by word of mouth that their verdict was rendered with a fair consideration of facts, and stating that rather those who decided to make certain charges against Caecilian, were guilty in the affair, so much so that after giving this verdict they forbade them to return to Africa. Therefore, on account of all this and an evaluation of the circumstances, I hoped that a fitting end had been made to all insubordinations and contentions. But when I read your "Reverence's" letters, which your Seriousness had deemed as necessary to send to Nicasius and the rest concerning the same false pretences, I plainly recognized that they would not place before their

12. Baynes, "Constantine the Great etc.," *op. cit.* 414, n. 46, sees no need for the emendation of "Aelafius" to "Ablabius," while Alföldi, *op. cit.* 49, accepts "Ablabius"; H. Kraft, *op. cit.* 182, rejects both "Aelafius" and "Ablabius," and suggests as a plausible choice the name of Aelius Paulinus, who was, indeed, the Deputy-Prefect of Africa about this time.

13. Optatus, *App.* III.

eyes either considerations of their own salvation or, what is more, the reverence that is due to Almighty God, since indeed they persist in doing what not only leads to their shame and infamy, but also gives an opportunity for scoffing to people who have long been known to turn their minds away from a most holy religion such as this. For it is appropriate for you to know that some of these men came, asserting that the same Caecilian is less worthy of the ministry of the most Holy Catholic religion, and in answer to my reply to them that they keeρ ιying it to no purpose, since in fact the matter had been terminated in the city of Rome by capable and most excellent bishops, they considered it necessary to answer with a steady obstinacy that the whole case had not been heard, but that the same bishops preferred to shut themselves up in a certain place and give judgement according to their own conscience. Therefore, since I perceived that these matters, so many and important, were being persistently protracted by dissensions, so that it appears that they cannot be ended in any way unless the same Caecilian and some of those who owe him concord, but also some of those who are opposed to Caecilian and are making a schism against him, come to the town of Arles for judgement, I deemed it proper to impose upon your carefulness to see to it, as soon as you receive this letter of mine, that the above-mentioned Caecilian with some of those whom he shall personally choose – but some from each of the provinces of Byzacium, Tripolis, the Numidias and the Mauritanias, who will have to bring with them some of their clergy of their own choice – and some as well of those who are opposed to Caecilian shall, after they were provided with public transportation through Africa and Mauritania, sail over by a short route to the Hispanias. Then, you shall also, similarly provide each of these bishops with individual travel provisions, so that they may arrive at the above-mentioned place by the first day of August. You will, without delay, impress on them their duty to make arrangements, before they depart, so that, in their absence, there may be appropriate discipline and there may, perchance, arise no sedition or strife amongst any of them – a thing that tends to cause the greatest scandal. Once full information is gathered about what is hidden let there be an end to this matter. For when all are present, those things which are now known as contentious should all with a good cause receive a timely conclusion, so that they might forthwith be terminated and laid to rest. Since in my court they are certain that you also are a worshipper of the most High God, I confess to your Seriousness that I consider it by no means allowable that contentions an quarrels of this kind should be overlooked by us, because perchance as a result of these the Highest Divinity may be aroused not only against the human race but also against me personally, to whose care by His heavenly will He entrusted the government of all earthly affairs, and He may be so far aroused as to take some untoward step. For I shall be able to feel really and completely secure and always to hope for the fullest prosperity and happiness from the most willing kindness of the most mighty God, only, when I see all

65

worshipping the most holy God in the proper cult of the Catholic religion with harmonious brotherhood of worship.

It is clear from these last two letters how Constantine really felt about the current situation, and about schisms in general in the Catholic Church. Just as clearly, these two letters show that if ever there was one who cared for the true welfare of the Christian Church, and, particularly, for its unity, and who truly believed in it with all his heart, it was Constantine himself. He sincerely associates the welfare of all humanity, of the whole Empire, and that of his own person with the happy unity of the Holy Catholic Church! In fact, he regards as being against Divine Law the over-looking of quarrels and contentions that were festering in the Catholic Church at that time. Therefore, since he received his power from the Supreme God, he believed that it was his duty to do his utmost for the welfare of the Catholic Church, for, other-wise, he might himself feel the wrath of God, would not be really secure and could not hope for prosperity and happiness.

The Council of Arles met, as scheduled, on August 1, 314 A.D. It confirmed the verdict of the Council of Rome and thus Caecilian was once more confirmed in his position as the Bishop of Carthage. The Council also produced twenty-two canons, and among them it renounced the baptizing of once fallen but reconciled Christians; it declared ordinations even by a *traditor* as valid, and it also pre-scribed a strict procedure for deciding whether anyone was a *traditor*. All these decisions and some others were reported by the Council of Arles to Pope Silvester, their duly recognized head:[14]

To the most beloved Pope Silvester: Marinus, Acratius, Natalis, Theodorus, Proterius, Vocius, Verus, Probatius, Caecilianus, Faustinus, Surgentius, Grego-rius, Reticius, Ambitausus, Termatius, Merocles, Pardus, Adelfius, Hibernius, Fortunatus, Aristasius, Lampadius, Vitalis, Maternus, Liberius, Gregorius, Crescens, Avitianus, Dafnus, Orantalis, Quintasius, Victor, Epictetus send endless greetings! Bound together by the common tie of charity and the unity of our Mother, the Catholic Church, and being brought to the City of Arles by the wish of the most faithful Emperor, we send you greetings from this place with the reverence which is your due, most glorious Pope. Here we have endured to the end men of unruly mind, both harmful and dangerous to our law and tradition, whom both the powerful authority of our God and

14. Optatus, *App.* IV.

66

tradition but also the rule of truth reject because there is no oderly system in their arguments nor do they possess any proper method of accusation or any proof. Therefore, by the judgement of God and of Mother Church, who knows and acknowledges her own children, they have been either condemned or rejected. And if only, most beloved Brother, you had thought it important enough to be present at this great spectacle. We certainly believe that a more severe sentence would have been delivered on them, and that our assembly would have rejoiced with a greater gladness, if you had been passing judgement together with us. But because you could not by any means withdraw from that region, where the Apostles hold court daily, and their blood unceasingly bears witness to the glory of God, it was still our opinion, dearest Brother, that we ought not only to discuss those matters, on account of which we had been summoned, but we decided that we should also look into our affairs, and because the provinces from which we have come here are different, and therefore there are various things taking place to which we think we ought to pay attention. Therefore we decided, in the presence of the Holy Spirit and His Angels, that from among the topics which concern everyone of us we make decisions with a view to the present state of peace. We also decided that before all else these should be written to you, who hold the greater jurisdictions, so that they may be, especially through your instrumentality, communicated to all. As for our decisions, we append them to this writing of our insignificance. Of course, the topic concerning the usefulness of our life had to be discussed in the first place, so that He who, all by himself died for the many and rose from the dead, might be honoured at the proper time by all with such a religious mind that divisions and dissensions might not arise at such a great religious observance. We resolve, therefore, that the Passover of the Lord be observed throughout the whole world on the same day. Also, concerning those who were ordained ministers in any places whatever, we resolve that they stay in the same places. Concerning those who throw down their arms in time of peace, we have decreed that they be kept from communion. Concerning charioteers who belong to the Faithful, we have decreed that, as long as they continue to drive, they be debarred from communion. Concerning theatrical players, we decreed that as long as they act, they be debarred from communion. Concerning those who are stricken by illness and wish to believe, we decreed that hand be laid upon them. Concerning governors who belong to the Faithful and reach the governorship, we decreed that when they are moved to the office, they should indeed receive ecclesiastical letters of communion, but in such a way that in whatever places they perform their office, the bishops of these places should watch over them, and if they begin to act against discipline, they be then finally excluded from communion. We decreed similarly concerning those who wish to have office in the administration of the state. But concerning Africa, because they use their own law for the purpose of rebaptizing,

67

we decreed that if any heretic comes to the Church, they should question him about the Creed, and if they found that he had been baptized in the Father and the Son and the Holy Spirit, hands will only be laid upon him. But if questioned about the Creed, he does not name this Trinity in his answer, let him rightly be baptized, and the rest.

Then getting tired of the matter, he commanded all to return to their sees. Amen.

In the meantime, Constantine initiated his own investigation through an official inquiry as to whether, according to the Donatist claim, Felix, the Bishop of Aptunga, Caecilian's consecrating bishop, was in fact a *traditor.*

A somewhat worn and corrupt, but still sufficiently well pre-served manuscript clearly shows what really happened. This document is made up of the *Acts* of proceedings that took place, *first*, before Aelius Paulinus, the Deputy-Prefect of Africa, on August 19, 314 A.D., and, *then*, before Aelianus, Proconsul of Africa, acting on behalf of Verus, the current Deputy-Prefect of Africa, on February 15, 315 A.D. By the testimony of Alfius Caecilianus, one of the *duoviri* of Aptunga in 303 A.D., the year of the Imperial edict that ordered, *inter alia,* the handing over and the destruction of Christian Sacred Scriptures, it became clear that the document on the basis of which the Donatists pretended that Felix had been a *traditor* was in fact a childish fabrication of Ingentius, one of the Donatist crew. Here is the text of the records of this inquiry:[15]

The Acts of the Vindication of Felix, Bishop of Aptunga ... In the town of Aptunga, Gallienus the Duovir said: 'Since you are present, Caecilianus, listen to the letter of my lord, His Excellency Aelius Paulinus, deputy-prefect, and hear what he has deigned to command according to the letter addressed to us, which charges you, and the clerk you had at that time during your administration, and your recorder to make a declaration. But because the recorder of that time has died, you will have to bring with you all the acts of your administration in faithful compliance with the letter of this my Lord, and you will be obliged to travel to the town of Carthage. The Curator is present and it is in his presence that we charge you. What do you answer to this?'

Caecilianus said: 'As soon as you delivered to me the letter of His Excellency Aelius Paulinus, deputy-prefect, I, without delay, sent word to the clerk

15. Optatus, *App.* II.

Miccius that he should come and bring me the Acts made during that very time, and he ist still searching for them, understandably, since no small space of time has passed since I held the office of Duovir, actually, eleven years. For this reason, when he finds them I will obey a command of such great importance!'

The Duovir Gallienus said: 'It is in your interest to obey the command, for, you see, the command is Imperial.'

Caecilianus said: 'I am faithful to such a great command.'

Moreover, when, a short time later, the clerk Miccius came over, the Duovir Fuscius said: 'Have you too, Miccius, heard that you have to go with Caecilianus to the office of His Excellency the deputy-prefect, taking with you the records of that time? What do you say to this?'

Miccius answered: 'The magistrate, after the completion of his year of office, took home all his acts. I am searching ...'

And since he was searching, the Duovir Quintus Sisenna said: 'He has answered what the court has been inquiring.'[15a]

(The Inquiry before the Proconsul Aelianus:)

Apronianus said: 'If the magistrate had taken away all his acts, whence do we, after such a long time, obtain records which were at that time lost or destroyed?'

And, when he said this, the Proconsul Aelianus said: 'Both my questions and the answers of each person are contained in the acts.'

Agesilaus said: 'Besides, there are also other documents indispensable for this case. It is important that they be read.'

The Proconsul Aelianus said: 'Read in the hearing of Caecilianus, so that he may recognize whether he dictated it.'

Agesilaus read aloud:

'During the consulship of Volusianus and Annianus, on the nineteenth of August, in a lawsuit before Aurelius Didymus Spretius, priest of Jupiter the Best and the Highest, duovir of the splendid town of Carthage, Maximus said: "I speak in the name of the presbyters of the Christian people of the Catholic Rule. The case will have to be pleaded before the Supreme Emperors against Caecilian and Felix, who are trying with all their power to assail superiority of that same Rule. Documentary proofs of the charges against them in this matter are being collected. For when persecution was proclaimed against the Christians, that is, when they were ordered to offer sacrifice, hand over whatever Scriptures they might have, for burning, Felix, who was then Bishop of Aptunga, had given his consent for Scriptures to be handed over by the hand of Galatius that they might be consumed by fire. And at

---

15a. Here the text of one inquiry ends, and a later one before the Proconsul Aelianus begins or continues.

that time Alfius Caecilianus was a magistrate and it pleases you to see him here present. And since at that time it was his official duty to see to it that, in compliance with the proconsular order, all should sacrifice, and that, in accordance with the Imperial law, they hand over any Scriptures they might possess, I ask him, since he is here, and you see he is an old man and cannot go to the Imperial court, to make his deposition for records as to whether, according to the Acts held by him, he, as a result of a pact, authored a letter, and as to whether things what he stated in the letter are true, in order that the actions and the truthfulness of these persons may be ascertained at the Imperial trial".'

The Duovir Spretius said to Caecilianus who was standing by: 'Do you hear, what are the depositions in the Acts?'

Alfius Caecilianus said: 'I had gone to Zama to buy linen with Saturninus, and when we returned to the town, the Christians themselves sent to me and asked: "Has the Imperial order reached you?" I said: "No, but I have seen copies already, and at Zama and Furni I saw the churches being pulled down and the Scriptures being burned. Therefore, if you have any Scriptures, bring them out, that the Imperial command may be obeyed." Then they sent to the house of Felix the Bishop to take out the Scriptures from there, so that they could be burnt according to the Imperial order. So Galatius went with me to the place where they used to hold their prayer meetings. We took out the throne and the letters of greeting, and all the doors were burnt according to the Imperial order. And when we sent to the house of Felix the bishop, the town officials reported that he was away. And when, at a later time, there arrived Ingentius, the clerk of Augentius, with whom I served as aedile, I dictated this same colleague a letter for the same Bishop Felix.'

Maximus said: 'He is here, let this letter be shown him, so that he may recognize it.'

He answered: 'This is it.'

Maximus said: 'Since he has recognized his own letter, I shall read it, and ask that it be introduced in the Acts in full.'

And he read it aloud: "Caecilianus to his Father Felix, greetings. Since Ingentius met my colleague Augentius, his friend, and inquired whether, in accordance with the Imperial law, any Scriptures of your Rule had been burnt during the year when I was Duovir ... my friend Galatius, a follower of your Rule, publicly brought forth letters of greetings from the church. I wish you good health. This is the proof that the Christians and he who owns the official residence sent [you] to intercede with me, and that you said: "take away the key and take the rolls you will find on the throne and the books which you will find on the stone. Of course, see that your officials do not take the oil and wheat." And I said to you: "Do you not know that the very building in which the Scriptures are found is to be demolished?" And you said: "What are we to do then?" And I said to you: "Get one of your men to take them into the yard where you hold your prayers, and let them be put there. And I come with my officials and remove them." And we came there and removed them all according to the Imperial order."

Maximus said: 'Since the text of his letter, which he himself has acknowledged that he sent, has been read into the records, we ask that what he has said be part of the records.'

The Duovir Spretius said: 'What you have said is written down.'

Agesilaus said: 'He has examined the letter; he says that the last part which he has just now read is spurious.'

Caecilianus said: 'My Lord, I dictated up to this place where its says: "I wish you, my dearest Father, good health."'

Apronianus said: 'Those who have refused to be in harmony with the Catholic Church, have always acted falsely by resorting to terror, pretext, and irreligious mentality. For when Paulinus was here the deputy-prefect, a certain man without official position was suborned to play the part of messenger to go to those united in the Catholic Church for deceiving and terrorizing them. Thus, the plot has been discovered. For a false story was being concocted against the most faithful Bishop Felix, in order that it might appear that he had handed over and burnt the Scriptures. Indeed, Ingentius, since all this activity of his was directed against the holiness and religious faithfulness of Caecilian, was suborned to come with a letter purported to be from the Bishop Felix to Caecilianus the Duovir, and to pretend to him that he was commissioned by Felix. Let him give us the very words in which the story was concocted.'

The Proconsul Aelianus said: 'Tell us.'

Apronianus said: '"Tell," he said, "tell my friend Caecilianus that I took to my possession eleven sacred books of great value and because I have now to return them, say that you burnt them during the year of your magistracy, lest I should have to return them." On account of this, therefore, Ingentius must be questioned as to what extent this was invented and fabricated, and to what extent he wanted to trick his master into lying, so that he might bespatter Felix with infamy. Let him state by whom he was sent ... For he is the person who was sent by the opposite side as an ambassador throughout Mauritania and Numidia.'

To Ingentius, who was present there, the Procunsul Aelianus said: 'At whose bidding did you undertake to do these things that are being brought against you?'

Ingentius said: 'Where?'

The Proconsul Aelianus said: 'Since you pretend not to understand what you are asked, I will speak more plainly: Who sent you to the magistrate Caecilianus?'

Ingentius said: 'No one sent me.'

The Proconsul Aelianus said: 'How was it then that you came to the

71

magistrate Caecilianus?'

Ingentius said: 'When we arrived and the case of Maurus who purchased the episcopate for himself was being tried, Felix, the Bishop of Aptunga, came to the city to take a hand in it, and said: "Let no one communicate with him, because he committed a fraud." But I answered him: "Neither with you, nor with him, because you are a *traditor*." For I was grieved by the case of Maurus, a host of mine, since I had communicated with him when I was away from home, because I fled from the persecution. Afterwards I went to the country of Felix himself, taking with me three prebyters, so that they might see whether or not it was true that he had given up books.'

Apronianus said: 'It was not so. He went to Caecilianus. Ask Caecilianus.'

The Proconsul Aemilianus said to Caecilianus: 'How did Ingentius meet you?'

Caecilianus answered: 'He came to my home. I was taking a meal with the workmen; he came there and remained in the doorway. "Where is Caecilianus?" said he. I answered: "Here." I said to him: "What is it? Is everything all right?" "Yes," said he. I answered him: "If you are not averse to taking meal, come and eat." He said to me: "I will return." He came alone. He began with saying this to me: "My request is that you take the trouble and see whether any Scripture was burnt during the year when I was Duovir." I said to him: "You are troublesome to me, You are a man acting for someone else. Get out from here." And I chased him away from me. And he came there again, in the company of my colleague with whom I had been aedile. My colleague said to me: "Felix, our Bishop, sent the man in order that you might write him a letter, because he had received books of great value and is unwilling to return them. Write, therefore, that they were burnt in the year when you were Duovir." And I said: "Is this the honour of the Christians?"'

Ingentius said: 'My Lord, let Augentius also come here. I too hold a title of honour ...'

The Proconsul Aelianus said to Ingentius: 'You are being convicted under a different title.'

The Proconsul Aelianus said to an attendant: 'Get him ready.' And when he was made ready, the Proconsul Aelianus said: 'Let him be drawn up.' And when he was drawn up, the Proconsul Aelianus said to Caelilianus: 'How did Ingentius meet you?'

He answered: '"Our friend Felix" – so he spoke – "has sent me here that you should write to him since there is an abandoned man who owns some very valuable books which are in his possession and he is unwilling to return them. In order, therefore, that he may not take them back, write letter saying that they were burnt." And I said: "Is this the honour of a Christian?" And I began to rebuke him, but my colleague said: "Write to our friend Felix." And so I dictated the letter which is here in evidence as far as it was dictated by me.'

The Proconsul Aelianus said: 'Listen without fear to the reading of your letter. Take notice how far you dictated it.'

Agesilaus read it: ' "... I wish you, dearest Father, good health for many years'."

The Proconsul Aelianus said to Caecilianus: 'Did you dictate it up to this point?'

He answered: 'Up to this point, the rest is spurious.'

Agesilaus read it aloud: '" This is the proof that the Christians and he who owns the official residence sent (you) to intercede with me, and that you said: "Take away the key and take the rolls which you will find on the throne and the books which you will find on the stone. Of course, see that your officials do not take the oil and the wheat." And I said to you: "Do you not know that the very building in which the Scriptures are found is to be demolished?" And you said: "What are we to do then?" And I said to you: "Get one of your men take them into the yard where you hold your prayers, and let them be put there. And I come with my officials and remove them." And we came there and removed them all according to the Imperial order. Maximus said: 'Since the contents of his letter, which he himself said to have recognized and sent, has also been read into the records, we ask that this should be part of the records.' Spretius said: 'What you have said is written down.' Caecilianus answered: 'It is spurious from there, it is my letter up to this point where I said: "Farewell, dearest Father." ' '

The Proconsul Aelianus said: 'Who do you say added to the letter?'

Caecilianus said: 'Ingentius.'

The Proconsul Aelianus said: 'Your declaration is part of the records.'

The Proconsul Aelianus said to Ingentius: 'You will be tortured in order that you may not lie.'

Ingentius said: 'I did wrong. I did indeed add to this letter, because I was grieved on account of Maurus, my host.'

The Proconsul Aelianus said: '(Constantine) Maximus ever Augustus and Licinius, Caesars, deign to show favour to the Christians in such a way that they do not wish their discipline to be corrupted, but they rather want this religion to be observed and cultivated. Therefore, do not delude yourself into believing that, since you tell me that you are a worshipper of God, you cannot for this reason be tortured. You will be tortured that you may not tell lies, which is, it seems, foreign to Christians. And, for this reason, speak honestly, that you may not be tortured.'

Ingentius said: 'I have already confessed without torture.'

Aproninaus said: 'Be pleased to ask him by what authority, by what deception, by what madness he went around in all the Mauritanias and also the Numidias, and by what method he stirred up sedition against the Catholic Church.'

The Proconsul Aelianus said: 'Have you been to the Numidias?'

He answered: 'No, my Lord. Let one prove it.'

The Proconsul Aelianus said: 'Nor in Mauritania?'

He answered: 'I was there on business.'

Apronianus said: 'In this he also lies, my Lord, for to Mauritania one can get only through the Numidias, and he says he was in Mauritania, but not in Numidia.'

The Proconsul Aelianus said to Ingentius: 'What is your rank?'

Ingentius answered: 'I am a decurion of the Ziquenses.'

The Proconsul Aelianus said to an attendant: 'Lower him.'

When he was lowered, the Proconsul Aelianus said to Caecilianus: 'You have given false evidence.'

Caecilianus answered: 'No my Lord. Let him who wrote the letter appear; he is his friend; he will tel you to what point I dictated the letter.'

The Proconsul Aelianus said: 'Who is it whom you wish to come here?'

Caecilianus said: 'Augentius, with whom I was aedile. I can prove my case only through Augentius himself who wrote the letter. He can tell you to what point I dictated to him.'

The Proconsul Aelianus said: 'Is it then certain that the letter is falsified?'

Caecilianus answered: 'It is certain, my Lord. I do not lie, upon my life.'

The Proconsul Aelianus said: 'Since you held the office of Duovir in your country we must believe your words.'

Apronianus said: 'It is not unusual for them to do this. Besides, they added what they pleased to the Acts. This has been their ingenuous art.'

The Proconsul Aelianus said: 'Through the evidence of Caecilianus, who says that the Acts have been falsified, and that many additions have been made to this letter, the purpose of Ingentius in doing this is clear. Let him, therefore, be committed to prison. He is needed for a closer interrogation. On the other hand, it is clear that Felix the faithful Bishop had nothing to do with burning sacred writings, since no one was able to prove anything against him with regard to the charge that he had given up or burnt the most holy Scriptures. For through the previously written interrogation of all (witnesses) it is evident that no holy Scriptures were disclosed or damaged or burnt (by him). It is recorded in the Acts that Felix the holy Bishop neither was there nor was aware of, or ordered, any such thing to happen.'

Agesilaus said: 'What is your Lordship's order concerning these people, who came to provide your Lordship with evidence?'

The Proconsul Aelianus said: 'Let them return to their homes.'

Thus the Proconsul Aelianus declared Bishop Felix of Aptunga innocent of the charge of being a *traditor*, and sent Ingentius to prison for more examination.

Constantine, on being informed of the results of this inquiry, sends a letter to Probianus, the next proconsul of Africa, and orders that Ingentius be sent, under proper escort, to his court, to be a living proof to the Donatists that it is futile for them to try to resort to false pretences and, then, to appeal to his judgement, as they kept doing. The full text of this letter of Constantine to Probianus, the Governor of Africa,[16] is as follows:

The Emperors Constantine Maximus and Valerius Licinianus Licinius, Caesars, to Probianus the Proconsul of Africa. Aelianus, your predecessor, as long as his Excellency Verus, the Deputy-Prefect of Africa at that time, was incapacitated by ill-health, was officially acting on his behalf and, while acting in this capacity, he rightly decided that he should, among other matters, submit to his own investigation and disposal that bussiness or hateful affair that seems to have been stirred up concerning Caecilian, a Bishop of the Catholic Church. For after he had summoned to his presence the Centurion Superius, and Caecilianus, a magistrate of the people of Aptunga, and Saturnius, a former Curator, and Calidius the Younger, Curator of the same city, and Solus, a public slave of the same city, he gave a proper hearing, so that, although it was objected against Caecilian that the episcopate had reportedly been conferred on him by Felix, who was, it seems, accused of handing over and burning sacred Scriptures, the innocence of Felix was, as a result proved. Finally, when Maximus contended that Ingentius, a decurion of the town of the Ziquenses, had falsified the letter of Caecilianus, a former Duovir, this Ingentius, as we read it in the Acts in my possession, was drawn up and escaped being tortured only because he maintained that he was a decurion of the town of the Ziquenses. Therefore, we want you to dispatch this same Ingentius, under proper escort, to my, Constantine Augustus', court, in order that those who are in my presence and never cease appealing, day in day out, may hear and be actually present while it is proved and demonstrated to them that it is futile for them to wish to create prejudice against the Bishop Caecilian and to rise violently against him. For so it will come about that such quarrels will be abandoned, as they should be, and the people will without any dissension devote themselves to their own religion with due reverence.

In another letter, Constantine writes to the bishops assembled at Arles to inform them that the Donatists have again appealed to him:[17]

Constantine Augustus to the Catholic Bishops, his dearest Brothers, greetings! The ever-loyal and incomprehensible faithfulness of our God does not in any

16. Augustine, *Ep.* 88, 4.
17. Optatus, *App.* V. About the genuineness of this letter, see H. Kraft, *op. cit.* 185 ff.

way allow human nature to wander unduly long in darkness, nor does it suffer the hateful dispositions of some people to prevail so far as not grant, by at last opening to them through its most splendid light the word to salvation, that they return to the rule of righteousness. In fact, I know this by many examples, I make this same conclusion from my own case. For at first there were in me things which seemed to lack righteousness, and I did not think that a power above saw any thoughts which I was harbouring in the secret places of my heart. Honestly, what fortune did these thoughts, being such as I have mentioned, should have received? Surely one abounding with every calamity. But Almightly God, sitting on high, has granted me what I did not deserve. Certainly now the blessings which He has granted in His heavenly kindness to me His servant cannot be told or counted, most holy Bishops of Christ the Saviour, dearest Brothers. Therefore, I rejoice, indeed, I do rejoice in a special way, because at last, thanks to a most equitable inquiry just held, you have recalled to a better hope and fortune those whom the malice of the devil seemed by his wretched persuasion to have turned from the most glorious light of the Catholic Law. O truly victorious providence of Christ the Saviour, that He was mindful even of those who, already deserting from the truth, and in a way taking up arms against it, joined themselves to the pagans. For, if they even now are willing with unadulterated faith to offer their obedience to the most holy Law, they will be able to understand how greatly they had been cared for by the will of God. I was, my most holy Brothers, to tell the truth, hoping that this would be found even in those who by nature had in themselves the greatest hardness of heart. But upright judgement has not been profitable to them, nor has the gracious Divinity entered their dispositions. In truth, not undeservedly will the indulgence of Christ withdraw from those, whose character is clearly and manifestly such, that we conclude that they are hated even by the heavenly providence, which keeps acting against them with such great fury, while they with incredible arrogance convince themselves of things which must not be spoken or heard and they are rejecting your upright judgement just delivered, through which, as if by heavenly providence, I have learnt that they are appealing to my judgement. What force of malice is persisting in their hearts! How often have they already been rebuffed by myself in an answer they fully deserved for their most shameless approaches to me. If they would only have kept this before their eyes, they would in no way have taken this very step. They appeal to my judgement, who am myself waiting for the judgement of Christ. For I say, and this is the truth, that the judgement of Bishops ought to be regarded as if the Lord Himself were sitting in judgement. For these may not believe, nor proclaim anything, except what they have been taught by the teaching authority of Christ. Why then, as I in truth have said, are malicious people influenced by the favours of the devil? They seek the things of this world, abandoning heavenly things. What frenzied audacity! As is customarily done in the lawsuits of the pagans, they have interposed an appeal. For the pagans sometimes, to avoid the lower courts, where justice can be quickly obtained, customarily prefer to have recourse to higher courts by interposing an appeal. What shall I say of these detractors of the law, who, rejecting the judgement of Heaven, have thought it fit to demand mine? Is this the way how they think of Christ the Saviour? Behold, they are now betrayers! Behold, they, of their own accord, have themselves betrayed their wicked deeds, without any rather severe investigation! What do those feel about humanity, who, like monsters, made an attack on God Himself?

Although, my dearest Brothers, these things seem to have been detected in them, nevertheless to you, who follow the way of the Saviour, show patience by still granting them a free choice to determine for themselves what they ought to choose. And yet if you see them persevere in this same course, set out forthwith with those whom the Lord has deemed worthy of His worship, and return to your own sees, and remember me, so that our Saviour may always have mercy on me. Otherwise, I have directed my men to conduct immediately these abominable deceivers of religion to my court, there to live, and there to see before them something worse than death. I have also sent a suitable letter to him who holds the office of deputy-prefect in Africa, ordering him to dispatch without delay to my court all and every person showing the characteristics of this madness, lest in the future, under so great a glory of our God, such things may be done by these very persons as could excite the greatest anger of the heavenly Providence. May Almighty God keep you safe, my dearest Brothers, through the ages, in answer to my prayers and yours.

Was the appeal by the Donatists made in good faith?[18] Constantine at least did not think so. In this letter, the Emperor expresses his belief that the Devil has turned them away from the most glorious light of the Catholic faith. He upbraids the schismatics for their arrogance in appealing from the right decision of the Council of Arles to his personal judgement! Nevertheless, he encourages the bishops of the Council of Arles to "show patience" in the spirit of the Saviour by granting the schismatics "a free choice to determine for themselves what they ought to choose." Finally, Constantine tells the bishops to return to their sees, and he informs them that he has ordered his Deputy-Prefect of Africa to send to his court all persons showing the characteristics of the Donatist "madness," and that he has ordered that "these abominable deceivers of religion," i.e. the Donatist bishops, be brought to his

18. As was suggested by Jones, op. cit. 116.

court, "there to live, and there to see before them something worse than death." Was all this nothing more than blustering hot air?

The Emperor Constantine's preoccupation was soon interrupted by war – with Licinius.[19] Licinius was probably from the beginning jealous of young Constantine's ascendency to the position of the Senior Augustus. It would seem that Bassianus, Constantine's newly appointed Caesar and the husband of Anastasia, Constantine's half-sister, was involved in a conspiracy with Senecio, a half-brother of his, who was in the service of Licinius. Constantine had Bassianus put to death and demanded the extradition of Senecio. Licinius promptly refused and then both Augustuses prepared for war. In the late summer of 314 A.D., Constantine marched to the East. The first battle was at Cibalae between the rivers Save and Drave, in October 314, and Licinius, despite his numerical superiority, was heavily defeated. The beaten Augustus withdrew, concentrated his forces around Hadrianople, and then proposed peace. Efforts for peace failed, and then a second battle was fought and, this being undecided, further peace talks were more successful. According to the terms of this peace conference Licinius retained only Thrace in Europe, all his other European territories coming under the rule of Constantine.

Constantine returned to Rome on July 21, 315 A.D. From a letter he soon wrote to the Donatist bishops it is clear that he had given permission to these bishops to return to Africa, and that he had at the same time promised to rehear their case right there – in Africa. But he obviously changed his mind:[20]

> Constantine Augustus to the [Donatist] Bishops. A few days ago, it is true, I decided that, in accordance with your request, you should go back to Africa, so that the whole case, which according to you, is due against Caecilian, should be investigated there by my friends whom I would choose, and duly come to its conclusion. But I have been thinking about the matter for a long time and, while, not without a good cause, I was pondering it, I decided that the best thing to do is – since I know that some of your party are quite turbulent and obstinately have hardly any respect for an appropriate verdict and for finding the honest truth, and that for this reason it might come about that if the case is investigated on the spot, the affair is not terminated as it

19. For a simple narrative of the story, see Jones, *op. cit.* 126-128.
20. Optatus, *App.* VI.

should and as the business of searching for the truth demands, and that through your excessive obstinacy something happens that may displease the heavenly Divinity and would be greatly embarrassing to my good name, which I desire always to preserve spotless, – I have decided, as I said, that Caecilian should rather, as previously arranged, come here, and I believe that he will, in compliance with my letter, soon come here. But I promise you that if in his presence you prove by yourselves anything on one single charge or crime against him, I shall regard this as if all the accusations which you bring against him were proved. May Almighty God grant us perpetual safety.

Thus still detaining these Donatists, Constantine apparently summoned Caecilian, and promised these Donatists that if in his presence they proved anything on one single charge or crime, he would regard all the accusations against Caecilian as proved. It must have been at approximately this time that Constantine heard about the results of the investigations before the high magistrates of Africa, and of the conviction of Ingentius for forging a document incriminating the Bishop Felix of Aptunga as a *traditor*. Somehow Caecilian did not arrive in Rome in time to meet Constantine, whom we find on October 19, 315 A.D. in Milan. However, Caecilian finally arrived at Milan and Constantine was apparently ready to retry the whole case. Claiming however that the case had gone against Caecilian by default, the Donatists tried to escape,[21] but Constantine had them arrested and brought to Milan, while 'for the sake of peace' Caecilian was being detained at Brescia.[22] In the meantime, the Bishops Eunomius and Olympius were sent to Africa to replace the 'two bishops' with a newly consecrated one. But this plan was brought to an abrupt end by the riotous resistance of the Donatist party.[23] Then, first Donatus escaped and returned to Africa, and then, hearing of this, Caecilian followed him back to Carthage.[24] Constantine heard of this at Trèves and released the other few remaining Donatists and, then early in 316 A.D., in a very curious travel document, provided them with safe conduct, state transportation, and full board first up to Arles and then from there to Africa:[25]

21. See letter of Constantine to Domitius Celsus, Optatus, *App.* VII, below; also Augustine, *Ep.* 43.
22. Optatus, I, 26.
23. *Ibid.*
24. *Ibid.*
25. Optatus, *App.* VIII.

Petronius Annianus and Julianus to Domitius Celsus, Deputy-Prefect of Africa.

Since the Bishops Lucianus, Capito, Fidentius and Nasatius, and the priest Mammarius, who in accordance with the heavenly instruction of the Lord Constantine Maximus, the Unconquered, ever Augustus, had gone to the Gauls with other men of their Rule, were commanded by his Majesty to return to their homes, we have, Brother, in accordance with the command of the Eternity of our most kind Emperor, supplied them with transportation and proper provisions up to the port of Arles, so that from there they may sail for Africa, a fact which your Carefulness must learn from this letter. We wish you, Brother, the greatest happiness and good health. Given at Trèves on April 28, by Hilary, the Chief Officer.

The Emperor then first ordered Domitius Celsus, the Deputy-Prefect of Africa, to investigate the riotous situation. But perhaps not wishing to create 'so-called' martyrs for the Donatists, he once again wrote to Domitius Celsus in order to suspend the proceedings against the Donatists and promised to go to Africa to pronounce clear judgement in the matter:[26]

To Celsus, Deputy-Prefect of Africa.

The latest reports of your Excellency show that Menalius, who has long been suffering from madness, and the others, who have departed from the truth of God and given themselves over to a most perverse error, are persisting in their course of action. In these reports you have also mentioned, my dearest Brother, that you follow my command concerning the punishment of their insurrection and that the upheaval which they were preparing was thus checked. Since, that they had abominable plans has become clear from the fact that, when I decided to hold a full investigation into the various allegations they and Caecilian were making against one another, they endeavoured to slip away from my presence by taking to flight, by this most disgraceful act of theirs they have admitted that they were hurrying back to their previous activities which they even now persist in doing. But since there is no doubt that no one can draw any profit from deeds which are thoroughly wrong, even though their punishment has been put off for a short while, I have thought it right to command your Excellency, that in the meantime you stop proceeding against them, and that you recognize the necessity of discretion in dealing with them. But after you read the letter, make it plain to both Caecilian and to them as well that when by the favour of Divine Love I come to Africa, I shall most fully demonstrate, by pronouncing a clear judgement, to all, both Caecilian and those who appear to oppose him, what kind of veneration

26. Optatus, *App.* VII.

is to be rendered to the Highest God and what sort of worship appears to please Him. Moreover, I will, by employing careful examination, learn to the fullest extent, and bring to light, things which some, misled by their ignorance of mind, now, fancy they can keep in the dark. Those persons who are the cause of this situation and bring it about that the Supreme God is not being worshipped with the reverence that is His due, I shall destroy and disperse. And since it is obvious enough that nobody can gain the beatitudes of martyrdom if he is one of that brood which seem to be alienated and divorced from the truth of religion, I shall without any hesitation cause those whom I judge hostile to the divine law and religion itself, and find guilty of violence against the proper worship, to pay with their destruction they deserve for their madness and reckless obstinacy ... I am going to make plain to them what kind of worship is to be offered to the Divinity. For I believe that I can in no other way escape a most serious guilt than by absolutely refusing to connive at this wickedness. What more important business is there for me to do in virtue of my policy and Imperial office than to dissipate errors and banish rash opinions and so ensure that all offer Almightly God true religion, guileless concord and due worship?

Reading this letter, one just might agree with Jones,[27] who accuses Constantine of "moving fast to Caesaro-papism." Nobody can truly object to Constantine's promise: "... I come to Africa, I shall most fully demonstrate, by pronouncing a clear judgement, to all, both to Caecilian and to those who appear to oppose him, what kind of veneration is to be rendered to the Highest God ..." Is this not the zeal of the neophyte or rather the catechumen in the person of the Roman Emperor feeling responsible for the House of the Lord as well as the civil order of his Empire? When he says: "those persons who are the cause of this state of affairs and bring about a situation in which the Supreme God is not being worshipped with the reverence that is His due, I shall destroy and disperse (*perdam et discutiam*)" is Constantine not threatening those who are threatening the Church with destruction? But even Jones and perhaps Frend as well might agree[28] that Constantine uttered sound theology and common sense in saying that "it is obvious enough that nobody can gain the beatitudes of martyrdom if he is one of that brood which seem to be alienated from the truth of religion ..."

27. Jones, *op. cit.* 120.
28. Frend, *op. cit.*, 157-159.

However, Constantine never went to Africa to continue the futile and completely fruitless arguments with the Donatists. Tired of the affair, and most understadibly so, he passed his own personal judgement, no doubt on the basis of previous investigations by proper ecclesiastic authorities and civil courts. This final judgement of Constantine is expressed in a letter, dated November 10, 316 A.D., which he wrote to Eumalius, the Deputy-Prefect of Africa:[29]

[At the trial] I clearly perceived that Caecilian was a man possessed of all innocence, who observed all the duties that were owing to his religion and devoted himself to it as it was required of him. It also became evident that no crime could be found in him, as indeed it was fabricated against him by the hypocrisy of his enemies although he was absent [from the place of the crime].

It is worth noticing that Constantine neither took nor threatened any punitive measures against those found guilty in these disruptive activities of the Donatist party.

It was about three and one half years later that the real face of Donatism was even more completely unmasked. Silvanus,[30] Donatist bishop of Cirta, and, importantly, one of the bishops who had consecrated Majorinus as bishop in opposition to Bishop Caecilian of Carthage, had quarreled with one of his deacons called Nundinarius. Having detailed knowledge of Silvanus' discreditable acts of the past concerning, among others, *traditio*, and, having failed to receive satisfaction from Bishop Silvanus, Nundinarius was determined to go to the judgement seat of Zenophilus, Consular of Numidia. Other Numidian bishops, particularly Purpurius of Limata, afraid of the disclosure of his own crimes, desperately tried but failed to bring about a reconciliation between the Bishop Silvanus and the Deacon Nundinarius.

The *Acts* of the proceedings that took place on December 13, 320 A.D.[30a] against Bishop Silvanus give, on the one hand, a lively picture of one of the many scenes from the first year of the Great Persecution, and, on the other hand, they reveal the discreditable way in which Silvanus became a bishop; how he took money in

29. Augustine, *Contra Cresc.* III, 82.
30. For a brief account read Jones, *op. cit.* 121-123; Frend, *op. cit.* 161.
30a. Optatus, *App.* I.

exchange for the office of priesthood; that he kept the money which Lucilla had given for the poor; that he was truly a *traditor*; etc.:

The Commencement of the Proceedings, in which it is established that Silvanus, who, with the assistance of others, consecrated Majorinus, was a *traditor*.

During the consulship of Constantine Maximus Augustus and Constantine the younger, the most noble Caesar, on the thirteenth of December ... after Victor the Grammarian was brought in and placed before the judgement seat, His Excellency Zenophilus, a man of consular rank assisted by the Deacon Nundinarius, said: 'What is your name?'

He answered: 'Victor.'

His Excellency the Governor Zenophilus said: 'What is your position?'

Victor said: 'I am a professor of Roman Literature, a Latin grammarian.'

His Excellency the Governor Zenophilus said: 'What is your rank?'

Victor said: 'My father was a decurion of Cirta, my grandfather a soldier, and as such he served as an Imperial escort. For our family is of Moorish blood.'

His Excellency the Governor Zenophilus said: 'Mindful of your rank and honour, plainly describe what was the cause of dissension among the Christians?'

Victor said: 'I do not know the origin of the dissension. I am one of the Christian population. Only, when I was in Carthage, and once the Bishop Secundus after all came there, it was said that they discovered that Caecilian had been by some improperly established as a bishop, and in opposition to him they set up another bishop. The dissension over there at Carthage began at that time, but I cannot have a full knowledge of that dissension, because our city has always had only one Church, and if there was dissension, we do not know anything about it.'

His Excellency the Governor Zenophilus said: 'Are you in communion with Silvanus?'

Victor answered: 'Yes.'

His Excellency the Governor Zenophilus said: 'Why is he then in a separation from him whose innocence has been vindicated?' And he added: 'Besides it is being positively stated that you know something else with the greatest certainty, namely, that Silvanus is a *traditor*. Acknowledge this.'

Victor answered: 'This I do not know.'

His Excellency the Governor Zenophilus said to the Deacon Nundinarius: 'Victor denies that he knows that Silvanus is a *traditor*.'

The Deacon Nundinarius said: 'He must know, for he himself surrendered books.'

Victor answered: 'I had run away from this storm and may I perish if I lie.

When we were hit by the sudden onset of the persecution, we fled to the mountain of Bellona. I was lying low there with the Deacon Mars and so was the Priest Victor. When this Mars was asked for all the books, he denied that he had them. Then Victor gave the names of all the lectors. They came to my house when I was not there. The magistrates went in and took away all my books. When I returned, I found that all my books were removed.'

The Deacon Nundinarius said: 'But then at the public investigations you answered that you gave up the books. Why deny these when they can be shown in writing?'

His Excellency the Governor Zenophilus said to Victor: 'Simply confess that you may not be examined more severely.'

The Deacon Nundinarius said: 'Let the Acts be read.'

His Excellency the Governor Zenophilus said: 'Let them be read.'

And Nundinarius gave them to the notary and he read them: "During the eighth consulship of Diocletian and the seventh consulship of Maximian, on the nineteenth of May, from the Acts of Munatius Felix, perpetual flamen, Curator of town of Cirta. Upon arrival at the house in which the Christians were accustomed to come together, Felix, perpetual flamen and Curator, said to Bishop Paul: 'Bring out the Scriptures of your Law and anything else you have here, as has been directed, so that you may obey the order.'

Bishop Paul said: 'The lectors have the Scriptures. But we surrender what we have here.'

Felix, perpetual flamen and Curator, said to Bishop Paul: 'Show us the lectors or send word to them.'

Bishop Paul said: 'You all know them.'

Felix, perpetual flamen, Curator of the community said: 'We do not know them.'

Bishop Paul said: 'The public officials know them, that is the clerks Edusius and Junius.'

Felix, perpetual flamen, Curator of the community said: 'The consideration of the lectors will wait, since officials will point them out. As for you, do you surrender what you have.'

Sitting there were Bishop Paul and the priests Montanus and Victor Deusatelius and Memorius, standing were the deacons Mars and Helius, the subdeacons Marcuclius, Catullinus, Silvanus and Carosus, the grave-diggers Januarius, Meraclus, Fructuosus, Migginis, Saturninus, Victor and the others, while Victor of Aufidus was writing in front of them the following short catalogue: "two golden chalices, also six silver chalices, six silver pots, a silver cooking vessel, seven silver lamps, two torches, seven short candlesticks with their lamps, also eleven brass lamps with their chains, eighty-two tunics for women, thirty-eight veils, sixteen tunics for men, thirteen pairs of shoes for men, forty-seven pairs of shoes for women, eighteen country pattens."

Felix, perpetual flamen, Curator of the community said to the grave-diggers Marcuclius, Silvanus and Carosus: 'Bring out what you have.'

Silvanus and Carosus said: 'All that was here we have thrown out.'

Felix, perpetual flamen, Curator of the community, said to Marcuclius, Silvanus and Carosus: 'Your answer is in the Acts.'

When the chests in the book-rooms were found empty, Silvanus brought there a silver container and a silver lamp, and said that he had found them behind a large vessel.

Felix, perpetual flamen and Curator of the community, said to Silvanus: 'If you had not found them you would be a dead man.'

Felix, perpetual flamen and Curator of the community, said to Silvanus: 'Search more carefully, lest anything should be left behind.'

Silvanus said: 'Nothing has been left behind. We have here thrown out everything.'

And when the dining-room was opened, four jars and six jugs were found there.

Felix, perpetual flamen, Curator of the community, said: 'Bring forth whatever Scriptures you have, so that we may obey the instructions and the order of the Emperors.'

Catullinus brought forth an extremely large book.

Felix, perpetual flamen and Curator of the community, said to Marcuclius and Silvanus: 'Why have you given up only one book. Bring forth the Scriptures which you have.'

Catullinus and Marcuclius said: 'We do not have more, since we are subdeacons, but the lectors have the books.'

Felix, perpetual flamen, Curator of the community, said to Marcuclius and Catullinus: 'Point out the lectors.'

Marcuclius and Silvanus said: 'We do not know where they are staying.'

Felix, perpetual flamen, Curator of the community, said to Catullinus and Marcuclius: 'If you do not know where they are staying, tell us their names.'

Catullinus and Marcuclius said: 'We are not traitors. We are here. Order us to be killed.'

Felix, perpetual flamen, Curator of the community, said: 'Let them be seized.'

And on arrival to the house of Eugenius, Felix, perpetual flamen, Curator of the community, said to Eugenius: 'Bring out the Scriptures which you have, so that you may obey the order.'

And he brought out four books.

Felix, perpetual flamen, Curator of the community, said to Silvanus and Carosus: 'Point out the other lectors.'

Silvanus and Carosus said: 'The Bishop has already said that the clerks Edusius and Junius know all of them. Let them point out their houses to you.'

The clerks Edusius and Junius said: 'We will point them out to you, my

85

Lord.'

And on arrival to the house of Felix, the worker in marble, this brought forth five books. And on arrival to the house of Victorinus, this brought forth eight books. And on arrival to the house of Projectus, this brought forth five large and two small books. And on arrival to the house of the Grammarian, Felix, perpetual flamen, curator, said to Victor the grammarian: 'Bring forth the Scriptures which you have, so that you may obey the order.'

Victor the grammarian presented two books and four *quinions.*

Felix, perpetual flamen, curator of the community said to Victor: 'Bring forth the Scriptures. You have more.'

Victor the grammarian said: 'If I had possessed more, I would have handed them over.'

And on arrival to the house of Euticius of Caesarea, Felix, perpetual flamen, curator of the community, said to Euticius: 'Bring forth the Scriptures which you have, so that you may obey the order.'

Euticius said: 'I have none.'

Felix, perpetual flamen, curator of the community said to Euticius: 'Your declaration is recorded.'

And on arrival to the house of Codeo, his wife brought forth six books. Felix, perpetual flamen, curator of the community, said: 'Have a good look, lest you should have more, and bring them forth.'

The woman answered: 'I have no more.'

Felix, perpetual flamen, curator of the community, said to Bos, the public slave: 'Go in and see whether she has more.'

The public slave said: 'I have searched and found none.'

Felix, perpetual flamen, curator of the community, said to Victorinus, Silvanus and Carosus: 'If anything has been withheld, you are threatened with danger." '

After this was read, His Excellency the Governor Zenophilus said to Victor: 'Confess with sincerity.'

Victor answered: 'I was not there.'

The Deacon Nundinarius said: 'We have read letters written by Fortis to Bishops.' And he read a copy of the accusation handed in to the Bishops by the Deacon Nundinarius:

"Christ is my witness and His Angels that they with whom you have been in communion surrendered books, that is, Silvanus of Cirta is a *traditor* and a thief of the goods of the poor; that all you Bishops, priests, deacons, elders have knowledge of the four hundred *folles* given by Lucilla, a most noble woman, for the sake of which you conspired that Majorinus might become Bishop, and this resulted in the schism. Moreover, Victor the fuller, before you and the people, gave a gift of twenty *folles* so that he might be made a priest, and Christ and His Angels know this."

And a copy of a letter was read aloud: "The Bishop Pupurius to his fellow

Bishop Silvanus greetings in the Lord! Our son, the deacon Nundinarius, has come to me and has begged me to send this letter to intercede with your Holiness, so that there may, if it were possible, be peace between you and himself. For I want this to be brought about, in order that nobody should know what is going on between us, by a letter from you, if you please, asking me that I, by myself, come to your place concerning this matter, and that I may put an end to this dissension between you. For he himself handed to me a statement of what happened, explaining why he was, by your order, assaulted. It is not right for a father to chastise his son unjustly, and I know that the things listed in the statement handed over to me are true. Look for a salutary solution by which this ill-will over there may be extinguished before the flame could flare up which, afterwards, may be impossible to put out without the shedding of spiritual blood. Summon your fellow clerics and the elders of the people who belong to the church and let them look into these dissensions, so that what is decided may be decided according to the precepts of the Faith. You will not deviate either to the right or to the left. Do not willingly lend your ear to evil teachers who do not want peace. You slay us all ... Farewell."

Again, a copy of a letter: "Bishop Purpurius to the Clerics and Elders of the People of Cirta, eternal health in the Lord! Moses cried out to the whole assembly of Israel and told them what the Lord wanted to be done. Nothing was being done without the counsel of the Elders. Therefore, you, too, my beloved, who, I know, have all heavenly and spiritual wisdom, investigate with all your strength the nature of this dissension, and return to peace. For the Deacon Nundinarius says that you know full well the origin of this dissension between our dearest Silvanus and himself. For he has handed to me a statement in which everything is listed. He said that you are well aware. I know that nobody is listening. Look for a good solution, so that this matter may be extinguished without danger to your soul, that you may not suddenly come under indictment for having regard to personalities. Bring a just verdict between the parties in accordance with your gravity and justice. Do not deviate either to the right or to the left. This business concerns God, who is closely examining the thoughts of every single man. See to it that nobody knows the nature of this conspiracy. The matters contained in the statement concern you. This is an unhappy affair. For the Lord says: Out of thy mouth thou shalt be condemned and out of thy mouth shalt thou be justified."

Again, another one was read out: "Fortis to his beloved Brother Silvanus, eternal health in the Lord! Our Son the Deacon Nundinarius has come to me and related the matters which have taken place between you and him, as if by the intervention of the Enemy, who wishes to divert the souls of the just from the way of truth. When I heard this I was unable to comprehend that such a dissension arose between you. ... Now, therefore, beseech him that, while it is possible, the peace of the Lord Saviour Christ may be with him, lest we go out in public and be condemned by the Gentiles. For it has been written: See to it that while you are biting and accusing each other, you may not be devoured by each other. I therefore ask the Lord that this scandal may be removed from our midst, so that the business of God may be celebrated with the giving of thanks, since the Lord says: My peace I give to you, my peace I leave to you. What kind of peace can be there, where there is dissension and where there are rivalries? For when I was by the soldiers *roasted and singled out* and due to such violence I got into that situation, I commended my soul to God and I forgave you because God sees the minds of men ... But God has delivered us and we serve Him with you. Therefore, as we have been forgiven, so you too be reconciled in peace, that we may be able to celebrate the peace of Easter with joy in the Name of Christ. Let no one know ...

(Again, another was read out:) "Fortis to his brethren and sons, to the clergy and the elders, eternal health in the Lord! My son Nundinarius, your deacon, has come to me and related to me the things that were done against you. The matter should of course have been settled by you before you could have undergone such great madness that people were assaulted by you for telling the truth, a thing which both you and we know, as you reported it to us. And it is written: Is there no wise man among you who can judge between brethren? But even brother goes to court with brother, and this among the unbelievers, just as you now are disputing before the court. Has the situation got to this that we give such an example to the Gentiles, that those who used to believe in God through us, now speak evil of us, when we go out in public? Therefore, in order that it may not develop to this, you who are spiritual see to it that nobody may have the knowledge, so that we may celebrate Easter with peace, and do exhort them to be reconciled in peace, and let there be no dissension, lest, when this matter goes out to the public, you too may start being exposed to danger, if this really happens, and afterwards blame yourselves. You will take very special care, you, priest Donatius, who possess, Valerius and Victor, each of you, who know, the Acts – take care that you have peace amongst you."

Again, another letter was read out: "(Sabinus to his brother Silvanus,) eternal health in the Lord! Your son Nundinarius has come to us, not only to me but also to our brother Fortis, making a firm and serious complaint. I am surprised that your Gravity dealt in such a manner with your son, whom you reared and ordained. For if an earthly building has been built, is not something heavenly added that it is built by the hand of the priest? But one must not be surprised at you, for the Scripture says: I will destroy the wisdom of the wise and I will reject the prudence of the prudent, and it says again: Men have preferred darkness to light, just as you too are doing. Let it be enough for you to know the facts. Concerning this our Brother Fortis has also written to you. Now I would ask of your charity, my most kind Brother, to make good of the saying of the prophet Isaiah: Remove malice from your souls, and come, let us discuss, says the Lord. And again: Remove evil from your midst. You too act in similar fashion: suppress and avert the rebellion of those who have been against peace between you and your son. On the contrary, let your son Nundinarius celebrate Easter in peace with you, so that the matter may not, beyond the fact that it is already known to all of us, become public. I would ask you, my kindest Brother, to fulfil the request of my mediocrity. Let nobody know about it."

Again, another letter was read out: "Sabinus to his brother Fortis, eternal health in the Lord! How charity is among all our colleagues I know very well, but that Silvanus is devoted to you according to the disposition of God, who said: Some I love above my soul, I am certain. Therefore I have not hesitated to send you these writings, because I had your writings sent to him for the sake of Nundinarius. If we act diligently God's business always advances vigorously. Do not put forward an excuse. Business is urgent these days and it leaves us with no let-up in taking care of these matters up until the most solemn day of Easter, so that through you there may be a most abundant peace, and we may be found worthy co-heirs with Christ, who said: My peace I give unto you, my peace I leave to you. And I ask again that you do what I ask." And in another hand: "I wish you good health in the Lord and that you are mindful of us. Farewell, but I ask you not to let anyone know about it."

After these have been read, His Excellency the governor Zenophilus said: 'According to the Acts and letters which have been read out, it is clear that Silvanus is a *traditor.*'

And he said to Victor: 'Frankly confess whether you know that he surrendered anything.'

Victor said: 'He did, but not in my presence.'

His excellency the Governor Zenophilus said: 'What was Silvanus' office at that time among the clergy?'

Victor answered: 'The persecution began under the episcopate of Paul; Silvanus was then a subdeacon.'

The Deacon Nundinarius answered: 'When he went there, as he said, to be made Bishop, the people responded: "Let some one else be made Bishop; God, hear us." '

His Excellency the Governor Zenophilus said to Victor: 'Did the people say: "Silvanus is a *traditor*?" '

Victor said: 'I myself fought against his being made Bishop.'

His Excellency the Governor Zenophilus said to Victor: 'Then you knew he was a *traditor*? Admit this.'

Victor said: 'He was a *traditor.*'

The Deacon Nundinarius said: 'You elders kept crying out: "Hear us, God! We want our fellow-citizen. He is a *traditor.*" '

His Excellency the Governor Zenophilus said to Victor: 'Then you shouted with the people that Silvanus was a *traditor* and that he ought not to be made Bishop?'

Victor said: 'I shouted it and so did the people. For we were asking for a fellow-citizen, a man of integrity.'

His Excellency the Governor Zenophilus said: 'For what reason did you believe him to be undeserving?'

Victor said: 'We were asking for a man of integrity and a fellow-citizen. For I knew that for this we would go to a trial at the Emperor's Court, as long as the office is given to such men.'

Then, when the grave-diggers Victor of Samsuricum and Saturninus were brought in and *placed before the judgement seat*, His Excellency the Governor Zenophilus said: 'What is your name?'

He answered: 'Saturninus.'

His Excellency the Governor Zenophilus said: 'What is your position?'

Saturninus answered: 'Grave-digger.'

His Excellency the Governor Zenophilus said: 'Do you know that Silvanus is a *traditor*?'

Saturninus said: 'I know that he handed over a silver lamp.'

His Excellency the Governor Zenophilus said to Saturninus: 'What else?'

Saturninus answered: 'I do not know of anything else, except that he threw it out from behind a cask.'

And when Saturninus was removed, His Excellency the Governor Zenophilus said to one standing next: 'What is your name?'

He answered: 'Victor of Samsuricum.'

His Excellency the Governor Zenophilus said: 'What is your position?'

Victor said: 'I am a artisan.'

His Excellency the Governor Zenophilus said: 'Who handed over the silver table?'

Victor answered: 'I did not see. What I know I will tell.'

His Excellency the Governor Zenophilus said to Victor: 'Although it has now become clear from the answers of those who have been questioned before you, confess nevertheless whether Silvanus is a *traditor*.'

Victor said: '... I heard from the mouth of the Bishop himself: "I was given a silver lamp and a silver casket, and these I handed over."'

His Excellency the Governor Zenophilus said to Victor of Samsuricum: 'From whom did you hear that?'

Victor said: 'From Bishop Silvanus.'

His Excellency the Governor Zenophilus said to Victor: 'Did you hear it from himself that he had handed them over?'

Victor said: 'I heard it from himself that he had handed them over with his own hands.'

His Excellency the Governor Zenophilus said: 'Where did you hear that?'

Victor said: 'In the Basilica.'

90

His Excellency the Governor Zenophilus said: 'At Cirta?'

Victor said: 'There he started to talk to the people saying: "Why do they say I am a *traditor*? Because of the lamp and the casket?".'

His Excellency the Governor Zenophilus said to Nundinarius: 'What else do you think these should be questioned about?'

Nundinarius said: 'About the casks belonging to the Treasury. Who took them?'

His Excellency the Governor Zenophilus said to Nundinarius: 'What casks?'

Nundinarius said: 'They were in the temple of Serapis and Bishop Purpurius took them away. The vinegar that they contained was taken by the Bishop Silvanus, the priest Dontius and Lucianus.'

His Excellency the Governor Zenophilus said to Nundinarius: 'Do these who are standing by know that this was done?'

Nundinarius answered: 'They do.'

Deacon Saturninus said: 'Our parents told us that they were taken away.'

His Excellency the Governor Zenophilus said: 'By whom are they said to have been taken away?'

Saturninus said: 'By Bishop Purpurius, the vinegar by Silvanus, and the Priests Dontius and Superius, and the deacon Lucianus.'

Nundinarius said: 'Did Victor give twenty *folles* and was he made a priest?'

Saturninus said: 'Yes.'

And when he said this, His Excellency the Governor Zenophilus said to Saturninus: 'To whom did he pay?'

Saturninus said: 'To Bishop Silvanus.'

His Excellency the Governor Zenophilus said to Saturninus: 'Did he then give the twenty *folles* to Bishop Silvanus that he might be made a priest?'

Saturninus said: 'He did.'

His Excellency the Governor Zenophilus said to Saturninus: 'Was the money placed before Silvanus?'

Saturninus said: 'Before the throne of the Bishops.'

His Excellency the Governor Zenophilus said to Nundinarius: 'By whom was the money taken away?'

Nundinarius said: 'The Bishops divided it among themselves.'

His Excellency the Governor Zenophilus said to Nundinarius: 'Do you want Donatus to be brought here?'

Nundinarius said: 'By all means let him come. For it was about him that the people cried out two days after peace arrived: "Hear us, God, we want our fellow-citizen."'

His Excellency the Governor Zenophilus said to Nundinarius: 'Is it certain that the people shouted this?'

He answered: 'Yes.'

His Excellency the Governor Zenophilus said to Saturninus: 'Did the people shout that Silvanus was a *traditor*?'

Saturninus said: 'Yes.'

Nundinarius said: 'When he was made Bishop, we did not have communion with him because he was said to be a *traditor*.'

Saturninus said: 'What he says is true.'

Nundinarius said: 'I saw Mutus, a worker in sand-quarries, carry him on his shoulders.'

His Excellency the Governor Zenophilus said to Saturninus: 'It happened like this?'

Saturninus said: 'It did.'

His Excellency the Governor Zenophilus said: 'Is everything that Nundinarius says true — that Silvanus was made Bishop by the quarry-men?'

Saturninus said: 'True.'

Nundinarius said: 'Prostitutes were there.'

His Excellency the Governor Zenophilus said to Saturninus: 'Did quarry-men carry him?'

Saturninus said: 'They and the people carried him. For the citizens were enclosed in the cemetery of the *Martyrs*.

Deacon Nundinarius said: 'Were the people of God there?'

Saturninus said: 'They were enclosed in the large house.'

His Excellency the Governor Zenophilus said: 'Is it certain that everything Nundinarius says is true?'

Saturninus said: 'It is.'

His Excellency the Governor Zenophilus said: 'And what do you say?'

Victor said: 'Everything is true, my Lord.'

Nundinarius said: 'Bishop Purpurius took one hundred *folles*.'

His Excellency the Governor Zenophilus said to Nundinarius: 'Which people do you think should be questioned concerning the four hundred *folles*?'

Nundinarius said: 'Let Deacon Lucianus be brought here, because he knows the whole story.'

His Excellency the Governor Zenophilus said to Nundinarius: 'Do these men know it?'

Nundinarius said: 'They do not.'

His Excellency the Governor Zenophilus said: 'Let Lucianus be brought here.'

Nundinarius said: 'These people know that four hundred *folles* were received, but they do not know that the Bishops divided them among themselves.'

His Excellency the Governor Zenophilus said to Saturninus and Victor: 'Do you know that the *folles* were received from Lucilla?'

Saturninus and Victor said: 'We do.'

His Excellency the Governor Zenophilus said: 'Did the poor not receive them?'

They said: 'Nobody received anything.'

His Excellency the Governor Zenophilus said to Saturninus and Victor: 'Was anything taken away from the sanctuary of Serapis?'

Saturninus and Victor said: 'Purpurius took away the casks, and Bishop Silvanus and the priests Dontius and Superius and the deacon Lucianus took away the vinegar.'

His Excellency the Governor Zenophilus said: 'From the replies of Grammarian Victor and of Victor of Samsuricum and of Saturninus it is clear that all the alleagations of Nundinarius are true. Let them be dismissed and leave.'

His Excellency the Governor Zenophilus said: 'Who else do you think should be questioned?'

Nundinarius said: 'The deacon Castus, to tell us whether he (Silvanus) is not a *traditor*, for he himself ordained him.'

After the deacon Castus was brought in and placed before the judgement seat, His Excellency the Governor Zenophilus said: 'What is your name?'

He answered: 'Castus.'

His Excellency the Governor Zenophilus said: 'What is your position?'

Castus said: 'I have no dignity.'

His Excellency the Governor Zenophilus said: 'Although the charges of Nundinarius have now been admitted by the Grammarian Victor as well as Victor of Samsuricum and Saturninus, still state whether Silvanus is a *traditor*.'

Castus answered: 'He said that he had found a lamp behind a cask.'

His Excellency the Governor Zenophilus said: 'Give evidence also about the casks taken from the sanctuary of Serapis and the vinegar.'

Castus replied: 'Bishop Purpurius took away the casks.'

His Excellency the Governor Zenophilus said: 'Who removed the vinegar?'

Castus answered that the Bishop Silvanus and the priests Dontius and Superius removed the vinegar from there.

His Excellency the Governor Zenophilus said to Castus: 'Tell us how many *folles* did Victor give in order that he might be made a priest.'

Castus said: 'My lord, he offered a little bag, but I do not know what it contained.'

His Excellency the Governor Zenophilus said to Castus: 'To whom was the little bag given?'

Castus said: 'He brought it to him in the large house.'

His Excellency the Governor Zenophilus said to Castus: 'Was the money not divided among the people?'

Castus answered: 'I did not see any money given.'

His Excellency the Governor Zenophilus said to Castus: 'Did not the poor receive any of the *folles* that Lucilla had given?'

Castus said: 'I did not see anybody receive any.'

His Excellency the Governor Zenophilus said to Castus: 'What did then become of the money?'

Castus said: 'I do not know.'

Nundinarius said: 'You must have either heard or witnessed if it was said to the poor: "Lucilla gives this also to you from her property."'

Castus said: 'I did not see anyone receive anything.'

His Excellency the Governor Zenophilus said: 'The evidence of Castus makes it clear that he does not know that the *folles* which Lucilla donated were distributed to the people. Let him therefore be dismissed.'

Again, after the subdeacon Crescentianus was brought in and placed before the judgement seat, His Excellency the Governor Zenophilus said: 'What is your name?'

He answered: 'Crescentianus.'

His Excellency the Governor Zenophilus said to Crescentianus: 'State plainly, as the others have also done, whether you know that Silvanus is a *traditor*.'

Crescentianus said: 'Those before me, who were clerics, related every detail.'

His Excellency the Governor Zenophilus said to Crescentianus: 'What did they relate?'

Crescentianus said: 'They related that he was a *traditor*.'

His Excellency the Governor Zenophilus said to Crescentianus: 'Did they say that he was a *traditor*?' And he added: 'Who said it?'

Crescentianus said: 'Those people who were in his company said that he had one time been a *traditor*.'

His Excellency the Governor Zenophilus said to Crescentianus: 'Were they saying this of Silvanus?'

Crescentianus said: 'Yes.'

His Excellency the Governor Zenophilus said to Crescentianus: 'Were you there when he was made Bishop?'

Crescentianus said: 'I was present with the people, though shup up in the large house.'

Deacon Nundinarius said: 'People from the country and the quarry-men made him Bishop.'

His Excellency the Governor Zenophilus said to Crescentianus: 'Is it certain that Mutus the quarry-man carried him?'

He said: 'Without doubt.'

His Excellency the Governor Zenophilus said to Crescentianus: 'Do you know that the casks were taken away from the sanctuary of Serapis?'

Crescentianus said: 'Several people were saying that Bishop Purpurius himself removed the casks and the vinegar, which got to our Senior Bishop Silvanus, as the sons of Aelion were saying.'

His Excellency the Governor Zenophilus said to Crescentianus: 'What did you hear?'

Crescentianus said: 'That the vinegar was taken away by the Senior Bishop Silvanus and the priest Dontius and Superius and the deacon Lucianus.'

His Excellency the Governor Zenophilus said to Crescentianus: 'Did the people receive anything of the four hundred *folles* that Lucilla donated?'

Crescentianus said: 'I do not know of anyone receiving anything of them, nor do I know who spent them.'

Nundinarius said: 'Did old women never receive any of them?'

Crescentianus said: 'No.'

His Excellency the Governor Zenophilus said: 'Surely, whenever anything of this kind is donated, all the folks there publicly share in it?'

Crescentianus said: 'I neither heard nor witnessed that he had given to any of them.'

His Excellency the Governor Zenophilus said to Crescentianus: 'Then, nothing of four hundred *folles* was given to the people?'

Crescentianus said: 'Nothing. Some small amount would have certainly come our way.'

His Excellency the Governor Zenophilus said: 'Where then were they taken?'

Crescentianus said: 'I do not know. Nobody received anything.'

Nundinarius said: 'How many *folles* did Victor pay, so that he might be made a priest?'

Crescentianus said: 'I saw baskets with money brought in.'

His Excellency the Governor Zenophilus said to Crescentianus: 'To whom were the baskets given?'

Crescentianus said: 'To Bishop Silvanus.'

His Excellency the Governor Zenophilus said: 'Were they given to Silvanus?'

Crescentianus said: 'Yes, to Silvanus.'

His Excellency the Governor Zenophilus said: 'Nothing was given to the people?'

He answered: 'Nothing. We too should have received something if the distribution had been made in the usual way.'

His Excellency the Governor Zenophilus said to Nundinarius: 'What else do you think should be asked of Crescentianus?'

Nundinarius said: 'What he has said is all that is required.'

His Excellency the Governor Zenophilus said: 'Since the subdeacon Crescentianus has given evidence about everything with sincerity, let him be dismissed.'

Again, after Januarius was brought in and placed before the judgement seat, His Excellency the Governor Zenophilus said: 'What is your name?'

He answered: [The rest is missing.]

Although the *Acts* end abruptly, we know from Saint Augustine[31] that Silvanus was sentenced to exile. Thus, although it was Silvanus who was on trial, was convicted and discredited, this case at the same time helped to have the real face of the Donatist movement unmasked. The Donatist leaders were found convicted of having committed the very sin they had alleged against the Catholics.

Not only Silvanus but also other Donatist leaders were banished. It was perhaps at this time, but probably earlier, *i.e.* just after the conviction of Donatist Ingentius for forgery in framing Bishop Felix of Aptunga, or perhaps only after his final verdict on November 10, 316 A.D., in favour of Caecilian and against the Donatists, that the Emperor Constantine brought a severe law against the schismatics and had their places of assembly and basilicas confiscated.[32] Very soon however Constantine realized the futility of his anti-Donatist measures, and on May 5, 321 A.D., he sent a letter to Verinus, Deputy-Prefect of Africa, ordering that he should restore the exiles and granting the Donatists toleration:[33]

... the Donatists] showed a letter of the same Constantine which he sent to the Deputy-Prefect Verinus, in which he severely denounced them and said that they were to be released from exile and forsaken by his anger, because God had already begun to take vengeance against them. But even by this very letter of the Emperor, they confirmed that they had spoken falsely in saying that Caecilian was condemned by the Emperor, although the Emperor, on the contrary, demonstrated that they had been proved wrong by Caecilian, seeing that it was only after violently cursing them that he ordered that they should be released from exile, so that they might be punished, as indeed they have already begun being punished, by God the judge.

Constantine thus gives up his efforts to stop the destructive movement of the Donatists and ends all coercive measures against them, leaving them to the judgement of God!

In an unusually short letter to the Bishops and Laity of Africa[34] the Emperor sums up his efforts in attempting to put an end to this terrible schism: He endeavoured, "within the bounds of prudence," to do what *'our Faith'* demanded, but did not succeed in subduing that criminal violence; a clique, a few of criminal

31. *Contra Cresc.* III, 30, 34.
32. Augustine, *Ep.* 105, 8-9; esp. *Ep.* 93, 13-14.
33. Augustine, *Ep.* 141, 9; *Ad Don.* 31, 54; 33, 56.
34. Optatus, *App.* IX.

mentality, are still trying to prevent the confiscation of places so that they may have locations "where they may gloat over their criminal conduct." However to say that the Emperor is obliged to admit defeat[35] would probably be far wide of the mark. Instead, he waits for the grace of God to change the hearts of these rebels. Like a good Christian, he exhorts the Bishops of the Holy Catholic Church, perhaps in spite of themselves, to exercise patience towards the schismatics, and urges them not to pay back injury with injury. Fittingly, he shows great wisdom, and in closing the affair he concludes that it is "in the nature of a fool to usurp the right of vengeance" which is reserved to God ... The judgement of God should be an ominous enough prospect for these enemies of the Catholic Church. But there is Constantine's letter to the Bishops and Laity of Africa:

Constantine Augustus to all the Bishops throughout Africa and to the people of the Catholic Church.

You know very well that, using every means of humanity and moderation, I endeavoured, within the bounds of prudence and so far as the limits of its purity allowed, to do what our Faith demanded, so that, in accordance with the teaching of our Law, the peace of the most Holy Brotherhood – and the supreme God has infused in the hearts of His servants a grace for this peace – should, through complete harmony, remain firmly established. But since the measures taken by me have not succeeded in subduing that stubborn criminal violence that is firmly implanted in the minds of only a few of them, while a clique still zealously supports this villany in trying to prevent by every means the forceful confiscation of places where they could gloat over their criminal conduct, we must see to it that while all this evil has ensnared a few, it may be, by the mercy of Almighty God, made harmless towards the people. For we must hope for a relief from it when all our good promises and deeds are repaid. But, until the heavenly medicine presents itself, our plans must be moderated to the extent that we cultivate patience and with the virtue of serenity we tolerate everything that according to their habitual intemperance they insolently attempt or make good. Injury should not be repaid with injury. It is in the nature of a fool to usurp the right of vengeance which we must reserve for God, especially since our faith ought to be sure that whatever it suffers from the fury of such men, will count before God for martyrdom. For what is the meaning of victory in this world in the Name of God unless it means to endure with a steadfast heart the savage violence of men harassing the people of the Law of Peace. If you observe this sincerely,

35. Jones, *op. cit.* 125.

by the grace of the supreme Deity you will quickly bring it about that those, who behave as standard-bearers of this most miserable strife, may come to recognize that, as their rules and morals decline, they should not, through the persuasion of a few, all perish and offer themselves to everlasting death, although they could, through repentance and by having corrected their errors, be healed for eternal life. Farewell in common prayer forever by the will of God, my dearest Brothers.

Constantine, rightly, had no doubt that the Donatists were heretics as well as schismatics, and he believed that their father was the devil himself and that they submitted to devilish falsehood and wickedness. Since he also believed that people infected with the evil of an impious mind ought to be separated from *"our"* Catholic Community, Constantine heartily approved of the action of some Numidian bishops when they, after vainly trying to keep it for themselves against Donatist efforts, let the schismatics have the basilica Constantine had built for the Catholics in the city of Constantine. In a letter to these Numidian bishops, written probably some years later, perhaps as late as 330 A.D., the Emperor gladly accedes to the bishops' request that the Custom House may be passed over to them in exchange for the basilica they had lost to the schismatics. Generous as ever, Constantine also instructs the Consular of Numidia to have a new basilica built right there for the Catholics, at the expense of the Imperial treasury, which has been made to disgorge copiously for the building of this new basilica:[36]

Constantine, the greatest Victor and always triumphant Augustus to the Bishops Zeuzius, Gallicus, Victorinus, Sperantius, Januarius, Felix, Crescentius, Pantius, Victor, Babbutius, and Donatus.

Since it is clearly the will of the Supreme God, who is the Author and Father of this world, through whose kindness we live, look up to heaven, and rejoice in the society on men, that the whole human race should have a common agreement and be joined together in a certain loving companionship by, as it were, mutual embraces, there is no doubt that heresy and schism have come from the devil, who is the source of wickedness. Therefore there is no doubt that what ever heretics do, is done by the inspiration of the one who has taken possession of their senses, minds and thoughts. For when he brings such people under his power, he lords over them in everything. Then what good can be achieved by one who is insane, faithless, irreligious,

36. Optatus, *App.* X.

unholy, hostile to God, an enemy of the Holy Church, who – departing from God the Holy, the True, the Just, the Supreme, and the Lord of All, from Him who has created and brought us forth in this life and gave us spirit for the life we are living and who, because he wanted us to be his, has, by His Will, made us and all things perfect – runs, with a deep delusion, over to the side of the devil? But, because the soul once possessed by the Evil One – for it must pursue the works of its teacher – does perform things which seem to be opposed to fairness and justice, consequently, they who are possessed by the devil submit to his falsehood and wickedness. Moreover, it is not surprising that the wicked depart from the good. For this has been expressed by the proverb which says that birds of a feather flock together. Those who have been infected with the evil of an impious mind must be separated from our community. For, as the Scripture says, if it is true that a wicked man brings forth wicked things from a wicked treasure, a good man certainly brings forth good things from a good treasure. But since, as has been said, heretics and schismatics, who, abandoning good and pursuing evil, perform things that displease God, are clearly shown as keeping close to the side of the devil, who is their father, your Gravity has acted most properly and wisely and in accordance with the holy precept of the Faith, by keeping out of their perverse contentions and by surrendering them which they claim for their use although they have no right to it and it does not belong to them, so that they may not, according to their malicious and perfidius perversity, burst out in seditious strifes and, at their turbulent meetings, stir up men like themselves, and that thus there may not result a situation, which would have to be checked. For their criminal mind always requires them to perform the works of the devil. Therefore when, through their patience, the Bishops of God overcome them and their very father, let those who are the worshippers of the Supreme God receive glory for themselves, but the others condemnation and appropriate punishments. Indeed, may the judgement of the Supreme God emerge all the more glorious and just, because He bears with them in the spirit of fairness, and, while He is patient, He condemns everything that has taken place through their agency, and while He waits, God has indeed promised that He would be the Avenger of all. And, therefore, while vengeance is reserved to God, punishment is inflicted on His enemies the more strictly. I have learned that you, the servants and priests of God, have willingly done this at the present time, and I have been quite happy that you are demanding no punishment for the impious, the polluted, the sacrilegious, the profane, the perfidious and the irreligious, for those who displease God and are hostile to the Church, and that you ask that they rather be pardoned. This is to know God truly and deeply, this is to walk in the commandments, this is to believe abundantly, this is to understand truly, this is to know that greater punishment is being called forth against the enemies of the Church when they are treated with forbearance in this world.

Having received the letter of your Wisdom and Gravity, I have learnt that the heretics or schismatics, with their usual impudence, decided to seize the basilica of the Catholic Church, which I had built in the city of Cirta, and that, although they had been warned by us and, at our command, by our judges, to return what was not theirs, they refused. I learnt that you nevertheless, imitating the patience of the Supreme God, with a peaceful mind, relinquish what is yours to their malice and rather ask for another place to replace it, namely, the Custom House. According to my custom, I have gladly accepted this petition of yours and immediately sent a suitable letter to the Treasurer that he see to it that our Treasury building be transferred with all its rights to the ownership of the Catholic Church. And I have donated this with unreserved generosity and ordered that it be handed over to you without delay. However, I have commanded that on this place a basilica be built at the expense of the Treasury, and ordered that a letter be sent to the Governor of Numidia, telling him to help your Holiness in everything in the construction of this church. I have also decreed that lectors and subdeacons of the Catholic Church, and the others who, through the instigation of the above-mentioned, have been called, an account of their character, to perform public services or the office of the decurions, should, according to my statute law, be exempt from all public service. But we have also ordered that those who have been inducted by the instigation of the heretics should be without delay freed from vexatious duties. For the rest, I have also ordered that my law which I had issued concerning Catholic ecclesiastics, be observed. All these things have been written down in full for your patience, as the present letter bears witness, in order that they may become clear. On the other hand, if only the heretics or schismatics would finally provide for their salvation and if only they would, by dispelling their blindness, open their eyes to the vision of true light, and if only they would depart from the devil and, at least at this late hour, take refuge with God, who is One and True, and the Judge of all. But, because it is obvious that they wish to remain in their malice and to die in their crimes, our warning and continual exhortation in previous times is enough for them. For if they had been willing to obey my commandments, they would be free from all trouble. Let us, Brothers, nevertheless attend to what are our affairs, let us walk in the commandments, let us observe the Divine Precepts by good actions, let us free our life from errors and, with the favour of the merciful God, let us steer it along the straight path. Given on February 5 at Sardica.

Was Constantine, once again, admitting defeat? Or was he practising Christian patience, or rather the evangelical counsel advising true followers of Christ to keep separate from those who do not accept the doctrine of Christ?[37]

37. John, *Ep.* II, 9-10.

THE LICINIAN INTERMEZZO: DISSONANCE REMOVED

After the 314 A.D. skirmishes, ending in an apparent draw but with a very definite territorial and psychological advantage for Constantine, an uncertain peace lasted for five to six years.[1] The facts that Constantine, first in 321 A.D. and then again in 322 A.D., appointed consuls of his own choice without first obtaining Licinius' agreement might be regarded[2] as the first very definite signs of discord between the two Augustuses. Then it was early in 323 A.D., a year of consuls without the agreement of Licinius, that Constatine successfully campaigned against the Goths, after the latter had invaded and caused much destruction both in Moesia and Thrace, Constantine's and Licinius' respective territories. In repelling the invading Goths Constantine, perhaps as a military necessity and unavoidably, crossed into Licinius' dominion. Licinius, perhaps unreasonably and just looking for a *casus belli*, protested but did not receive satisfaction.

Early next year, 324 A.D., the two Augustuses went to war.[3] In the light of Constantine's and Licinius' relationship, especially during the few years before this fateful year, it becomes quite clear that the Milan conference and its major product, the Edict of Milan, were for Licinius a *tour de force*, and that it must have been Constantine who represented the Christian interests, and not Licinius, as suggested by Henri Grégoire, and that it was Licinius who represented pagan interests. Soon enough after the conference

1. For a simple account of the estrangement and the final battles of the two Augustuses, see A.H.M. Jones, *Constantine and the Conversion of Europe* (London, 1968) 128-135; also, Sir Edwin Pears, "The Campaign against Paganism," *English Historical Rev.* 24 (1909) 1-17; *et al.*
2. Jones, *op. cit.* 129.
3. For a discussion of the date of this war, see N.H. Baynes, *J. of Roman Studies* 18 (1928) 218-220; E. Gerland, "In welchem Jahre gelangte Konstantin d. G. zur Alleinherrschaft?" *Byzantinische Zeitschrift (Festgabe A. Heisenberg)* 30 (1929-30) 364-373; *et al.*

they were evidently following opposite policies towards Christianity. Constantine's laws increasingly show the influence, and indeed the entrance of Christianity into his legislation, especially with regard to prohibition or limitation of the practice of divination, soothsaying, magic, and the like.[4]

Constantine's favour to Christianity showed itself very particularly when he was extending privileges to the Catholic clergy and building great churches in Rome, Palestine and other holy places.[5]

In contrast to Constantine's generosity, Licinius, in the other half of the Roman Empire, granted no favours to Christianity. This fact, coupled with the fact that his rule became increasingly vexatious to the Church, shows that he was, at this later stage, an open enemy to Christianity, but it implies as well that at earlier times he had not been a friend to the Church and that Eusebius' rhetorical praises of him were hasty and probably entirely unfounded. It may be true[6] that, as the ever-increasing and practically unlimited generosity and the frequent and open confession of Christianity by Constantine made Licinius' Christian subjects cast envious eyes upon their more fortunate brethren of the Western Empire, Licinius simply could not help feeling estranged or even increasingly hostile to the Christian Church. Licinius may have been — and probably was — envious of Constantine[7] on account of his higher position in the Empire as well as in the estimation of his Christian subjects.

It is however difficult to say when Licinius' perhaps only diplomatic neutrality changed into open hostility.[8] But when it did it manifested itself not only in petty and vexatious legislation to hamper normal Church activities, but also in open hostility resulting in a number of martyrdoms. Details of the Licinian persecution are reported by Eusebius.[9] He expelled Christians

---

4. For a short review, see B.J. Kidd, *A History of the Church* (Oxford U. P., 1922) v. 2, 5-10.

5. *Ibid.* 6-7.

6. According to N.H. Baynes, "Constantine the Great and the Christian Church," *Proceedings of the Brit. Acad.* 15 (1929) 354; Jones, *op. cit.* 130; *et al.*

7. See e.g. Eusebius *H.E.* X, viii, 3.

8. Perhaps, not before 319 A.D.; H.M. Gwatkin, *Studies in Arianism* (Cambridge, 1882) xxiii; *et al.*

9. *H.E.* X, viii; ix; *Vita Constantini* I, 51-54; II, 1 ff.; L.S. Le Nain de

from his court and residence,[10] and prohibited the holding of bishops' councils,[11] thereby partly paralyzing Church life. Then, pretending to act in the interest of public morality, he prohibited women and men from worshipping together in churches, and ordered that Christian assemblies take place not inside the cities but outside, in the open country.[12] It was perhaps then that some churches were pulled down while others were simply shut up to prevent Christian assembly, particularly in Amasea and elsewhere in the Pontus.[13] Licinius also seems to have singled out Christians serving in his army by preventing them from what was called "honourable rank."[14] How far persecution reached into the army seems to be uncertain,[15] though the Passion of the Forty Martyrs of Sebaste may have been part of such a persecution.[16] Whether owing to direct orders or to administrators' zealousness in trying to please their Imperial master, bishops were arrested and put to death.[17] Indeed, the great *Acta Sanctorum* of the Bollandists would testify to many martyrdoms at this time in the Empire of Licinius.

At last, ready for a final battle against his envied colleague and acting like Maximinus Daia before his final battle, Licinius openly declared himself a champion of the old gods of the Empire. He summoned[18] to him pagan priests and diviners, and magicians from Egypt, he conciliated the gods through prayers and sacrifices, and, then, he inquired about their will to be disclosed in oracles. His speech on this occasion, quoted by Eusebius,[19] is most remarkable, and there is no good reason for declaring it to be fictitious.

Tillemont, *Memoires etc.* (Paris, 1712) V, 502-514; F. Görres, "Kritische Untersuchungen über die Licinianische Christenverfolgung," *Zschr. f. wiss. Theologie* 19 (1876) 159-167; "Die Religionspolitik des Kaisers Licinius," *Philologus* 72 (1913) 250-262.

10. Eusebius, *H.E.* X, viii, 10; *Vita Constant.* I, 51.
11. *Ibid.* I, 51.
12. *Ibid.*
13. Eusebius, *H.E.* X, viii, 15.
14. *Ibid.* viii, 15.
15. See Baynes, "Constantine the Great etc.," *op. cit.* 354, n. 53.
16. Kidd, *op. cit.* v, 2, 5.
17. Eusebius, *H.E.* X, viii, 14; X, viii, 17; *Vita Constant.* II, 2; Theodoretus, *H.E.* I, vii, 5; Tillemont, *op. cit.* V, 515-517.
18. See Jones, *op. cit.* 132 f. Eusebius, *Vita Constant.* II, 4.
19. Jones, *op. cit.* 132 f. Eusebius, *Vita Constant.* II, 5.

Eusebius heard of this from members of the audience: 'He was a worshipper of the old gods, Constantine and his followers were atheists; this coming battle between him and Constantine would decide whether the old gods or Constantine's God was the true saviour; and in either case, he would join the winning side.'

After the first battle on July 3, 324 A.D., Licinius was obliged to retreat to Byzantium. At this point, Constantine blockaded Byzantium but supplies still kept coming to Licinius by sea. Constantine had to put and end to this, and accepted, therefore, that the supremacy of the straits had to be decided. He put Crispus, his son, in charge of these operations, and Crispus did not disappoint his father. With brilliant manoeuvres and despite the great superiority of the forces of the Licinian fleet, he dealt Licinius a crushing defeat by destroying a great part of his navy. Licinius was forced to abandon Byzantium, and crossed over the Bosporus to Chrysopolis. At Chrysopolis, on September 18, 324 A.D., was fought the final battle. Constantine's forces again prevailed, and Licinius fled to Nicomedia. Constantia, his wife and half-sister of Constantine, was sent by him to the victor to plead for his life. Constantine spared his brother-in-law, and even received him at a dinner, but then sent him to Thessalonica, where, however, according to some evidence, Licinius plotted against Constantine and was put to death. According to other reports, Licinius gave no provocation to Constantine to deserve execution.

That both Augustuses regarded the final battle as a supernatural event, cannot be doubted. Licinius, as mentioned above, just like Maximinus Daia and other persecutors before him, lined up on his side the gods of old Rome. There can be hardly any doubt that Constantine believed that ever since he began his campaign against Maxentius all his victories, including this very last one against Licinius, were won with the help of Christ's Cross. On a coin[20] e.g. the *labarum* is seen severing the serpent, which clearly indicates that it was viewed as a symbol that overcomes the forces of the Devil. Again,[21] the same event is clearly commemorated and graphically celebrated on the gable of the entrance to Constantine's palace in Constantinople. Here, with the Emperor and his sons standing by, the Cross is above their heads, while the infernal dragon is at their feet, slain and falling into the abyss. That the

20. H. Dörries, *Constantine the Great* (New York, 1972) 59.
21. *Ibid.*

war was that of religion and that it was, as far as Constantine was concerned, a veritable Crusade, a war of liberation for the Christian Church, is admitted by Constantine himself.

Edicts that soon followed his victory over Licinius attest that Constantine believed that the Eastern provinces had until now been truly oppressed, and that he was going to undo all the wrongs done against the Church (and the Christians had suffered not only under Licinius but also during the time of all the recent persecutions), for the injustices done to the Church and the Christians had not yet been in most cases rectified in the Eastern Empire. The toleration that Galerius had granted in 311 A.D. was grudging and far from being perfect. It left many injustices un-rectified and many wounds still open. Then Maximinus Daia for example never really implemented the Edict of Galerius in his empire. What he did in apparent compliance with this edict left the Christians in doubt regarding his sincerity. The Edict of Milan should have healed all wounds and undone almost all or most wrongs suffered by the Church and its individual members. But there may be some very serious doubts whether Licinius carried out all the measures of the Edict of Milan. Then came Licinius' own persecution of the Church and Christians, and this, once again, left many things to be corrected.

To dispel all doubts, to heal all injuries, to make up for all sufferings, and leave no wrong undone, Constantine issued an edict, or perhaps more properly a constitution, by which he meant to do all this. Constantine issued this edict obviously on behalf of his new Christian subjects of the Eastern provinces, and, by the measures enunciated in it, he goes beyond even those of the Edict of Milan: This edict was to guarantee full religious freedom for the practice of Christian worship; it ordered that all displaced persons and all those banished to islands and foreign lands for confessing Christianity were free to return to their homes; that all goods and estates that had been confiscated for the same reason were to be returned; that all those who had been condemned to hard labour in public works and other places were to be released; that all those who had lost their military ranks, privileges of high or simply free birth should be reinstated; and there were other provisions as is clear from the edict itself:[22]

22. Eusebius, *Vita Constant.* II, 24-42.

To those who have correct and sound opinion of the Supreme Being, it has been from the beginning and is even now eminently clear and beyond any shadow of doubt how great a difference there has been between those who carefully observe the hallowed worship of the Christian religion, and those who would hold towards it a hostile and scornful attitude. But now it has been, by more manifest deeds and more splendid acts of success, even more clearly demonstrated how unreasonable it is to doubt and how great is the power of the Great God: because those who faithfully observe His most holy law and do not attempt to break His commandments received abundant benefits and, also, great power with good hopes, but those who had impious attitude received what corresponded to their own course of action. For who could obtain any good who would not recognize God the author of all good things or give him the proper worship? But let the facts give credence to what I have [just] said.

If, for example, anyone retraces in his mind history from the earliest times up to the present and examines the actions in the past, he will find that those who made justice and excellence the foundation of their business carried their undertakings to a favourable end and reaped a good harvest as a natural result, so to say, of some good root. On the other hand, those who were engaged in unjust enterprises, or insanely raged against the Supreme Being, or had no consideration for the human race but dared to inflict them with exile, degradations, confiscations, massacres and many similar things, without ever having regrets or turning their minds to a better course, these he will find to have received fitting retribution. Indeed, this might come about not without reason and expectation.

All those who go into any business with an upright mind and have, at all times, the fear of the Supreme Being in their minds, keeping their faith in Him steadfast, and do not consider present fears and dangers of greater weight than their hopes of future blessings, – these people, though may, for a while, experience some vexations, would, through their hope of greater rewards in store for them, suffer their misfortunes without ill feeling and would, in addition, acquire a glory the brightness of which is proportionate to the severity of the difficulties they experience. But all those who held the principle of justice in disdain or did not acknowledge the Supreme Being, and dared to subject those who faithfully worship Him to barbarous insults and punishment and yet did not, on the one hand, regard themselves as wretched in comparison to those whom they punished on such pretexts, and did not, on the other hand, regard as happy and most blessed those who maintained their faithfulness towards the Supreme Being even under such circumstances as mentioned above – all those people had many of their armies defeated and put to flight, and all their war preparations ended in a most shameful defeat.

As a result of this, grievous wars arise and ruinous destructions, and then there arise scarcities of things necessary for life, but also, in association with them, a multitude of sufferings. Then, the originators of such ungodliness as mentioned either had the misfortune of dying amidst the most terrible sufferings, or of living a most shameful life, and they acknowledged that this life was worse than death. Thus, they received, as it were, punishments in proportion to their injustices. For each one found misfortune in proportion to the degree in which he was led by his blindness to war against the Divine Law, so that they had not only the weight of this life on them, but they were also grievously terrorized by the thought of punishment under the earth.

So then, with such grievous impiety reigning in human affairs, and the public affairs in danger of being utterly destroyed as if by a pestilential disease and in need of powerful saving help, what relief, what deliverance did the Divinity provide for the sufferings? This Divinity must by all means be conceived of as the one who alone and truly is and possesses almighty and everlasting power. To acknowledge, on the other hand, in solemn terms the beneficence of the Supreme Being is by no means boasting. He searched for and chose my service to carry out his purpose. Starting then at the faraway sea of the *Britanni* and the regions where the sun, as ordained by some force, sets, by the help of some Supreme Power, I drove out and scattered all the prevailing evil things, in order that the human race, reared with my assistance, might, at once, call upon the service of the most holy law, and, at the same time, our blessed faith might grow, led by the mighty hand of the Supreme Being. For I would never be arrogant about the grace I owe Him. Believing that this most noble ministry was given to me freely as a gift, I have come to the regions of the East, which cried out to us for even greater help since they were oppressed by more grievous calamities. I am most firmly convinced that I owe my life and my every breath, and, in short, if anything is turned about in my innermost mind, even this I owe to the Supreme God. I am well aware that those who sincerely pursue the heavenly hope and firmly place it to God's heaven as their heart's desire have no need of the favour of men, and the more they separate themselves from the inferior and worthless things of the earth the greater are the rewards they reap. Nevertheless I still believe that it is proper that, as far as possible, I remove from those not guilty and free of liability the constraints placed upon them for a while, and the improper punishments. Indeed, it would be very strange if under those who were zealous in persecuting men for their worship of God firmness and constancy of soul of these were sufficiently known, yet their glory were not raised into more illustrious blessed height under the Servant of God.

Therefore, let all those who exchanged their own home for a strange one, because they would not deny the faith towards God to which they dedicated themselves with all their hearts, and who were, at different times, subjected to harsh judicial trials, let all those who were enrolled in municipal registers, although earlier they did belong to their number, let all these give thanks to God, the Liberator of all, for being restored to their ancestral properties and

107

customary comforts. Let those also who have been deprived of their goods and up till now lived a life of utter degradation since they were inflicted with the loss of all they owned, let these be restored to their ancient homes and families and possessions and enjoy with gratitude the kindness of the Supreme God.

But we also command that those, too, who are detained on islands against their will benefit from this provision, in order that they who till now have been closed in on all sides by rugged mountains and surrounded by the waters of the sea may, being freed from their gloomly and desolate isolation, fulfil their fond desire by rejoining their dearest associates. Let these who have for a long time lived a miserable life in disgusting squalor, regarding their return as a prize and being relieved for the future from their anxieties, let these live without fear. That life under our government should be fearful, though we boast and believe ourselves to be the servants of God, would be a most extraordinary thing even only to hear, not to mention to believe, for we are here to put right the errors of others.

All those who were condemned to hard labour in the mines or to do service in the public works let all these have an enjoyable time instead of long-lasting toils, and let them finally live a life of more ease and abundance, ending their interminable and unpleasant labours for quiet relaxation. And if there are any who were deprived of their civic rights and suffered loss of honour, let them just like those who have been abroad for a long stay, hurry back to their home countries, and, with becoming joy, take up their former position.

Nevertheless, let those wo are proved to have once possessed honourable military positions and then deprived of them for the harsh and unjust reason that they preferred the worship of the Supreme God to the rank they held, let these [I repeat] have a free choice to decide whether to remain in their former situation, in case they are content with military life, or to lead, after an honourable discharge, a life of undisturbed peace. For it would be proper and consistent that one who displayed such greatness of soul and endurance with regard to dangers which were brought upon him should, if he so wished, enjoy, according to his own free choice, either leisure or his rank.

Then, also, let those who were forcefully deprived of the privileges of high birth and were subjected to a judicial judgement that had them either thrown into women's and linen-making establishments to suffer harsh and cruel labour, or made use of as slaves of the public treasury, their superior birth being of no help to them, – let all these people delight in the honours they previously enjoyed and the blessings of liberty, resume their customary dignities and live, for the future, in complete happiness. Let him who has been deprived of his free status and made, instead, a slave by some injustice and, no doubt, inhuman madness, who has lamented over his unusual duties and been aware of being, unexpectedly, a slave instead of a free man, let him,

108

on the basis of our edict, regain his freedom, rejoin his family, and let him be engaged in those bodily labours which befit his free status and dismiss from his memory duties which he found distressing and unbecoming.

Nor must we ignore the case of those estates of which some individuals were, on various pretexts, deprived. If any were deprived of their goods because they engaged, with a fearless and undaunted mind, in the noble and divine contest of martyrdom, or if any confessors, standing firm, provided eternal hope for themselves, all these who were forced to settle elsewhere and in addition were deprived of their goods because they did not yield to the persecutors by betraying their faith, or if there are any who, though not suffering the sentence of death, suffered the confiscation of their goods, we order that the estates of these be assigned to their kinsmen. But since, at any rate, the laws simply speak of the nearest kin, it will be easy to decide to whom the estates belong. This is the case also because, according to reason, those would have succeeded to the inheritance who would also have been the nearest kin if the persons in question had died of natural causes.

But if there should be no kinsmen left who would normally succeed to the estate of any one of the above-mentioned, *i.e.*, martyrs, confessors, or those who on some similar pretext were banished from their home-country, let it be ordained that, in each instance, the local church receive the estate. And it will be by no means offensive to the departed that the Church should inherit their estates, since for its sake they submitted to all sorts of sufferings. It is, of course, necessary to add that if any of the above-mentioned donated any of their goods to persons of their own choice, it is reasonable that the sole title should remain with these persons.

That, however, the edict may not be erroneously interpreted, but all readily learn what is right, let all men know that if they have in their possession a piece of land, or a house, or a garden, or anything else which belongs to the above-mentioned persons, it is fair and it is their duty to acknowledge it and to restore it will all haste. For if it should, for the most part, appear that some made abundant profits from this unjust possession, we do not consider a demand on their behalf as just. Nevertheless, let them declare how much they gained, and from what sources, and let them ask us for pardon for this, in order that their convetousness may first be set right by such atonement, and the Great God, at the same time, may accept this as some measure of penance, and be gracious to those who had done wrong.

But those who became masters of such properties (if it is proper or possible to attach to them this title) will perhaps say by way of apology that it could not be avoided at a time when arbitrariness was visible everywhere, people were cruelly banished, killed without mercy, thoughtlessly cast out, when confiscations of property were common, and when the persecutions and plunder of the goods of innocent people were increasing, – if any should justify themselves with such arguments as these, and persevere in their greedy inclinations, they will learn that such conduct of theirs will not be un-punished, and all the more since this is how the Supreme God is served by our government. From now on, therefore, it will be dangerous to retain what deadly necessity earlier made it imperative to take. Besides, it is necessary by every means to lessen greediness, both by reasoning and exemplary lessons.

Nor will the treasury be allowed to hold on to anything that it might possess that belongs to the above-mentioned people. But, without even venturing as much as to speak against the holy churches, the treasury will rightly give up, in favour of the churches, the possession of all those things which it for a while retained without just cause. Therefore, we order that all things that appear rightfully to belong to the churches, whether the posses-sion happens to be houses, or some fields, or gardens, or whatever else, shall be restored, without exception and in their entirety, and with an undiminished right of their possession.

Also, who would doubt that the very places which have been held in honour on account of the bodies of the martyrs and have become memorials of their glorious departure, rightly belong to the churches, and who would not issue an edict to that effect? For surely there could be no offering more noble, no labour more pleasing and more profitable than, by the prompting of the Divine Sign, to be zealously engaged in such matters as these and to secure, as is just, the restoration and safe return to the holy churches of those things which were taken away from them under false pretenses by unjust and most wicked men.

But since it would be wrong in an all-inclusive provision to pass over in silence those who either obtained anything from the treasury by the right of purchase, or retained it after they got it as a gift, let those who, rashly, went so far as to indulge their insatiable greed in such acts as these be in-formed that even though, especially by daring to make these purchases, they risked the alienation of our goodwill to them, they shall nevertheless not fail in obtaining this, within the limits of possibility and proper fashion. For the time being, let this much be determined.

But since it became clear by the most manifest and plainest proofs that, through the goodness of the Almighty God and also through the counsels and the aid which He deigns, on so many occasions, to administer on my behalf, the ill temper that earlier afflicted the whole human race is now banished from everywhere, let all people, one by one, recognize after earnest meditation how mighty and how gracious He is who utterly wiped out and destroyed a race, so to say, of the most wicked and evil men, but who restored joy to the good people and is now diffusing it in abundance to all countries, and, moreover, gives full freedom to honour the Divine Law, as it should be honoured with all reverence, and to pay due homage to those who dedicated themselves to the service of this Law. They, as if rising out of some abyss of darkness and possessing a clear insight into matters, will in the future demon-

110

strate the worship and honour that is proper and due to the Divine Law. Let this be published in our Eastern provinces.

Curiously, Constantine orders, though grudgingly, a limited restitution only in cases when the 'new owners' of Christian properties had actually purchased them from the treasury or received them as gifts. Clearly, this edict went beyond the provisions of the Edict of Milan, particularly, in that it provided for restitution not only to the corporate Church but also to its individual members.

That the edict's historicity has been denied is not suprising,[23] for some modern historians simply have not been able to accept the possibility that so many injuries still remained, even after the Milan conference, to be healed. Whether or not there was real need for all these elaborate provisions for making up for all the wrongs done not only under Licinius, but also under all his persecuting predecessors ever since 303 A.D., the fact is that this edict has been proved to be completely historical thanks to a papyrus discovered recently.[24] Indeed, this edict intended to liquidate, once and for all, the persecutions, this time in the Eastern provinces. Once again, Constantine is acting on behalf of the Holy Catholic Church as God's chosen one, whom the Supreme God had led all the way from Britain to the East to ensure His Worship in His Holy Church!

Constantine, in his relatively brief reference to his pagan subjects does not hold out much goodwill towards them, for "who could obtain any good who would not recognize God as the author of all good things or give Him proper worship?" Constantine has only reproach for all those, including his predecessors in the Imperial purple who persecuted the Church, although by doing so and as the punishment of God, they brought ruin and suffering on themselves and their subjects.

In this edict Constantine openly confessed Christianity as his faith, declared Christianity to be the favoured religion, and manifested only an ominous snarl at those who persisted in

23. Concerning the edict's historicity, see Baynes, *Constantine the Great etc., op. cit.* 354 f.; n. 55; also Dörries, *op. cit.*, 59-61.

24. See A.H.M. Jones, "Notes on the Genuineness of the Constantinian Documents in Eusebius' Life of Constantine," *J. Eccl. Hist.* 5 (1954) 196-200.

refusing the Supreme God of Christianity. The pagans no doubt felt uneasy and even apprehensive about their status in this newly established Christian Empire. In another edict, or constitution, Constantine had to say something concerning this, if only to allay their fears. Furthermore, there had also been some panicky rumours flying around "that the rites of the temples and the power of darkness" were being abolished. Once again, reviewing, therefore, and condemning the great persecution and its originators, but particularly Diocletian, as barbarous and as a shameful stain on the history of Rome, and proclaiming his conviction that the perpetrators of this "abomination are gone forever" after a shameful death and that "they are consigned to ever-lasting punishment in the depths of hell", Constantine declares that, in the interest of the peace of the Roman world and the whole of mankind, he grants religious freedom to all non-Christians: "Let those who delight in error have the same enjoyment of peace and quiet as those have who believe!" Though the peace he grants to his pagan subjects is grudging, nevertheless, in most exemplary Christian spirit, he tells his subjects: "Let no one molest the other! Let everybody follow what his soul prefers ..., so that the equal privileges may bring about their conversion and restoration to the straight path." Here is the whole constitution guaranteeing religious freedom to his pagan subjects:[25]

Victor Constantinus, Maximus, Augustus, to the People of the Eastern Provinces.

All things that are under the control of the most compelling laws of nature, provide for men an adequate idea of providence and planning in the Divine dispensation. And those whose minds are on the right road that leads to knowledge in order to reach this end, do not have any doubt that the correct application of sound reasoning and one's very eyesight lead, through the power of true virtue alone, to the knowledge of God. Accordingly, not one wise man will be disturbed if he sees that the masses are driven by opposite plans. For the beauty of virtue would remain hidden and unattractive if vice had not, by contrast, made manifest the perversity of senseless life. This is why a crown awaits virtue, while the most high God Himself hands out the condemnation.

But I will try to explain to you all, as clearly as possible, my personal thoughts.

25. Eusebius, *Vita Constant.* II, 48-60.

I used to regard the former emperors as repulsive on account of the brutality of their methods. In fact, my father was the only one who practised the deeds of humanity, and in all his actions he called on God the Saviour with admirable reverence. But all the others, not being sound of mind, pursued deeds of cruelty rather then humanity, they cultivated their disposition without restraint, they distorted the True Doctrine, each in his own time, and their violence became so harsh that, although relations in religious and political matters were peaceable, they rekindled the flames of civil wars.

At that time, they say that Apollo speaking from the inmost part of a dark cavern but without the medium of any human being declared that the righteous people of the earth were preventing him from speaking the truth, and that, therefore, the oracles of the tripod were made false. For his priestess consequently let her locks down because she was deprived of the oracular spirit, and lamented the harm that it meant for the human race. But let us see what consequences this had.

Now, I call on you, Most High God, to be my witness that when I was a young man I myself heard him who at that time was the Senior Emperor of the Romans, a wretched, truly wretched man, suffering from delusion and deceit, making serious enquiries from his bodyguards as to who the just of the earth were, and that one of the soothsayers in his company answered that they were undoubtedly the Christians. Swallowing the answer like some honey, he unsheathed the swords, which were to serve for the punishment of crimes, against irreproachable holiness. He therefore immediately drew up edicts by points of swords stained by bloodshed, and ordered the judges to strain their natural brain-power for the invention of newer ways of punishment.

Then, indeed, one could see with what violence that holy religion of God's worship was daily subjected, with sustained fierceness, to the most shocking outrages, and how a modesty, which no enemy would ever wrong, became the object of the enraged citizens' drunken frolic. There was no form of punishment by fire, torture or any kind of torment that was not applied to anyone without any regard to age. It was then that the earth openly shed tears, and the all-encompassing universe was in deep mourning because it became polluted by the bloodshed, and the very light of the day, pained by the spectacle it was exposed to, covered its face.

But what is the meaning of these events? Now, the barbarians are boasting that, in contrast to the events just mentioned, they received and guarded in humane captivity those who at that time were fleeing from us, and that they guaranteed for them not only personal safety, but also the practice of the holy religion in security. And now the Roman nation bears this lasting stain on its honour, which the Christians, driven from the Roman world at that time, and fleeing to the barbarians, branded on them.

But what need is there for me to dwell any longer on these sad events and the general misery of the Roman world? Those perpetrators of that abomination are gone for ever; experiencing a shameful death, they are consigned to never-ending punishment in the depths of hell. For they were entangled in civil wars against each other, and left neither their names nor families behind. This would never have happened to them if that impious practice of issuing prophesies by the Pythian Apollo had not exercised a deceitful influence on them.

Now, I call upon you, most high God. Be kind and gracious to your people of the Eastern provinces crushed by long-lasting misfortune, bring them healing through me, your servant. Nor do I, Holy God, ask you, the Lord of All, for this without reason. For it was with your guidance that I instituted and accomplished saving measures, and, keeping your emblem everywhere before me, I led my army to glorious victory, and if ever there is a call in the interest of public necessity, I set out against the enemy by following the same emblem of your goodness. This is why I dedicated to You my soul purified by love and fear, for I truly love your name, and I revere your power, which you demonstrated with many signs and thus made my faith ever firmer. Therefore, I hasten to devote all my strength to the restoration of your most holy house, which those abominable and most impious men outraged with their defilement and destruction.

In the interest of the Roman world and the whole of mankind, it is my desire that Your people live peaceably and without civil strife. Let those who delight in error have the same enjoyment of peace and quiet as those have who believe. For the equal enjoyment of common privileges will bring about their conversion and restoration to the straight path. Let no one molest the other. Let everybody follow what his soul prefers, let him make full use of this. Those of sound judgement must, however, be persuaded that only those will live a holy and pure life whom You call to a dependence on your holy laws. But let those who separate themselves have their shrines of falsehood if they wish. We have the glorious house of Your truth. What You gave us as birth-right we pray that you give them too, so that they, too, may receive in their hearts the joy that is the manifest fruit of the unity of minds.

For in our system, from the time when we believe the order of the universe was firmly established, there has been nothing new nor any recent innovation but You ordered it for the glory that befits Your Name. But although the human race fell and was led into all sorts of errors, You, in order that the evil one should not oppress it any longer, You, through your Son, held up to us pure light and gave testimony of Yourself to all men.

The truth of this is supported by Your works. Your power makes us free of guilt, and makes us faithful. The sun and the moon follow a course prescribed for them, nor do the stars follow an irregular orbit in their cosmic revolution. The cyclic changes of the seasons are established by law. The steady position of the earth is settled by Your law, and the wind is brought into motion according to prescribed law, the rushing movement of the waters goes on with an unlimited flow, the sea is surrounded with fixed boundaries, and whatever is stretched out on the earth and the ocean, all this is contrived for some wonderful and useful purposes. If this were not produced by Your device and will, such diversity and such a great variety of powers would unquesntionably bring ruin on all life and its works. Otherwise, those beings that fight among themselves and, though unseen, do injury to the human race even now, would do even greater injury to human kind.

Very many thanks to You, Lord of the universe and Mighty God, for the more human nature becomes known through its diverse pursuits, the more are the teachings of Your Divine Word confirmed to those who think rightly and care for true virtue. But as for anyone who refuses to be cured, let him not attribute this to anyone else, for the medicine that surpasses all medicines is placed in the open, at the disposal of all people. Only let no one injure this religion, which experience has shown to be without blemish. Let us, therefore, all of us, enjoy the good, *i.e.*, the blessing of peace that has been given to us all by keeping our consciences clear from all strife.

But let no one use the faith he has received for hurting another; let everyone, if possible, help his neighbour with what he knows and believes in, but if that is not possible, let him leave him alone. For it is one thing to enter voluntarily into conflict for the prize of immortality, and another to use force with the threat of punishment.

I have said this, and discussed it in a more detailed fashion than the purpose of an ordinary letter of mine would demand, because I am unwilling to conceal from you my faith in what is the truth, but mostly, because, as I hear, there are some who say that the rituals of the temples and the power of darkness have been removed. We would have advised this removal to all people, if the violent and rebellious spirit of wretched error were not still firmly implanted in the souls of some for the frustration of the salvation of all.

Clearly, this edict is a public confession of the Christian faith: "Let those who separate themselves have, if they wish, their precincts of falsehood. We have the glorious house of Your truth!" The fervent confession of Christianity and, indeed, the entirely feverish interest the writer shows in its protection are so typically Constantinian that there can be no serious doubt that this letter to the Eastern Provinces was also that of Constantine.[26]

26. Concerning doubts about its authenticity, see Baynes, "Constantine the Great and the Christian Church," *op. cit.* n. 56. While Baynes defends its genuine Constantinian authorship, A. Crivelucci, "I documenti della 'Vita

Constantine made some other laws that he thought were necessary for the establishment of a flourishing Church in the newly acquired Empire of Licinius, by bringing about the enlarging and rebuilding of the old churches and the building of new ones.[27] His letter to Eusebius and other bishops envisages exactly this programme for which, as was his custom in his Western Empire, he offers the unlimited resources of the Empire.[28]

Victor Constantinus, Maximus, Augustus to Eusebius.

Since tyranny has by its unholy council, until now, persecuted the servants of God the Saviour, I am fully satisfied and convinced, my dear Brother, that the buildings belonging to all the churches either became delapidated through indifference, or, through fear of the constant threat of violence, received less attention than they should. But now that liberty is given back, and that that dragon is, by the providence of the Great God and through my ministry, driven out of the administration of public affairs, I believe that the power of God has become evident to all, and that those who, through fear or unbelief, embraced some errors recognize the true God, and will come to the true and right state of life. Concerning, then, all those churches over which you yourself preside and the other bishops, priests, and deacons whom you know to be presiding over them at different places, admonish these to be zealous about the buildings of the churches, and either to repair or enlarge the existing ones, or, wherever necessary, build new ones.

However, you, and the others through you, must demand all the necessary things from the provincial governors and the office of the Praefect. For these have been commanded zealously to comply with your Holiness' orders. May God watch over you, beloved Brother.

With the dissonance of 'the dragon, by the Providence of God, driven out,' through these and other constitutions Constantine proved himself to be a most powerful protector of the Church — a Church that found itself completely unprepared for its newly found freedom, and in sore need of its Protector's faith, resources, and even at times almost overwhelming authority.

Constantini'," *Studi Storici* 7 (1898) 453-459 rejects it. See also H. Kraft, *Kaiser Konstantins religiöse Entwicklung* (Tübingen, 1955) 212 f.

27. Eusebius, *Vita Constant.* II; 45.

28. *Ibid.* 46.

ARIANISM AND CONSTANTINE:
WOLVES WITHIN THE FOLD IN SHEEP'S CLOTHING

Having joined the East to his Empire, Constantine at the same time proved himself to be a true son of the Holy Church and a true missionary of the true Christian faith. But he also had another great hope. The unity of the Western Church was, if not shattered, certainly disturbed by the persistent existence and even the violent activities of the Donatist Schism, and Constantine hoped that by the help of the bishops of the East the breach in the Western Church might be completely healed.[1] This was a vain hope. The Emperor had hardly arrived in Nicomedia when he learned that the Church in the East was suffering from a perhaps even more serious disunity. In fact, the cause of disunity in the East later spread even to the West and proved to be more disastrous than the Donatist schism had ever been. In fact, it seemed for a while to have conquered the whole Empire.

This disease, known as the Arian heresy, had its origins in Alexandria, in the dispute between Arius, an Alexandrian priest, and Alexander, the Bishop of Alexandria, or rather in the humanistic, materialistic, and down-to-earth logic of the Alexandrian priest. Arius,[2] a disciple of Lucian, the Antiochian philosopher who had been disowned by bishops of Antioch, drifted, like other pupils of Lucian, away from simple faith into the "intellectual" speculations of the so called Christian Platonism of his predecessors such as Origen and Dionysius. Not being able to understand the Christian doctrine concerning the relationship of God the Father and God the Son, Arius maintained that, since the son had to be posterior to the father, the Son was created by the Father out of

1. Eusebius, *Vita Constant.* II, 63 ff.
2. Socrates, *H.E.* I, 5; Sozomen, *H.E.* I, 15, 1 ff.; H.M. Gwatkin, *Studies in Arianism* (Cambridge, 1882); "Arianism," *Cambridge Med. Hist.* V. i (Cambridge U.P., 1957) 119 ff.; A.H.M. Jones, *Constantine and the Conversion of Europe* (London, 1968) 139 ff.; *et al.*

nothing, and that therefore He was not God in the same sense as the Father, and that thus the Father was not always a father. Not content with expressing his views to his regular congregation and among theologians, and badly in need of admiring crowds, Arius also expressed his heretical views in verse that had a great appeal to the common folk.[3] Arius' shocking views resulted in a few debates in which Arius expressed his opinions in an even more extreme fashion, which circumstance, in its turn, resulted in the convocation of a Council of Bishops. A great number, – about 100 – bishops subject to Alexander's authority assembled and they, with the exception of two of them, condemned and anathematized Arius and his doctrines. Consequently, the condemnation of the Arian heresy, its author, and his followers was published in a letter, perhaps of 319 A.D., by Bishop Alexander of Alexandria to his clergy.[4]

Arius, then, turned to Eusebius, recently Bishop of Berytus, but now of the prestigious place called Nicomedia, by writing to his "fellow student" of Lucian. However, this letter is nothing but a repetitive reaffirmation of the Arian heresy, with a request for support.[5] What we have of Eusebius' reply to Arius is short, and served only to confirm Arius in his heresy:[6] "Your thinking is all right, pray that all may think as you do. It is obvious to all that that which was made did not exist before it came into existence. That which came into existence has a beginning of its existence."

Arius soon left Alexandria and Egypt for Nicomedia and the East to seek support for himself and his cause.[7] His fellow Lucianists and other supporters of his wrote to Bishop Alexander of Alexandria in order to defend Arius and his heresy. Eusebius of Nicomedia, however, perhaps in answer to Arius' earlier excommunication by Alexander and the other bishops of Egypt and Libya, himself convoked a synod of the Bishops of Bithynia, and had Arius and his doctrine approved by them.[8]

3. E.g. in Athanasius, *De synodis* 15.
4. Socrates, *H.E.* I, 6, 4 ff.; Gelasius Cyz., *H.E.* II, 3, 1.
5. Theodoretus, *H.E.* I, 5; Epiphanius, *Haer.* 69, 6.
6. Athanasius, *De synodis* 17.
7. B.J. Kidd, *A History of the Church to A.D. 461* (Oxford U.P., 1922) v. ii, 16-19.
8. Sozomen, *H.E.* I, 15, 10.

It must have been at this time and in the company of Eusebius of Nicomedia that Arius and some of his followers sent a letter to Bishop Alexander of Alexandria formally stating what amounts to the Arian Creed.[9] This was a grave provocation to Bishop Alexander and the result no doubt of the encouragement of Eusebius of Nicomedia. The other Eusebius, the Bishop of Caesarea, seems to have supported Arius in a Council of Palestinian bishops, which council also passed a resolution that Arius should be permitted to assemble the people as before, but that he should submit to Bishop Alexander of Alexandria and be reconciled with him.[10]

But Bishop Alexander remained firm. He confirmed the orthodox position in innumerable letters.[11] One of the most important of these many letters was one he wrote, probably, to his namesake, Alexander, the Bishop of Byzantium.[12] In this letter[13] the Bishop of Alexandria bitterly complains about the activities of Arius and especially of Achillas, an Arian supporter, who built "dens of robbers," were incessantly raising riots and persecutions against him, and were discrediting Christianity through the activities of undisciplined females who were parading "around every street in indecent fashion."

It was about this time that Constantine, having just defeated Licinius in 324 A.D., came to the East with high hopes and expressed his profound disappointment that the Bishops of the East were indeed in no position at all to help him to heal the wounds of schism in the Western Church. Constantine's letter to Bishop Alexander of Alexandria and Arius is a clear testimony to Constantine's dismay at the outbreak of this new heresy:[14]

Constantine Victor Maximus Augustus to Alexander and Arius.

I call, if I may, on my helper in my undertakings, the Saviour of all, God Himself, to testify that I had a twofold reason for endeavoring the business which I have performed. Firstly, I planned to bring the opinions of all nations concerning the Deity to a condition, as it were, of uniformity, and secondly,

9. Athanasius, *De synodis* 16; Epiphanius, *Haer.* 69, 7; Jones, *op. cit.* 143.
10. Sozomen, *H.E.* I, 15; Jones, *op. cit.* 143; Kidd, *op. cit.* 18.
11. *Ibid.* 19; Epiphanius, *Haer.* 69, 4.
12. Theodoretus, *H.E.* I, 3. For a discussion of the identity of this other Bishop Alexander, see H.G. Opitz, *Athanasius Werke* v. iii, part i, p. 19.
13. Theodoretus, *H.E.* I, 3.
14. Eusebius, *Vita Constant.* II, 64-72.

to restore to health the body of the whole world suffering, as it were, from some grievous disease. With these plans in my mind, I was logically thinking out the first problem with the mystical eye of intellect, while I tried to rectify the second with the might of military intervention. For I knew that if I established, according to my aspirations, a unity of mind among all the servants of God, the business of public necessities would experience a happy change closely corresponding with the pious thoughts of all. When, then, the whole of Africa was seized by an intolerable madness, and since this happened through the agency of people daring, with a thoughtless frivolty, to split the worship of the people into various heresies, I, wishing to check this sickness, found no other therapy that would meet the problem than to send some of you to help restore unanimity among those who had the disagreement, after I removed the common enemy of the world who with his lawless judgement prevented your holy synods. For since the power of Light and the law of Sacred Worship, granted by the favour of God, as it were, from the bosom of the East, at once illuminated the world with its sacred light, I, believing that you were the chief promoters of the salvation of the nation, naturally undertook, with the determination of my mind and a forceful enquiry, to seek your help. Therefore, immediately after my great victory and true triumph over my enemies, the matter which I chose as my first subject of inquiry was the one which I believed to be the first and most important of all matters.

But, most glorious and Divine Providence, what a critical wound was inflicted on my heart when I heard the report that the dissension that existed among you was much more grievous than the one that seized the people in that other place, so that you, through whose aid I hoped there would be cure for the others, are in greater need of therapy. And yet, when I examined the origin and cause of all this, I found the pretext for it far too trifling and unworthy of such contentiousness as this. Being therefore compelled to write this letter to you about your unanimity and wisdom and calling upon Divine Providence to help me in this matter, I take upon me the role of the Chief Counsellor of peace to mediate in your disagreement among you. For with the help of a Higher Power, even though the occasion of the disagreement was greater, I was able, without much difficulty, to recall them to a more useful condition, by applying reason to the pious sentiments of those who heard me; this time, when the cause that is impeding the whole body is trifling and very insignificant, shall I not expect an easier and much speedier solution of the problem?

I understand, then, that the beginning of the present controversy was like this. When you, Alexander, enquired of the priests what each of them thought concerning a certain passage of the Scriptures, or rather, concerning frivolous questions, then you, Arius, inconsiderately rejoined with what was not proper, to begin with, even to consider, or, if considered, it should have been buried

120

in silence. Since dissension was aroused among you, communion was denied, and the holy people, split into two parties, lost the unity of the common body. Therefore, let each of you equally exhibit forgiveness, and accept the advice your fellow servant rightly gives. What is this advice? In the first place, it was not proper to ask such questions, nor was it proper to answer them. For those questions which are not enjoined by the authority of any law, but rather suggested by the contentious spirit that comes from useless leisure, even though it is for the sake of some philosophical exercise, should all the same be confined within our minds and not hastily carried to popular gatherings, nor should they be inconsiderately made the topic of popular talks. For how few are capable either to comprehend exactly or to explain worthily the nature of such sublime and very difficult topics? Even if one were believed to be able to do this easily, how many people would he convince? Again, in dealing with such a very subtle question, who can possibly avoid the danger of making a serious mistake? Therefore, in such topics as this, loquacity must be checked to prevent the people from the certain danger of falling either into blashphemy or schism, either because we are perchance not able to explain our subject, on account of the weakness of our natural faculties, or, because our listeners, on account of the slowness of their understanding, are perhaps unable to arrive at a correct comprehension of what has been said.

For this reason, let both the inconsiderate question and the answer receive forgivness equally from each of you respectively. For your contention did not come about in relation to any of the leading doctrines of the Law, nor has any new heresy arisen among you concerning the worship of God. On the contrary, you have the same conclusion, so that you can come together for the covenant of communion. It is believed that it is not becoming and by no means lawful that so large a portion of the people of God, which ought to flourish under your devout prayers, should be divided in their beliefs, and this on account of your strife concerning small and very insignificant matters.

At this point, I would like to bring to your mind a small thing as a lesson to you. You know that the philosophers, too, are united in one doctrine; nevertheless they often disagree in some part of their teachings, and though they differ with respect to the merit of knowledge, nevertheless they are indeed once again in agreement with regard to the unity of their doctrine. If this is so, would it not be much more fitting for you, the servants of the Supreme God, to be of one mind regarding the profession of religion?

But let us examine what I have said, more thoughtfully and with attention, and see whether it is right that, on account of some trifling and foolish verbal disagreements among you, brothers are hostile to brothers, and the venerable Synod is divided through impious dissension by you who are fighting among you about minor and altogether inessential matters. This is vulgar, and characteristic of childish foolishness rather than befitting the wisdom of holy and prudent men. Let us willingly keep away from the tempations of the devil. Our great God, the Saviour of all, extended his light to all alike. Let me, His Servant, under His Providence, bring to completion my task, so that I may be able, by my exhortation, my service, and insistent warning, to bring you, His people, to communion in the assemblies.

Since, then, as I said, you have the same faith, the one and same Church community among you, and since the commandment of the Law in both its parts obliges everybody to a spirit of concord, let not this affair which has caused this slight dissension among you, since it does not concern the nature of the complete Law, cause schism and faction among you in any way. And I do not say this to force you to come to a complete agreement concerning this very silly question, whatever its nature may be. For the honour of your synod can be preserved uncontaminated and your communion kept united, even though there may be among you some disagreement concerning some very insignificant matter. For we do not have the same inclinations in everything and we are not constituted to have the same nature and judgement. Therefore, concerning the Divine Providence let there be one faith and one judgement among you, and united consensus concerning the Almighty. But the very subtle disputations amongst you concerning these very unimportant questions, even though you may not come to agreement, should be kept guarded within the secret recesses of your thoughts and minds. Let, therefore, the virtue of mutual love, a faith in the truth, and the honour due to God and to the observance of his law remain among you undisturbed. Return then to mutual love and goodwill, let all the people embrace according to their custom. And as for yourselves, having, as it were, purified your souls, once again acknowledge one another. For friendship often becomes sweeter when it comes to reconciliation after the removal of hostility.

Give me back, then, my quiet days and untroubled nights, so that for me too there may be reserved some joy of tranquil life and the enjoyment of peace for the rest of my life. Otherwise, I will have no choice but to groan and be covered with tears, and I will not be able to live the rest of my life with a serene mind. For while the people of God, whom I call my fellow servants, are thus divided among themselves by an unjust and harmful strife, how is it possible for me to maintain my usual equanimity? But you should understand my excessive grief on account of this matter. When I recently visited the city of Nicomedia it was my intention to proceed immediately to the East. But while I was hastening toward you and had accomplished the greater part of the distance, the news of this matter reversed my plan, lest I should be obliged to see with my eyes what I did not think I could bear hearing with my ears. From now on, open to me then, by your unity, the road to the East which you obstructed with your dissensions among yourselves, and allow me to rejoice in beholding you and all the other people together soon, and to express in hymns of praise my thanks due to God for the general concrod and freedom of all people.

Coming to the East and at the same time seeing that his high hopes of having the Donatist schism healed with the help of the East were dashed, Constantine tries at least to stop the schism and the heresy that were quickly spreading in the Church in the East. His heart was no doubt wounded and suffered from excessive grief when he heard of the serious rift in the Church in the East. He therefore sent with this letter Hosius of Cordova to Alexandria[15] to restore unity. The Emperor's initial reactions and arguments may sound[16] like those of a 'plain man.' Saying however that the quarrel was about 'a very silly question'; that the cause of the split in the East was "trifling and very insignificant" and "unworthy of such contentiousness," Constantine rather betrays a lack of understanding of the problem involved in the controversy. He may also have wished to have "unity," of the kind desiderated by some ecumenical movements, at any price, without regard for deep and unchangeable traditional doctrine, sincere faith and conviction. But it is not likely that Constantine had this fatuous and false approach to Church unity. His suggestion that Bishop Alexander and Arius follow the example of pagan philosophers, who though united in one doctrine may still differ in some details, implies rather that he still did not quite understand Catholic doctrine and had much to learn. For it cannot be doubted that Constantine really possessed both the fervour and faithful orthodoxy of a sincere neophyte, or rather catechumen, though his understanding was still not deep enough.

There were two other schisms which, though still unknown to him, Constantine had to resolve. One was the schism of Colluthus, the other that of Melitius.

The schism of Colluthus[17] was the lesser evil. Though only a

15. The authenticity of this letter should be beyond question, but cf. P. Batiffol, "Les documents de la Vita Constantini," *Bull. d'anc. litt. et d'arch. chrét.* 4 (1914) esp. 83-86; N.H. Baynes, "Constantine the Great and the Christian Church," *Proceedings of the British Acad.* 15 (1929) 357; n. 59; also H. Kraft, *Kaiser Konstantins religiöse Entwicklung* (Tübingen, 1955) 217.

16. As Jones, *op. cit.* 144, believes.

17. See Athanasius, *Apologia c. Arian.* 12; 75; Epiphanius, *Haer.* 69, 2; Theodoretus, *H.E.* I, 8; Augustine, *Haer.* 65; Jones, *op. cit.* 146, *et al.*

priest of Alexandria, Colluthus was usurping the office of bishop by ordaining priests. Though he was known as strongly anti-Arian, the cause of the schism is not really known. Hosius, however, was able to trim down the revolt at a Council of about one hundred bishops at Alexandria, perhaps in 324 A.D., by declaring Colluthus was in fact only a priest. Colluthus' many followers remained nevertheless unreconciled and bitter, and, perhaps rightly, blamed the Emperor for the reversal in their fortunes.

The schism of Melitius, on the other hand, was very serious,[18] and its origins go back to the Great Persecution. Melitius, Bishop of Lykopolis, and Peter, Bishop of Alexandria, had been together in prison where they had argued about the future treatment of the *lapsed*, Melitius favouring a rather harsh treatment and Peter a more lenient one. Released in 306 A.D., the two bishops continued their sharp disagreement on the subject. Peter issued a list of rather mild prescriptions for the treatment of the *lapsed*. Consequently, Melitius formally revolted, and then ordained his own priests, and even a bishop, and when, despite warning, he continued this practice, he was excommunicated by Bishop Peter. After the martyrdom of Bishop Peter, the schism continued through the terms of office of Achillas and Alexander as Bishops of Alexandria.

Hearing from Hosius of these additional troubles of the Church in the East Constantine decided to convene a Council, and then sent out letters to bishops inviting them to assemble at Ancyra.[19] The future great Council of the Church, however, was to have an important forerunner in the important Council of Antioch, probably early in 325 A.D.

It would seem that the Council of Antioch[20] was summoned after the death on December 20, 324 A.D., of Philogonius, the Bishop of Antioch, a strong supporter of Bishop Alexander of Alexandria, in the Arian dispute, perhaps to ensure a successor like him. Bishops and representatives of the provinces subject to

18. See Athanasius, *passim*; Epiphanius, *Haer.* 68; H.I. Bell, *Jews and Christians in Egypt* (London, 1924) 38 ff.; F.H. Kettler, "Der melitianische Streit in Agypten," *Zschr. f. N.T. Wiss.* 35 (1936) 155-193; Jones, *op. cit.* 146-149; *et al.*

19. Opitz, *op. cit.* 41-42.

20. F.L. Cross, "The Council of Antioch in 325 A.D.," *Church Quarterly Rev.* 128 (1939) 49-76; Baynes, *op. cit.* 358 f. and n. 61 with a good bibliography; Jones, *op. cit.* 149 f.

Antioch elected Eustathius, the Bishop of Beroea, a strong anti-Arian, to succeed to the see of Antioch, but he was apparently left for the time being unconsecrated, perhaps to await the approval of the great Council.

The Council of Antioch, with Hosius presiding, produced a Creed,[21] which was orthodox and strongly anti-Arian and approved by all but three of the bishops of the Council.[22] If Constantine had expected from the Council of Antioch a consensus of opinion on the Arian question[23] he now obtained it. It was perhaps this result of the Council of Antioch that encouraged the Emperor to call a Great Council to resolve the Arian dispute, and it was perhaps only at this time that the Great Council was called by him. But Constantine was perhaps taken by surprise by the Council of Antioch's prejudging,[24] as may indeed have been the case, the matter to be placed before the future Great Council. Therefore he quickly issued a letter to *all* bishops in which he told them that they were to assemble in Nicaea in Bithynia, a place clearly more convenient than Ancyra would have been. The letter of invitation is as follows:[25]

Letter of Emperor Constantine Bidding the Bishops from Ancyra to Nicaea.

That there is nothing more highly valued in my eyes than the worship of God is, I believe, clear to all. As it was previously agreed that the synod of bishops should be at Ancyra of Galatia I have now decided for many reasons that it should be assembled in the city of Nicaea of Bithynia, both because the bishops of Italy and the rest of Europe are coming, and because of its pleasant climate, and also in order that I may be at hand to observe and participate in the proceedings. Therefore, I inform you, Beloved Brethren, that you are to be assembled in the above mentioned city, that is, Nicaea. Let every one of you, then, keeping in mind the common good, as I said above, hasten without delay and speedily, so that he may personally observe the proceedings that are going to take place. May God preserve you, Beloved Brethren.

We have no official record of this truly great ecumenical council

21. Cross, *op. cit.* 71-74.
22. H. Nordberg, *Athanasius and the Emperor* (Societas Scient. Fenn., Helsinki, 1963) 16.
23. *Ibid.*
24. Jones, *op. cit.* 150.
25. For the text in translation, see Opitz, *op. cit.* 41 f.

of the Church at Nicaea and although we still have many details from other sources, there are still tantalizing questions that remain unanswered. The only original documents we have of the Council are the Nicaean Creed, the twenty canons, the letter of the Council to the Church of Alexandria, and the two letters of the Emperor Constantine, one of which he wrote to the Church of Alexandria, and the other to the Churches at large.[26]

The total number of bishops present at the Council is unknown. It varies according to the sources, though the actual number must have been about three hundred. The overwhelming majority were from the Eastern part of the Empire, but some even came from outside, such as Armenia and Persia. The West was represented by only a few bishops. Even the Pope, aged and ill, was it seems represented only by two deacons.

Eusebius of Caesarea[27] describes in detail the opening ceremonies in the great hall of the Imperial palace in Nicaea, the Emperor's entrance, and the Emperor's unusually short opening address to the Council:[28]

My greatest desire, my Friends, used to be to enjoy the show offered by your gathering, and since this desire of mine is fulfilled, I confess that I am grateful to the King of All, because in addition to all His other blessings He granted me this blessing that is greater than the rest, namely, to see you all gathered together and to watch you professing the one, common and harmonious faith of all. May no malignant enemy destroy our blessings, and, now that the war of the tyrants against God has been, by the power of God the Saviour, liquidated, may the evil spirit that delights in wickedness, by using yet another trick, not surround the Divine Law with blasphemies. For it is my conviction that internal strife within the Church of God is more grievous than all terrible wars and strife, and our present troubles appear to be more distressing than those coming from outside. Therefore, when, by the will and co-operation of the Supreme God, I was victorious over my enemies, I was in the belief that nothing more was left for me but to give thanks to God and to share in the joy of those who had been liberated by Him through me. But

26. See Baynes, op. cit. 359, and notes 62; 63; 64; H.M. Gwatkin, Studies in Arianism, op. cit. 38 ff.; "Constantine and His City," Cambridge Med. Hist. v. i (Cambridge U.P., 1957) 13 ff.; "Arianism," op. cit. 121 ff.; Jones, op. cit. 152 ff.

27. Vita Constant. III, 6-11.

28. Ibid. 12; also, Socrates, H.E. I, 8; Sozomen, H.E. I, 17; etc.

as soon as I learnt of your strife, information which was against my expectations, and to which I attributed no mean importance, wishing that this
matter, too, should receive attention through my service, I summoned all of
you to me. I rejoice in seeing your assembly, but I believe that I will regard
my prayers answered to the highest degree when I see you all united in your
hearts and a common and harmonious peace reigning among you, that peace
which you ought to bring to others, since you are consecrated to God. Do
not delay, then, my friends, ministers of God, and faithful servants of the
common Lord and Saviour of us all, and begin from now on to bring into the
open the causes of your strife and, by obeying the demands of peace, remove
all causes that keep up the controversy. By doing this, you will accomplish
what pleases God, and you will confer upon me, your fellow servant, an
exceedingly high favour.

How Constantine had hoped that nothing more was left for him
to do except to give thanks to God and to share in the joy of those
who had been liberated by him! Once again, then, expressing his
deepest disappointment at finding dissension and strife in the
Church in the East, Constantine urges the Council members to
unity,[29] since 'strife within the Church of God is more grievous
than all the terrible wars ...'

The way in which the Council of Nicaea arrived at its all important achievement is rather mysterious.[30] It may be and it is
even likely that, perhaps at the encouragement of the Emperor
Constantine, Eusebius of Caesarea proposed what is regarded as
the traditional baptismal Creed of Caesarea, which after some
amendments, essential for some,[31] or minor according to others,
was accepted as the Creed of the Council. Therefore the letter of
Eusebius of Caesarea to his Church, though far from telling all the
truth, is most helpful in shedding some light on what was probably
the essential process by which the Nicaean Creed was formulated.
Here is the letter of the embarrassed Eusebius to the Church of
Caesarea:[32]

29. Not to unity at any price, nor merely to a 'unanimous decision,' as
suggested by Gwatkin, "Constantine and His City," *op. cit.* 14.
30. For simple accounts of the debate according to Eustathius, Eusebius
of Caesarea, and Athanasius, see the somewhat biassed, but useful notes in
Jones, *op. cit.* 158 f.
31. *Ibid.* 160 ff.
32. Athanasius, *De decretis Nic. App.*; Socrates, *H.E.* I, 8; Theodoretus,
H.E. I, 11; etc.

You have probably learned, Beloved, even from other sources about the transactions at the great Council assembled at Nicaea concerning the Creed of the Church, since rumour usually precedes the accurate account of the events that have taken place. But that the truth, as a result of such rumour, might not be falsely reported to you, it was necessary for us to transmit to you, first, the outline of the Creed instituted by us, and then a second one, which, after adding qualifications to our pronouncements, they promulgated. Our outline, which was read in the presence of our most pious Emperor and was proclaimed to be good and acceptable, has the following form:

Even as we inherited it from the bishops before us and heard it in our first instruction, and when we received the baptism, and as we have learned from the Divine Scriptures, and as we believed and taught in discharging the office of priest and even bishop, so believing even now, we bring to you our Creed. It is this:

'We believe in One God, the Father Almighty, the Maker of all things visible and invisible, and in One Lord, Jesus Christ, the Word of God, God from God, Light from Light, Life from Life, only-begotten Son, first-born of all creation, begotten from the Father before all ages, by Whom also all things were made; Who on account of our salvation became flesh and lived among men, and who suffered, and rose again on the third day, and ascended to the Father, and will come again in glory to judge the living and the dead. And we also believe in the Holy Ghost: believing that each of these exists, that the Father in truly father, and that the Son is truly son, and that the Holy Ghost is truly Holy Ghost, even as Our Lord also, when he sent forth his disciples to preach, said: Go and teach all nations, baptizing them in the name of the Father, and of the Son, and of the Holy Ghost. Concerning these doctrines we confirm that they are true, and that this is our understanding, and that this is how it has been of old, and that we will remain like this concerning this faith until death, anathematizing all godless heresy. That this has always been our understanding in our heart and soul, ever since we have known this of ourselves, and that, even now, this is our understanding, and that we say this is truth, we testify, in the presence of God the Almighty, and of Our Lord Jesus Christ, and we are able to demonstrate with proofs, and to convince you that in times past we have thus believed and also preached.'

When this Creed was proposed, there was no occasion for anyone to contradict it. On the contrary, our most pious Emperor was the first to testify that it was most orthodox. He confessed that this was his own understanding, and he exhorted all present to agree to it, and to subscribe to its doctrines, and to express their agreement with them after one single word, *Consubstantial*, was inserted. This word he himself interpreted, saying that the Son is said *Consubstantial* not according to the properties of the bodies, and that the Son subsists neither according to a division, nor any excision from the Father; that because the immaterial, and the intellectual, and bodiless nature cannot

128

have any bodily property subsisting in it, and that it becomes us to think of divine and ineffable ideas in such terms. And this is how our most wise and most religious Emperor discussed the matter. They, however, on the pretext of the addition of the *Consubstantial*, prepared the following outline:

'We believe in One God, the Father Almighty, Maker of all things visible and invisible; and in One Lord Jesus Christ, the Son of God, begotten from the Father, Only-begotten, that is, from the substance of the Father, God from God, Light from Light, true God from true God, begotten not made, Consubstantial with the Father, by Whom all things were made, both things in heaven and things in earth, who for us men and for our salvation came down, became flesh, was made man, suffered, and rose again on the third day, ascended into heaven, and is coming to judge the living and the dead. And in the Holy Ghost.

But those who say "there was time when He was not," and "He was not before He was begotten" or that "He was made from things not existing," or those who say that the Son of God is of another substance or essence, or created, or changeable, or subject to alteration, the Catholic and Apostolic Church anathematizes.'

After this outline was dictated by them, we did not leave the matter with them without inquiring in what sense they said the phrases "from the substance of the Father" and "Consubstantial with the Father." Therefore, questions were asked and answers given, and the deliberation clarified the meaning of the phrases. And it was admitted by them that the phrase "from the substance" was indicative of the Son's being from the Father, but of his not subsisting as a part of the Father. In this way, it seemed right to us to give full assent to the interpretation of the pious meaning which suggests that the Son is from the Father, but has no part of His substance. We, therefore, agreed to the interpreration, without even deprecating the term "Consubstantial," since before our eyes we had the aim of peace, and the wish not to deviate from the correct interpretation. In the same way, we also accepted the phrase "begotten, not made," since they said that "made" was a designation for all the other creatures which were made by the Son, and to whom the Son had no likeness. Therefore, He is not a creature resembling the things which were made by Him, but has a substance greater than any creature. And the Divine Revelations teach that this substance was begotten from the Father although the manner of the begetting is beyond the expression and consideration of all created nature. So, too, when its meaning is examined, the phrase "the Son is Consubstantial with the Father" is approved, not according to the way of the bodies, nor at all like mortal beings, for it is not by a division of the substance, or by an excision, nor even by any property, or changing, or alteration of the Father's substance and power, since the unbegotten nature of the Father has nothing in common with all these; and that the phrase "Consubstantial with the Father" indicates that the Son of

God bears no resemblance to created things; but that He is, in every way, only like the Father who begat Him, and that He is not from any other essence and substance but from the Father's. It seemed right to assent to this very phrase also, when it is interpreted in this manner, since we knew that some learned and illustrious bishops and writers among the ancients used the term "Consubstantial" in their theology concerning the Father and the Son.

Let this, then, be said about the Creed that was put before us, and we all assented to it, not without inquiry, but according to the interpretations that were given them, when they were examined in the presence of the most religious Emperor himself, and that were agreed upon for the considerations already mentioned. We thought that the anathematization that was put by them at the end of the Creed was not offensive, since it bars the use of words that were not written in the Scriptures, which caused the existence of almost all the confusion and disorder in the Church. Since no divinely inspired Scripture used the phrases "from things not existing" and "there was time when He was not" and phrases mentioned with them, it seemed to be groundless to use them in speech and teaching. We assented also to this very point as being a sound decision, since it was not customary for us before the present time to use these terms.

Moreover, it was not believed to be improper to anathematize the phrase "before He was begotten He was not" because it is agreed by all that the Son of God existed before His generation according to the flesh. As a matter of fact, even our most religious Emperor argued in a speech that He existed according to His divine generation as well, before all ages, since He, even before actually begotten, existed potentially in the Father, even though unbegotten, since the Father was always Father as well as always a King, and always a Saviour, being potentially all things, being always according to the same respects and in the same condition.

It was necessary for us to transmit this to you, Beloved, making clear to you our reasoning in the inquiry and for our assent and showing how reasonably we resisted to the last moment when strange propositions offended us, but we accepted them when they were not distressing, when, on a prudent examination of the interpretations of the expressions, they appeared to us to concur with our own which we proposed in the Creed we had earlier outlined.

It is quite obvious that if the Arians could accept the Eusebian Creed, it then had to be amended in such a way that it would not be capable of being interpreted in the Arian way. After some futile effort at such an amendment, it was apparently at the Emperor Constantine's suggestion that the "*homoousios*" or "Consubstantial" was added to the Creed to make it proof against the

Arian interpretation of the Second Person of the Holy Trinity. After the acceptance of this 'amendment' the whole Eusebian Creed was rewritten. How distressing all this was to Eusebius of Caesarea! And how dishonest his letter to his own people seems to be in explaining away the true importance of the word *Consubstantial*, as if the insertion of this word had made no difference! Or, was he still fighting for the Arian meaning, without having the honesty and courage to say so with some others who had refused to sign this new Creed, the Creed of Nicaea?

The letter written by the Council of Nicaea to the Egyptian Church[33] was much more straightforward and of course much more informative about the Council's decisions than Eusebius of Caesarea's letter to his Church. From this letter we learn that the Arian heresy was, of course, anathematized, and that Arius himself and two of his followers, the Bishops Secundus of Ptolemais and Theonas of Marmarice were condemned and excommunicated. In addition to Eusebius of Caesarea, in the end even Bishops Eusebius of Nicomedia and Theognius of Nicaea signed.

The Council took, however, a lenient view in permitting Melitius to retain his title of bishop, though prohibiting him to excerise the office of bishop. Other Melitian bishops were treated even more leniently. The ruling of the Council on the Novatians, "those calling themselves Pure," was most lenient.

Constantine's letter to the Catholic Church of Alexandria,[34] though it adds nothing to the above information by Eusebius and the letter of the Council to the Egyptian Church, nevertheless shows the deep emotional and religious involvement of the Emperor, his delight at the condemnation of Arius, his hope that all schisms would end and that all would return to the true faith:

Constantine Augustus to the Catholic Church of Alexandria.

Greetings to you, my beloved Brothers, We have received a most abundant grace from the Divine Providence in order that, freed from all error, we may acknowledge the one and the same faith. No room has been left for the Devil to act against us, for whatever he attempted (against us) through his evil tricks has been completely destroyed. The brilliant splendour of the Truth

33. Socrates, *H.E.* I, 9, 1-14; Theodoretus, *H.E.* I, 9, 2-13; Gelas. Cyz., *H.E.* 34, 2.
34. Socrates, *H.E.* I, 9, 17-25.

has, by the command of God, conquered the discords, the schisms, those most familiar tumults and what I should call the deadly poisons of dissensions. Therefore we have all had expressed our belief in one God, and we prostrate ourselves before His Name. But that this may come true, I have, because of a warning from God, convoked most of the bishops in the city of Nicaea, with whom, as one of you, and exceedingly happy at being your fellow servant, I myself undertook the close examination of the truth. Accordingly, all questions which seemed to engender doubt or pretext for disagreement were scrutinized and strictly examined. May the Divine Majesty pardon the terrible and enormous blasphemies which some were indecently uttering about our Saviour, our hope and life, and voicing and admitting their belief in things contrary to the divinely inspired Scriptures and to our holy faith.

Although more than three hundred bishops, admired for their moderation and prudence, firmly established one and the same faith, which is a faith in strict agreement with the true teachings of the Divine Law, Arius, overcome by the power of the Devil, was alone revealed as disseminating, with an impious mind, this evil, first among you, and then among others also. Let us, therefore, accept the doctrine which the Almighty gave us. Let us return to our beloved Brothers, from whom a shameless servant of the Devil separated us. Let us go with all eagerness to the common body and our legitimate members. For this becomes your prudence, faithfulness, and holiness, so that, since the error of him, who has been proved to be an enemy of the truth, is refuted, you may return to the grace of God. For that which three hundred bishops approved at the same time is nothing else than the teaching of God, especially where the Holy Spirit, influencing the mind of so many men of such quality, made clear the Divine Will. Therefore, let no one have doubts, let no one delay, but let all with eagerness return to the truest path, so that when I come to you, which will be quite soon, I may, among you, give due thanks to God, the Overseer of all, because He revealed the genuine faith and restored to you the love for which you had prayed.

In another hand: May God preserve you, beloved Brothers.

Then there is the Emperor's famous letter to the whole Church,[35] the main purpose of which seems to have been to communicate to all the Churches the Council's decision on the new way the date of Easter was to be decided. The problem was[36] to fix the date of this greatest feast of Christianity on the same day throughout the Church. Though the question may be regarded as technical,[37] and

35. Eusebius, *Vita Constant.* III, 17-20.
36. See brief discussion in Baynes, *op. cit.* n. 64; Jones, *op. cit.* 166-168; *et al.*
37. Jones, *op. cit.* 166.

there can be no doubt that it involved very abstruse mathematical, astronomical and other problems, it was to the Emperor quite obviously a very important question. This is very clear from his letter to the Churches on this question.

Though the document may be regarded[38] as having a "strongly anti-Semitic flavour", (for the Emperor expresses often enough the idea that the Christian religion should not have anything in common "with the perfidy of Jews," "those impious murderers of the Lord," and others) nevertheless Constantine is more likely expressing the "neophyte" shock rather than any "anti-Semitic" tendency as such. More importantly, according to his "old wish, Constantine wanted *unity* in celebrating "a feast of such religious significance." He regarded disagreement in this matter an act of disloyalty. Whether or not it was he who put the question of the date of Easter on the agenda of the Nicaean Council, it was the Emperor who sent the dicision of the Council on this matter to the whole Church, together with his own exhortation that all receive it gladly as the "will of God."[39]

Taking the welfare of the Commonwealth as a proof to show how great the grace of God's power has been towards us, I have deemed it fitting that it should be my aim before all else that unity of faith, sincerity of love and unanimity in the worship of Almighty God be preserved among the most blessed nations of the Catholic Church. But since this object could not be firmly and securely established, unless all or at least most of the bishops had come together to the same place and everything concerning our most Holy Religion had been discussed, for this reason an assembly, as numerous as possible, was brought together. Even I myself, as one of you, was present, for I would not deny, and this is my greatest joy, that I am your fellow servant. Every question received the proper examination until a judgement that was pleasing to God, who is watching over everything, was published amidst the general demonstration of unity, so that there was nothing left for creating discord or controversy in matters of faith.

At that occasion, the problem concerning the most holy day of Easter being examined, it was decided by general opinion that it was proper that everyone everywhere celebrate it on one and the same day. For what can be more fitting, what more solemn to us than the unfailing observance, among all people, according to the same system and counting, of this feast from

38. E.g. by Jones, *op. cit.* 167-168.
39. Eusebius, *Vita Constant.* III, 17-20; Socrates, *H.E.* I, 9, 32; Theodore-tus, *H.E.* I, 9, 1.

which we have received our hope of immortality? And first of all, it seemed that it was not proper that celebrating that most holy feast we should follow the custom of the Jews, who defiled their hands with a heinous sin, and likewise polluted their souls and are blind. For having discarded their custom, it is possible for us to keep celebrating this observance till future ages by a more correct system, which we observed from the first day of the Passion up to the present time. Let us, then, have nothing in common with the most detestable mass of the Jews, for we have received from our Saviour a different way. There lies open to our most holy religion a lawful and appropriate course. Most highly honoured Brothers, let us with one voice adopt this course, and detach ourselves from that detestable association. For to tell the truth, it is very odd for them to boast that we are unable to observe this without their instruction. For in what matter will they be able to give a right counsel, who after their impious murder of the Lord, being deprived of their senses, are led, not by any reasoned thinking, but by an uncontrollable impulse, wherever their inherited madness may drive them. Therfore, it is for this reason that even in this matter they do not see the truth, so that being completely off the right path, they, instead of making the appropriate revision, celebrate the Passover a second time in the same year. Why, then, do we follow those who are, as is agreed, afflicted with a grievous error? Of course, we will never permit the holding of a second Easter in the same year. But even if these points were not laid before you, it would be necessary that your Prudence see to it at all times by your zeal and your prayer that the purity of your soul may never appear, through any similarity, to have anything in common with the customs of people so utterly evil. We must also consider that, in a matter of such great importance and with regard to a feast of such religious significance, disagreement is an act of disloyalty. For our Saviour left us one day for the commemoration of the day of our deliverance, *i.e.* the day of His most holy Passion, He willed that His Catholic Church be one, the members of which, even though scattered to many different places, are nevertheless likewise conforted in the one Spirit, *i.e.*, the Divine Will. But let your Holiness' Prudence consider how terrible and unbecoming it is that on the same day some are spending their time by fasting, others participating in banquets, and that after the days of Easter some are present at festivities and amusements, others give themselves over to prescribed fastings. Therefore, as I believe that you all agree, it is the will of God's Providence that this should receive proper correction, and a uniform practice be introduced.

Since, therefore, it was proper that this matter should be put right, so that we might have nothing in common with the nation of those impious murderers of the Lord, and since that system is a fitting one which all the churches of the western, southern, and northern parts of the world, and even some of the eastern places observe, all believed, on this occasion, that this system is worthy of adoption. I myself even endeavoured to ensure that it might be agreeable to your Prudence that what is being observed with one harmonious mind in the City of Rome, throughout Africa, Egypt, the Spains, the Gauls, Britain, Libya, the whole of Greece, the dioceses of Asia, Pontus and Cilicia, your wisdom as well might gladly accept, because you take into consideration not only that the number of the Churches at the places just mentioned is greater, but also that this especially is a most sacred duty of all to be united in wishing what right reason seems to demand and what has nothing in common with the perfidy of the Jews. Now then, to sum it up as briefly as possible, it was decided by a common agreement of all that the most holy feast of Easter be celebrated on one and the same day. For on the one hand it is not proper that there should be any dissension in such holy matter as this, and on the other it is more acceptable to follow an opinion in which there will be no room left for outside error and mistake.

This then being so, receive gladly the grace of God and truly Divine command. For everything that is achieved in the sacred synods of the bishops is to be ascribed to the will of God. Therefore, on communicating the above to our beloved brothers, you are obliged to accept the reasoning expressed above and to make arrangement for the observance of this most holy day, so that whenever, according to my old wish I come to see you face to face, I may be able to celebrate the holy feast with you on the same day, and that I may rejoice for the sake of all, seeing with you the cruelty of the Devil removed by the power of God through our actions, while your faith, peace, and concord everywhere flourish. May God preserve you, beloved Brothers.

To say that for Constantine Creed was only of secondary importance,[40] and that it was for him only an instrument of unity, is to misunderstand him very seriously. Unity was most important for him because it meant unity of Creed. His letter to the herectics of the Empire[41] well illustrates his zeal for orthodoxy, union in true faith. There are few letters of Constantine in which he uses stronger expressions or more derogatory and biting words against his addressees than he does in this letter against the herectics. Instead of simply "cutting out the pestilential disease" to prevent it from "bringing about the pollution" of the healthy, Constantine only orders the confiscation of the meeting places of the heretics, prohibits them from meeting in public as well as private places, and tells them to return to the "spotless religion" of the Catholic Church:

40. Jones, *op. cit.* 172 f.
41. Eusebius, *Vita Constant.* III, 64-65.

You Novatians, Valentinians, Marcionites, Paulians, and you who are called Phrygians, and, in a word, all you who, throughout your private assemblies, make up the number of heresies, you must understand, by this legislation, of what tissue of falsehood your pretence is constructed, and with what deadly poisons your teaching is held together, so that through you the healthy fall victims of disease, and the living the prey of eternal death. You, haters of the truth, enemies of life, and counsellors of destruction! Amongst you, everything is opposed to the truth, but in harmony with shameful acts of wickedness, and favourable to senseless acts, and by these you concoct lies, afflict the innocent, and deny the light to those who believe. Though always masquerading under the pretext of godliness, you pollute everything, you wound the consciences of the pure and innocent with death dealing blows, while, one can almost say, you snatch the very daylight from the eyes of men. But it is not necessary to be specific, since to discuss any of your evil deeds as it deserves takes no short time and certainly more than I can spare. So long and so immense is the list of your disgusting deeds, so hateful and so completely actrocious are they that a whole day would not be enough to list them. Otherwise, it is better to shun and turn away our ears and eyes from such topics as these, so that by treating each particular evil of theirs the pure and unpolluted zeal of our faith may not be defiled. Why then shall we still allow such great evils? This, in spite of the fact, that this long toleration is bringing about the pollution even of the healthy by what is like a pestilential disease. Why, then, do we not cut out, as soon as possible, the roots, as it were, of such great evil by a public demonstration of displeasure?

Accordingly, then, since it is not possible to suffer your deadly work of destruction, we publicly declare by this present law that none of you should, in the future, dare to assemble. Therefore, we have ordered that those houses of yours in which you hold your council meetings shall be taken away from you, and this concern of mine extends so far as to prohibit the holding of your meetings of superstition and folly, not only in the public, but even in a private house or in any places owned privately. What is even a better course is that all of you who heed the true and spotless religion enter the Catholic Church and share in its holiness, through which you will be able to attain to the truth. But the trickery of your perverted teaching, I mean the cursed and wretched deceitfulness of the heretics and schismatics, must altogether give way to yield to the happiness of our times. For it befits our happy condition, which we enjoy with the help of God, that we lead back those who live in dependence upon good hopes, from all lawless error to the straight path, from darkness to light, from vanity to truth, and from death to salvation. But in order that this measure may have the necessary force, we have commanded, as was said above, that the meeting places of your superstition, I mean the heretics' houses of prayer, if it is fitting to call them houses of prayer, should be taken away from you; and that, without any objections and without any delay, they be handed over to the Catholic Church; and that the remaining places be given to the treasury; and that, for the future, no opportunity be left for you for gathering, in order that from this day on you may not dare to hold your lawless meetings in any place, public or private. Let this edict be made public.

Considering then that this edict was written against minor heresies, and apparently not against major ones such as Arianism, which was presumed dead, and the Donatist schism, which was left to the judgement of God,[42] it is hard to believe that these words did not come from his desire for the unity of Creed. We know that a constitution of September 1, 325 A.D. excluded heretics from the immunities earlier granted by Constantine to the Christian clergy, but this law was not carried out against the fairly large body of Montanists, and the Novatians were expressly protected against the measure,[43] it seems, for a good reason. Although outside the unity of the Catholic Church, nevertheless they were orthodox and pious, though rigorous. Both orthodoxy and piety appealed to Constantine. About honest rigorism he was perhaps not sure, but he seemed to respect it.

Not being forgetful of the small fry of heresy, Constantine was certainly not forgetful of the important supporters of an important heresy, such as Eusebius of Nicomedia and some others. From a letter the Emperor wrote to the Catholic Church of Nicomedia[44] we learn that he eventually exiled both Bishop Eusebius of Nicomedia and Bishop Theognius. Despite the very troubled text and composition of this letter, it is clear enough[45] that we have here an explanation of the banishment of these two bishops. Apart from some dark and vague political references by Constantine to Eusebius' activities in the final war between him and Licinius,[46] it is clear enough that Constantine's reasons for exiling Eusebius of Nicomedia and Theognius were not political but eminently

42. On the genuineness of this document, see Baynes, *op. cit.* n. 71.
43. Sozomen, *H.E.* II, 32.
44. Athanasius, *De decretis Nic. 41*; Gelasius Cyz., *H.E.* III, *App.* i; see Kraft, *op. cit.* 228 f.
45. Jones, *op. cit.* 173-175.
46. Eusebius of Nicomedia came to Constantine as an ambassador; Philostorgius, *H.E.* App. V. According to Philostorgius *H.E.* I, 10, Eusebius of Nicomedia was exiled three months after the Council of Nicaea.

religious, *i.e.* the perversion by these bishops of the faith declared in Nicaea, and the facts that they were doing this by intriguing with Arian priests deported by him from Alexandria to Nicomedia, and conspiring against the declared faith. Here is this troubled letter:

Constantine Augustus to the Catholic Church of the people of Nicomedia.

You all clearly know, Beloved Brothers, that the Lord God and the Saviour Christ are Father and Son; I mean Father the Creator of the world, who is without beginning and without end, and I mean Son, *i.e.* the Will of the Father, which is neither comprehended through a mental process nor grasped as the perfection of His works by the means of an acquired substance. For he who is and will be considering this will have an untiring patience for the suffering of all sorts of torments. But Christ, the Son of God, the maker of all things and the giver of immortality, was, according to the Creed which we have confessed, begotten, — rather, He who was always in the Father came forth to govern the things which He had created — He was therefore begotten through coming forth but without separating. For the will is fixed to its dwelling place, and handles and administers those things, which are in need of diverse administration, each according to its own character. What is, then, between God the Father and the Son? Clearly, nothing. The plenitude of all things has received the command of the will through perception, and did not at all separate the will from the Father's essence.

(From this it follows:) Who is he who stands in awe of the suffering of Christ my Lord, more through reverence than folly? Does the Divine suffer when the habitation of the venerable body demands the recognition of Its holiness? Or, is that which is separated from the body exposed to touching? Is that not different which is without the baseness of the body? But are we not living even though the glory of the soul summons the body to death?

What point, worthy of consideration, leaves a pure and sincere soul in uncertainty about this? Or, do you not see that God chose a most venerable body so as to make manifest, through it, the proofs of faith and the signs of his own power? Did he not wish, through it, to shake off the perdition that, by a deadly deception, spread to the human race? And to give a new doctrine of worship? And to purify, through the example of chastity, the unbecoming acts of the mind? and then to put an end to the pain of death, and to announce the rewards of immortality?

But you, who, on account of the communion of love, are rightly called brothers by me, you know me as your fellow servant; you know the safety of your salvation, the case of which I have truly taken upon me, through which we have not only overcome the arms of our enemies, but also, while they are still alive in the soul, I shut them up together in order that the true faith of brotherhood might be manifested.

138

I was happy on account of these gifts, and especially for the renovation of the whole world. And it was truly wonderful to lead so many people to unanimity, who, even a short while before, it was said, did not even know God. But what will these peoples learn, peoples who have not yet acquired any love for dissension? What, then, do you think, Beloved Brothers, since it is yourselves I am accusing? We are Christians, and through a lamentable disposition, we dissent. Is this our faith, is this the teaching of the most holy Law? But what is the cause through which the plague of the present calamity arose? O what superabundance of wickedness, O what superabundance of hatred is beyond all indignation! What a terrible crime has come to light in denying that the Son of God came forth from the indivisible substance of the Father! Is God not everywhere, and do we not feel that He is always present in us? Has not the harmonious order of the universe been maintained through His power? Has it been without the discord of separation?

Has anything been done to you? Beloved Brothers, understand, I beg of you, the pains of this present suffering. You promised to be the confessors of Him whom you deny to be a God since this pernicious teacher persuaded you to it. Who, I beg of you, is he who taught this to an innocent people? Clearly Eusebius, a conspirator in the tyrant's cruelty. For that he was, in every way, a protegé of the tyrant can be made manifest from many facts. The killings of bishops bear witness to this – I am, of course, speaking of true bishops – but also the most serious persecution of the Christians clearly and loudly speaks of it.

I shall say nothing now about the outrages committed against me, namely, that when the attacks of the opposing factions were especially active, he even sent against me undercover observers, and he only failed to help the tyrant with armed assistance. Let no one believe that I am not prepared to prove this. A clear proof is in the fact that the priests and the deacons accompanying Eusebius were apprehended by me. But I omit these, and yet they have been brought up by me not out of anger, but to their disgrace. My only fear, my only concern is that I see that you are involved as accomplices in his crime. For, as a result of Eusebius' influence and perversion you have developed a conscience that is alien to truth. But the remedy is not too late if you at least now receive a faithful and irreproachable bishop and turn your eyes to God. This, at the present time, is in your power, and should have been the result of your decision long ago if the afore-mentioned Eusebius with a turbulent crowd of his supporters had not come to that place and shamelessly disturbed the proper order.

But since I had to direct a few words about this Eusebius to your Charity, your Forbearance remembers that a council took place in the city of Nicaea, at which I was myself present, as it was my obligation in conscience. My only wish was to bring about concord for all, and, before all, to refute and shake

139

off this troublesome matter which began through the madness of Arius of Alexandria, but was immediately established through the wicked and destructive zeal of Eusebius. But this very Eusebius, my Beloved and most honoured Friends, with what tumult, since he was convicted by his own experience, and with what shamelessness do you think he stood by that utterly refuted falsehood! He was, at the same time, sending people to me who were petitioning on his behalf, and he was also asking me for some support, so that, being convicted of such a sin, he might not be turned out of the office which he was holding. God is my witness of this, and may He remain gracious to you as well as to me. For he deceived me, and shamelessly took advantage of me, which you also will recognize. For everything was done at that time as he wished, since everything that was evil he kept hidden in his mind.

But to pass over the rest of his depravity, please hear especially what he, a short while ago, carried through with Theognius, the accomplice of his madness. I had ordered some Alexandrians who had fallen away from our faith to be sent to this place, because, through their activity, the torch of dissent was blazing up. But these excellent bishops, whom the truth of the council once brought back to repentance, not only received them, but also consorted with them in their depraved ways. Therefore, I decided to do this concerning these ungrateful people: I ordered them to be seized and banished to a place that is as far away as possible. Now it is your duty that you look to God with that faith which is known to have always existed, and ought to exist, and that you conduct yourselves in such a way that we may rejoice in having holy, orthodox and dutiful bishops. If anybody dares, thoughtlessly, to go so far as to revive the memory of or praise those destructive persons, he will be immediately restrained in his boldness by the power of the servant of God, that is, mine. May God preserve you, Beloved Brothers.

We know[47] that the people of Nicomedia and Nicaea listened to Constantine, and elected new bishops, Amphion and Chrestus, to replace Eusebius and Theognius.[48]

After dealing with Eusebius of Nicomedia and Theognius, Constantine continued his mission by trying to bring about the unity of Faith as declared by the Council of Nicaea. In a letter to Eusebius of Nicomedia,[49] Arius claimed that Bishop Theodotus

47. Athanasius, *Apol. c. Arian.* 7.
48. Cf. Socrates, *H.E.* I, 14; in 328 A.D., both Eusebius and Theognius were allowed to return to their sees, but only after they had submitted to Constantine, and fully accepted the Nicaean Creed and, particularly, the full meaning of the term "Consubstantial".
49. Theodoretus, *H.E.* I, 4; Epiphanius, *Haer.* 69, 6.

140

of Laodicaea was one of his supporters, a bishop who in fact was one of the bishops excommunicated[50] at the earlier Council of Antioch. It is not surprising then that we have a letter by Constantine to this same Bishop Theodotus[51] in which the Emperor simply instructs the Bishop in the Catholic faith and at the same time reminds him of what has just happened to his pro-Arian colleagues of Nicomedia and Nicaea:

How great the force of the Divine anger is you can easily learn from the plight of Eusebius and Theognius, who behaved like violent drunkards towards the Most Holy Religion, and even after receiving pardon defiled the Name of God the Saviour in the assembly of their own piracy. For when, especially after the harmonious union of the Council in coming to the same judgement, it would have been necessary to correct their former error, at that very time they were caught persevering in the same absurdities. For this very reason Divine Providence drove them out from her people. For she would not tolerate watching innocent souls being corrupted because of the senselessness of a few, and even now she demanded from them fitting atonement, but she will exact even more severe punishment hereafter throughout eternity.

I thought that this matter ought to be made clear to your Prudence in order that if any evil counsel of such men as these got implanted in your chosen course of action – and I do not think it will – you may remove this advice from your soul, and eagerly offer, as is fitting, your mind pure, and your devotion sincere, and your faith undefiled to God the Saviour. For it is essential that this be done by whomsoever plans to be worthy of the perfect prizes of eternal life. (And in an other hand: May God watch over you, beloved brother.)

As far as we can tell, Theodotus took the hint from Constantine by complying and disowning all heretical disagreement with the Creed of Nicaea.

There was still another whom Constantine wanted to return to the acceptance of the Nicaean Creed. It was Arius himself. It may, then, seem natural that Constantine should have sent Arius a letter,[52] inviting him to his court just for a talk:

50. Theodoretus, *H.E.* I, 5; *et al.*; see Opitz, *Athanasius Werke* III, i, pp. 36 ff.
51. Athanasius, *De decretis Nic.* 42; Gelasius Cyz., *H.E.* III, *App.* II; H. Dörries, *Das Selbstzeugnis Kaiser Konstantins* (Göttingen, 1954) 76.
52. Socrates, *H.E.* I, 25.

141

It was indicated to your Firmness a long time ago that you might come to our court to enjoy our presence. We are surprised that you did not immediately do so. Therefore now get on a public vehicle and come quickly to our court, so that you may receive our goodwill and company and return to your homeland. May God protect you, Beloved. Dated on November 27.

This letter was probably written in 326 A.D. But whether or not the "meeting" took place, Arius himself and an Arian friend, Euzoius, very soon after Constantine's letter of invitation to Arius, sent the Emperor a letter in which they offered him on their own part and on behalf of their followers as well a statement of faith:[53]

Arius and Euzoius to the Emperor Constantine, our most Pious Lord and most beloved of God. In accordance with the command which you, Lord King, issued in your faithfulness and love of God, we set forth our faith and confess in writing, before God, that we and all our followers believe as follows:

We believe in one God the Father Almighty, and in our Lord Jesus Christ His only begotten Son, who was begotten of Him before all ages, God the Word, through whom all things, both in the heavens and the earth, were made; who came down, and took up flesh, and suffered, and rose, and ascended into the heavens, and is coming again to judge the living and the dead. And in the Holy Ghost, and in the resurrection of the flesh, and in eternal life that is to come, and in the kingdom of heavens, and in one Catholic Church of God throughout the world.

This faith we have received from the holy Gospels, since the Lord says to His disciples: Go and teach all the nations, baptizing in the name of the Father, and of the Son, and of the Holy Ghost. But if we do not believe this and do not accept the Father, the Son, and the Holy Ghost, as the whole Catholic Church and the Scriptures teach, in which we believe in all points, God is our judge both now, and on the day that is coming. Therefore, we appeal to your piety, Emperor, most beloved of God, that we who are clerics and have the faith and the mind of the Church and of the Holy Scriptures, may, through your peace-making and God-fearing piety, be without doubt reunited to our Mother, the Church, since the questions and the strange arguments that resulted from them have been removed, so that both we and the Church, being at peace with each other, may all together make our accustomed vows for your peaceful and pious reign, and for your whole family.

53. *Ibid.* 26; Sozomen, *H.E.* II, 27.

This Creed is clearly weak and evasive, and omits all the critical phrases, not to mention the term *Consubstantial*, that made the Nicaean Creed proof against Arianism. This Creed does not clearly exclude any of the Arian beliefs, despite statements that they "hold the faith and mind of the Church and the Holy Scriptures".

It seems that after his meeting with Arius, for they obviously had a meeting, Constantine, despite the weakness of Arius' confession of faith, wrote a letter to Bishop Alexander of Alexandria to suggest the readmission of Arius. The reply of Alexander must have suggested delay, as is clear from the fragments which we have of Constantine's next letter to the Bishop Alexander. In this letter the emperor describes his meeting with the '*very Arius*' and begs Alexander to help him to accomplish the unity of the Church:[54]

Even now will abominable jealousy bark back with unholy and fallacious arguments for delay? What is that to the present occasion? Are we laying down opinions other than those defined through you by the Holy Ghost, dearest Brother? Arius, the Arius, I tell you, has come to me, the Augustus, on the recommendation of many people, professing that he has the same views concerning the Catholic faith as were defined and confirmed by you at the Council of Nicaea, I, your fellow servant, being present and deliberating with you. This man then, together with Euzoius, clearly knowing the purpose of the Imperial command, came to us. I have in the presence of several discussed with them the word of life. I am known as the man who dedicated his mind to God with a sincere faith. I am your fellow-servant who have taken upon myself all the care for (peace) and unity (among ourselves) ...

Therefore I have sent a dispatch to you not only suggesting but begging that you receive the men who come as suppliants. If then you find that they hold firmly to the true and ever-living apostolic faith set forth at Nicaea — and they have affirmed in our presence that this is their belief — I am begging that you take thought for all. For if you take thought for them, you will conquer hatreds by concord. Aid then unity, I am begging you, administer, at the same time, the blessings of friendship to those who do not discard the blessings of faith. Let me hear the things that I desire and long for, the peace and unity of all of you. God will protect you, dearest father.

All this correspondence between Constantine and Bishop Alexander of Alexandria must have taken place some time in 327 A.D.

---

54. Gelaius Cyz., *H.E.* III, 15, 1; the origin of the two fragments is not clear; nevertheless, their genuineness cannot be questioned; H. Kraft, *op. cit.* 243.

and very likely before the 'reconvened meeting of the Council of Nicaea' at the end of 327.[55] Just as the idea of contacting Arius came, perhaps mainly, from pro-Arian bishops, so the petition by Arius for readmission and the reconvening of a session of the "Nicaean Council" must have come from the same quarters.[56] Of this reconvened 'session' we only know that it must have been to this gathering that Bishops Eusebius of Nicomedia and Theognius addressed a petition for readmission.[57] In this letter they both expressed their unequivocal agreement with the Nicaean Creed and with the full meaning of the term *Consubstantial*. The two bishops also quite logically argued that since the principal figure, Arius, had by that time been recalled and reconciled by Nicaea II they should be restored as well. Therefore they besought the Emperor for this act of mercy. The Emperor agreed probably gladly to their return to their sees in Nicomedia and Nicaea.

Bishop Alexander of Alexandria did not go to the 'Second Session of the Nicaeac Council' and this is perhaps why Athanasius ignores it.[58] The Bishop was not happy about the 'Second Session's' decision to readmit Arius to the Church, because Alexander undoubtedly saw through Arius' 'conversion' and the spirit of 'NicaeaII'. It was very likely this attitude of the Bishop of Alexandria that provoked Constantine to write such a letter to the Bishop[59] concerning the latter's refusal to readmit Arius.

To say[60] that at this stage the whole Church unanimously accepted the Nicaean Creed and that Arius submitted and was reconciled with the Catholic Church[61] entails a gross oversimplification of the Catholic faith and of its acceptance. One has only to look at Arius' latest statement of Faith to see that he was in no way in agreement with the Nicaean Creed, nor reconciled to the

55. Unless, of course, it took place after the reconvened session.
56. See Nordberg, *op. cit.* 17, about the fact that a second session of the Nicaean Council was summoned in 327 A.D.; see Otto Seeck, "Untersuchungen zur Geschichte des Nicäischen Konzils," *Zschr. f. Kirchengesch.* 17 (1896) 1-71; 319; Jones, *op. cit.* 176 f.
57. Socrates, *H.E.* I, 14, 2 ff.; Sozomen, *H.E.* II, 16, 3 ff.; Gelasius Cyz., *H.E.* III, 13, 1.
58. Nordberg, *op. cit.* 17.
59. *Above.*
60. Jones, *op. cit.* 177.
61. *Ibid.*

Catholic Church. There were others like him, but for one reason or another, perhaps mainly out of fear of the Emperor, they subscribed to the letter of the Creed.

Bishop Alexander of Alexandria and Athanasius, his successor, did not, for quite obvious reasons, believe that Arius really accepted the Nicaean Creed, and they did not believe that he should be readmitted to the Church, but particularly in their own see, Alexandria. It seems though that those bishops,[62] who accepted the Nicaean Creed only grudgingly and probably for their fear of the strong arm of the Secular City, were waiting and watching for opportunities to make the position of their orthodox opponents impossible. There is much obscurity about the pro-Arian on-slaught against bishops which soon followed, but certainly many anti-Arian bishops were deposed and exiled, though the details about the disposal of the "lesser fry"[63] are not known.

Before turning to the pro-Arian fight to unseat, or rather undo Athanasius, the most orthodox of bishops, let the cases of the Bishops Marcellus and Eustathius illustrate, by way of anticipating, the pro-Arian bishops' tactics to destroy their orthodox opponents.

Marcellus,[64] the Bishop of Ancyra, a most loyal supporter of the Nicaean Creed, and one who refused communion with pro-Arian bishops, was in his "over-anxiety" determined to refute the Arian doctrines of an Asterius and the resulting book was inter-preted by Marcellus' opponents as itself heretical for entertaining "Paul of Samosata's sentiments." The few pro-Arian and anti-Athanasian bishops who (while most bishops of the Council of Tyre left for home) went to Constantinople at the command of Constantine and formed the "great Council" of Constantinople,[65] condemned and deposed Marcellus, who was subsequently exiled.[66]

---

62. Jones, *ibid.*, calls them Origenists.
63. *Ibid.* 178.
64. Socrates, *H.E.* I, 36; Sozomen, *H.E.* II, 33; Eusebius, *Contra Marcellum.*
65. A title used e.g. by Jones, *op. cit.* 178.
66. Later on, under perhaps more favourable circumstances, at the Synod of Sardica, Marcellus proved his orthodoxy, and that his writing was being misconstrued by his enemies; Sozomen, *H.E.* II, 33; Socrates, *H.E.* I, 36.

The case of Bishop Eustathius[67] is far more complicated but is also far more illustrative of the incredible methods used by pro-Arians against the orthodox. It is clear from our sources that Eustathius, the Bishop of Antioch, was condemned by the pro-Arian bishops such as Eusebius of Nicomedia, Theognius, Theodotus and others at a Council of Antioch, because Eustathius was strongly against their anti-Nicaean views and would not associate with them although the pretext for his deposition was 'immoral deeds.'

The composition of the Synod of Antioch must have been so clearly pro-Arian and anti-Nicaean that one source[68] stated that Eustathius was deposed as a supporter of the Sabellian heresy rather than of the tenets of Nicaea.[69] Eusebius of Caesarea makes[70] some references to this tragic affair, but, strangely, does not say anything on its merits, except that he reports on the riot[71] of the pro-Eustathian party, (though not so called by the historian) against the proceedings of those assembled in Antioch to elect a new bishop. Eusebius also transmits three letters of Constantine. In the first,[72] being sadly misled no doubt by some bishops of this assembly at Antioch on the true feelings of the people, the Emperor directs the people of Antioch not to take Eusebius away from Caesarea but to look for a candidate elsewhere; in the second,[73] to Eusebius himself, Constantine praises the Bishop of Caesarea for refusing the see of Antioch, and, finally, in the third,[74] to the assembled bishops in Antioch, the Emperor suggests that they should leave Eusebius in Caesarea and choose either George, a priest of Arethusa, or Euphronius, a priest of Caesarea in Cappadocia.

---

67. See Athanasius, *History of the Arians* 4; Socrates, *H.E.* I, 23, 8-24, 1; Eusebius, *Vita Constant.* III, 59-62; Sozomen, *H.E.* II, 19; Theodoretus, *H.E.* I, 22; 24.

68. Socrates, *H.E.* II, 24.

69. Cf. Jones' story, *op. cit.* 178 f.; Nordberg, *op. cit.* 21; E. Schwartz, "Zur Geschichte des Athanasius," *Nachrichten der Gesellschaft der Wiss. zu Göttingen* (1911) 404 t.; H. Kraft, *op. cit.* 138-140; Dörries, *op. cit.* 89-93.

70. *Vita Constant.* III, 59-62.

71. *Ibid.* III, 59.

72. *Ibid.* 60.

73. *Ibid.* 61.

74. *Ibid.* 62.

The case of Athanasius is the conclusive evidence in showing how far the pro-Arian Eusebians and their accomplices were willing to go to have Arius, and with him, no doubt, Arianism, accepted.

The long-lasting struggle between the pro-Arians and Athanasius started, if not as early as the Nicaean Council, then at the latest at the time when Athanasius became the Bishop of Alexandria on Alexander's death in 328 A.D., and it did not end with Athanasius' deposition by the pro-Arian bishops and his exile by the Emperor, who was tragically deceived by these bishops – an exile that lasted till the Emperor's death, and that was to be only the first in several exiles suffered by him in his fight for orthodoxy.[75]

Whatever the truth may be in the different pro-Athanasian and pro-Arian reports, there is nothing easier to believe than that the late Bishop Alexander *did* want Athanasius to succeed him; and that the people of Alexandria *were* very strongly in favour of Athanasius as the successor of Alexander in the see of Alexandria. It is just as easy to understand that pro-Arian bishops and clergy *did* want to replace Alexander with a pro-Arian bishop. Therefore it was quite natural and is indeed beyond question that the election of the successor was hotly contested by both the Catholics and the pro-Arians. Nevertheless, Constantine confirmed Athanasius' election.[76]

With this confirmation, the clash between the unshakable rock of Catholic orthodoxy and the Imperial will and power – the Emperor being misled by the unorthodox majority – was to begin almost immediately. At first everything seemed to be peaceful, but then about 330 A.D., or, perhaps somewhat earlier, the trouble started for Athanasius. It may have started with the alliance between the Arians and Melitians – an alliance that should not be surprising since the Melitians, with a considerable number of their bishops, appeared to have been siding with the Arians perhaps ever since as early as 328 A.D.

Arius, at that time, no doubt with the permission of the Emperor, who appeared satisfied by Arius 'confession of faith' and

75. Sources: Socrates, *H.E.* I, 27-35; Sozomen, *H.E.* II, 17-18; 21-23; 25-28; Theodoretus, *H.E.* I, 28-29; Athanasius, *Apol. c. Arian.* 59 ff.; Kidd, *op. cit.* v. ii, 56 ff.; Nordberg, *op. cit.* 18; Kraft, *op. cit.* 135-139; Dörries, *op. cit.* 99 ff.; and the very biassed and hostile Jones, *op. cit.* 180-203; *et al.*

76. For a fragment of Constantine's confirmation, see H. Kraft, *op. cit.* 252 (fragment 32A); Dörries, *op. cit.* 94.

the subsequent vote of readmission by Nicaea II, wanted to be readmitted to the Church in Alexandria. Athanasius refused to accept him however. Whether Constantine was making use of Eusebius of Nicomedia in this matter is not clear, although it is more likely that Eusebius of Nicomedia was using the Emperor to bring about the reinstatement of Arius in Alexandria. But Athanasius rebuffed repeated attempts by the Bishop of Nicomedia, who then must have complained to the Emperor.

It must have been under circumstances such as these that Constantine sent Athanasius a letter ordering him to grant unhindered admission to all those who wished to join the Church. We have a fragment of this letter:[77]

> Since, then, you have knowledge of my will, grant unhindered admission to all those who wish to join the Church. For if ever I learn that you hindered or denied admission to any of them, in spite of their expressed desire for the Church, I will immediately send someone who, by my command, will depose you and remove you from the area.

Athanasius answered this letter[78] by explaining that "anti-Christian heresy had no communion with the Catholic Church." The threat of banishment was however not carried out by the Emperor. He was perhaps realizing for the first time that he was faced by a rare and immovable rock of the Catholic Church. One unbeliever[79] has lately been surprised that Athanasius retained his position. It is conceivable that Athanasius received Constantine's threatening letter about the readmission of the Melitians[80] — a most unlikely supposition, since the Melitians had earlier been readmitted by the Council of Nicaea in 325 A.D. The further fact is[81] that the Arians were using the Melitians as willing tools to destroy Athanasius in the Emperor's estimation.

On the instructions of Eusebius of Nicomedia, Melitian bishops

---

77. Athanasius, *Apol. c. Arian.* 59; Socrates, *H.E.* I, 27, 4; Sozomen, *H.E.* II, 22, 5; Gelasius Cyz., *H.E.* III, 14; H. Kraft, *op. cit.* 252 f.; Dörries, *op. cit.* 95; Nordberg, *op. cit.* 19 f.; Baynes, *op. cit.* 360; *et al.*

78. Athanasius, *Apol. c. Arian.* 60.

79. Jones, *op. cit.* 184.

80. *Ibid.*; Athanasius, *Apol. c. Arian.* 59, clearly connects this letter of Constantine with his refusal to readmit Arius.

81. Athanasius, *Apol. c. Arian.* 60 ff.; Sozomen, *H.E.* II, 22-23; Socrates, *H.E.* I, 27; etc.

in 331 A.D. charged Athanasius with obliging the Egyptians to provide linen vestments, apparently for ecclesiastical purposes. The charge was refuted by two priests of Athanasius who happened to be at the court. In 332 A.D., Athanasius was next charged with having sent a purse of gold as a bribe to a man called Philumenus, perhaps master of the offices.[82] The Emperor personally tried Athanasius in the palace of Psammathia, a suburb of Nicomedia. He found the charges false, and drove Athanasius' accusers from his presence. It was charged on the same occasion that Athanasius, while making one of his regular visitations, had sent his priest Macarius to summon one of the pretended[83] priests of Colluthus named Ischyras, and that Macarius had burst in on Ischyras and broken a chalice used at a 'mass' by Ischyras. Athanasius' own version was that Macarius had been sent to Ischyras to summon him before Athanasius, since he, though a layman, had been acting as a priest; that Macarius had found him ill in bed in his home, and that Ischyras' father had promised to warn his son never to act as a priest again. The Emperor investigated this matter also at his palace of Psammathia and detected the falsehood of Athanasius' enemies. In a letter, to the people of Alexandria,[84] which he sent through Athanasius himself, Constantine reproved the people for their dissensions and expressed his belief that their bishop was truly a man of God.

Though he confessed in a letter that he was forced by Athanasius' enemies to make the false accusation,[85] Ischyras was not received into the Catholic Church, but then joined the Melitians.

The Melitians, however, just would not give up. According to Athanasius,[86] the Melitians, principally John Arcaph, the successor of Melitius and the new head of the schismatic church, accused Athanasius of murdering Arsenius, a Melitian bishop, and of cutting his hand off for purposes of magic. As proof they exhibited a severed hand. Constantine declined, against the wishes of the

82. Jones, *op. cit.* 186.
83. Kidd, *op. cit.* V. ii, 57; Jones, *op. cit.* 187, recognizes Ischyras as true priest.
84. Athanasius, *Apol. c. Arian.* 61; Nordberg, *op. cit.* 21; H. Kraft, *op. cit.* 253 f.; Dörries, *op. cit.* 96; *et al.*
85. Athanasius, *Apol. c. Arian.* 64.
86. *Ibid.* 65-70.

Melitians, to reopen the 'case of the broken chalice,' but commissioned his half-brother Dalmatius,[87] censor, to try the murder charge in Antioch.

In the meantime, Athanasius wrote from the trial at Antioch to his fellow-priests to investigate the whereabouts of Arsenius, and he was found alive and well. Constantine, hearing of this discovery, ordered the proceedings in Antioch stopped, and sent a letter to Athanasius with congratulations to him and with threats against the Melitians to the effect that if they were again found guilty of any similar offence, then they would no longer be treated according to Church law but according to the law of the state. The letter[88] was to be read frequently in public:

Having read the letters of your Prudence, I have decided to write back to your Firmness in order to exhort you to make an earnest effort to lead the people of God back to discipline and the practice of compassion. For in my mind my guiding principles are to cultivate truth, always to preserve righteousness in our thinking, and to rejoice with those who walk the way of life. But concerning people deserving every curse, I clearly mean the ill-starred and lawless Melitians, who as if seized by some stupidity are left in their insensibility, and, by their envious disturbing and tumultuous conduct, do nothing but create an undesirable situation, thus demonstrating their lawless disposition — concerning these people I will say only this. You, of course, see how the men whom these people claimed to have been slain by the sword are even now in our midst, and in the enjoyment of life. What stronger evidence could be advanced against their claim that so manifestly and clearly serves to bring about their condemnation than that those whom they alleged to have been slain live and are in the enjoyment of life, and will, quite obviously, be able to speak for themselves.

But the following, too, is relevant to activities of the Melitians. For they were maintaining that you rushed into the most holy place with lawless violence, and seized and broke a chalice deposited there. There could be no more serious charge or greater offence than this deed, if this sin was indeed committed.

But what sort of an accusation is this? What is the meaning of the shifting and variation of persons in this matter, so that they now transfer the accusation in this case to another person?

Evidently, this circumstance makes it, so to speak, clearer than the sun that they were eagerly plotting against your Prudence. After all this, who

87. Jones, *op. cit.* 188: Delmatius.
88. Athanasius, *Apol. c. Arian.* 68.

150

would be willing to follow those men, seeing that they were fabricating such charges to injure you? Seeing, especially, that they were following the path to ruin, and that they are accusing you of trumped up and false charges, as I have already said, who would follow them and go off headlong to the road of destruction? This is clearly the road on which they believe that they alone have the hope of salvation and help. For if they wish to attain to a pure conscience, and call to mind the best teaching, and arrive at a healthy disposition of mind, they will easily understand that there is no help for them from Providence, since they are zealously engaged in such activities, and are risking their own perdition. Therefore, I really believe it is fair to call this not a harsh opinion but the truth.

But, finally, I say this, too, that we wish this letter to be read frequently and publicly by your Wisdom, so that it might come to the knowledge of all, but, very specially, that whoever behave like this and thus turns the situation upside down, may come to understand that what is just being said for their improvement is being said in the service of the Truth.

Therefore, since there is such great offence in this upsetting activity, let them know that this is how I have judged and this is my decision, that if they start any such disturbance I will myself in the future look into their troublesome activities not according to the laws of the Church but according to the laws of the state, and that in future I will search them out, because they appear to be pirates, not with regard to mankind only but also to the very doctrine of God. May God preserve you, beloved Brother.

In this aftermath of the trial, Arsenius wrote a letter to Athanasius to beg him for peace and union with the Catholic Church.[89] Consequently he and his clergy were admitted to communion,[90] and he remained within this faithfully.[91] John Arcaph, too, was received back into communion with the Catholic Church, and then wrote a letter to Constantine admitting his misdeed, and received a reply, which no doubt expressed[92] the Emperor's genuine happiness at the peace that had become a reality:

The letter which I received from your Prudence was very satisfying to me, for I learned from it what I was desirous of knowing, that you have laid aside all pettiness, have joined, as was proper, the communion of the Church, and have come to the greatest harmony with the most reverend Bishop Athanasius. Be assured, therefore, that, in this regard, I praise you, because, giving

89. *Ibid.* 69.
90. *Ibid.* 8.
91. *Ibid.* 8; 50.
92. *Ibid.* 70.

up all quarrelling, you have done what was pleasing to God and returned into the unity of the Church. In order, then, that you may be convinced that you obtained what you desire, I thought that it was necessary that you should be permitted to board a public vehicle, and to hurry to the headquarters of my mercy. As for the rest, it is up to you not to delay, and since this letter grants you the authority to use a public vehicle, come to me immediately, so that you may both fulfill your desire and, by seeing us, joyfully participate in appropriate festivity. May God preserve you, beloved Brother.

Thus, with the exception of Arius, all who wished to return into the bosom of the Catholic Church were readmitted. That Arius, despite his 'readmission' by a second session of bishops in Nicaea in 327 A.D., was still refused readmission by Athanasius; that Arius threatened to establish a schismatic church if not granted his 'rightful readmission' to the Church in Alexandria, and that he like his like-minded supporters among the bishops, was still equivocal about and wanted to be readmitted with mental reservations about the Nicaean Creed, is clear from a letter which Constantine, the Emperor and "the man of God," wrote to Arius, in 333 A.D., according to the appendix of the letter itself. The text of this letter[93] is so extraordinary that it strains credulity:

Constantine Augustus to Arius and his Followers the Arians.

An unfaithful interpreter is a faithful picture and image of the Devil. For, just as skilful sculptors make him out as an image of deceitful cunning by putting on him, who, by nature, is simply and completely ugly, a goodly appearance of beauty, so that, by offering them error, he may destroy poor mortals, similarly, is, I believe, acting he who believes that for him, the only thing worthy of effort is to offer freely the harmful poisons of his own insolence. For he is introducing a new and unfaithful creed that has never been seen since men first existed. Therefore, what has long been said in the Word of God does not seem to be out of tune with the truth, namely, that they are believing the evil. What would anyone say when one has lost the gift to save oneself, and does not have the wish to find relief and help? Why am I, therefore, saying "Christ, Christ, Lord, Lord"? Why, then, is this band of robbers daily wounding us? There is opposed to us a violent recklessness and it rages and grinds its teeth, though ugly from its disgrace and covered with manifold reproaches. Though driven about by the law and the preaching about you, as if by some storms and mighty waves, it vomits forth pernicious

93. Preserved only in Athanasius, *De decretis Nic.* 40; Gelasius Cyz., *H.E.* III, 19.

words, and brings them to the public in writing, words which You, who are *with the Eternal Father, your origin*, never established in the teachings concerning Your person. It brings together and heaps up some strange and unlawful sacrileges, now, by boasting, and, again, by using jealousies of the unfortunate, whom it deceives and destroys in great numbers.

But I wish to examine the nature of its president. For what is he saying? *"Let us obtain"*, he says, that *which is already ours, or*, let it be the way we want it." He has fallen, and he has fallen for undertaking such things as this, "by trickery." he says, "or wicked intrigues." It makes no difference. He regards as holy only that which, through wicked designs flows to him. "We have," he says, "many with us." I will myself approach a little, so that I may witness the wars of madness. I shall, I said, move closer, personally, I, who used to put an end to the wars of senseless men. Come on, you Arian Ares, there is need of shields. But I beg you not to do this. Why, let rather the company of Aphrodite hold you back. But, would it not become you to abound in faithfulness to Christ just as much as you seem to try to win the approval of the masses? Do understand, I am coming, once more, as a suppliant, and I do not wish, in the abundance of my might, to fight with weapons, but, I want to cure you and the others, armed with the faith of Christ. Why do you profess, then, to do things which do not become your moral traits? But, tell me, how is your peace of mind, or what advantage have you gained, or rather, how far have you advanced in your recklessness? Such audacity deserves to be removed by thunderbolts! Listen, then, what he revealed to me, a short while ago, writing with a reed-pen oozing with poison. "This," he says, "is our faith." Then next he added, I believe, some imposing and very carefully expressed bombasts, and, going on, he did not omit any of his monstrosities, but opened up, so to say, all the vaults of his deranged mind. "We are driven away," he says, "they deny us permission to be re-admitted." However this is nothing really, but pay attention to what is coming next. For I am going to use his own words. "We ask," he says, "if the Bishop of Alexandria should remain steadfast in his disposition, we ask that we be given permission to bring about, according to the command of the Law, the lawful and indispensable worship of God." What a wicked shame-lessness that perverts the truth with fitting zealousness. Whatever he finds pleasure in he expresses in concise terms. What do you mean, madman? Are you in a hurry, with your sick and deranged mind, to devise a schism, with a façade that might please me, and are you rushing to destroy those who are implicated with you? "What am I to do," you say, "if nobody believes that I am worthy of being received." This is what you often yell from your godless throat. But, in return, I am asking you: where on earth did you give a clean demonstration and testimony of your meaning? You should have explained it, and made it clear to those in heaven and earth. But venomous reptiles are especially inclined to be very agitated whenever they come to understand that they are imbedded in the innermost part of their holes.

How very clever of him carefully to keep silence, as it were, under the false appearance of modesty. By putting on a false appearance, you show yourself meek and docile, but you deceive the crowd, although, inside, you are filled with numerous wicked schemes. What a misfortune! Just as the Evil One has wanted it, Arius became, in our eyes, a brothel of lawlessness. Come now and tell me the distinguishing mark of your own faith, and do not conceal it by silence, you, speaker of lies, with a nature all too ready for wickedness.

"One God", you say? You have my vote, too. Be minded like this. Do you say, "the Word, without beginning and without end, is from His substance"? I like this. Have a faith like this. If you attach to it anything further, I remove it. If you patch on to it anything concerning the impious idea of 'Separation', I confess that I neither see nor understand it. If you admit "the association of the body concerning the economy of God's operations," I do not reject it. If you say "their Spirit was, from all eternity, begotten in the superior Word," I accept it. Who knew the Father if not He who came from the Father? Whom did the Father know if not Him whom He has begotten, from Himself, from all eternity and without beginning? You, in your evil belief, think that it is necessary to assume a "different substance." But I believe that the fullness of the incomparable and all-pervading power of the Father and the Son is one substance. If, therefore, you take away anything from Him from whom nothing at all could ever be separated, not even by the thinking of those who lightheartedly argue for it, then you are inventing for Him accidental characteristics, and, generally speaking, in your search for signs of character, you are dividing Him who has given us, out of Himself, unending eternity and the idea of incorruptibility, and, He, by Himself, granted us belief in the resurrection and the Church. Put an end, therefore, put an end to this foolish lawlessness, you, who, with witty and elegant expressions, sing evil words bringing about loss of faith in those who are simple-minded. It was fitting that the Evil One recruited you to his evil work, and such a thing was equally pleasing to the people, for you have made the impression of being so witty, but this is altogether evil and destructive. Come, give up these absurd talks. Listen, you deluded Arius, I am talking to you. You surely appreciate what it means to be excommunicated from the Church of God. You are lost, you must know well, unless you look into yourself and renounce your current madness. But you will say that the masses are in your company, and relieve your anxieties.

Listen, therefore, and pay a little attention, you impious Arius, and do realize your madness. But You, O God, the Preserver of all, be agreeable to what I am saying, if it is in line with our faith. For I, "your servant," thanks to your gracious providence, will, from a very ancient Greek and Roman writing, clearly demonstrate that Arius' madness was predicted and prophesied

154

by the Erythraean Sibylla some 3000 years ago. For she said: "Woe to you, Libya, lying on the sea-shore. For a time will come for you when, together with your people and your daughters, you will have to enter into a terrible, savage, and most difficult battle and, as a result of this, the faith and piety of all will be tested, but an utter destruction will descend upon you. For you have dared to pull down the store house of heavenly flowers, then to tear it to pieces, and, indeed, to grind it into bits with your iron teeth."

What now, you, who are ready to do anything? In what part of the earth would you say that you are now yourself? Clearly, right in *that* place. As it is, I have in my hand the letter of yours which you, with the reed-pen of madness, wrote to me. In it you state that, with regard to salvation, the whole population of Libya is in agreement with you. But if you say that this passage is not true, God is my witness that I will indeed send to Alexandria the most ancient tablet of the Erythraean Sibylla composed in the Greek language, so that you might perish all the quicker. Then, will you be held unguilty, you abominable fellow? Then, will you not be clearly lost, you wretch, convicted by such mighty testimony?

We know, we do know of your undertaking. What care, what fear is troubling you?! This is no secret to us. O, you wretch, unfortunate and miserable, because you have such a dull mind, you do not even bemoan the sickness and helplessness of your own soul! O, you unholy man, who, with cunning words, undermines the truth, and being such a man, you are not ashamed now to censure us; next, you think, to prove us wrong, and, then, again, to admonish us. O, you, with a superabundance of faith and words, that the unfortunate hope to find, in your company, help for themselves! Of course, nobody should be in the company of such a man, not even to speak a word to him unless anyone thinks that it is concealed from the normal people that the hope of righteous living is in his deceitful words. But this is far from being true! That you are so senseless, all of you who associate with him! What insane frenzy drove you to suffer his unbearable tongue and endure his sight!

Very well. Now I will address you with my words, you madman, you chatterbox, you with a heart without faith. Give me, for speaking, not some very large and wide-ranging field, but a well-outlined arena, with not soft but with firm ground, you godless, most evil, and deceitful man. For I am coming out to speak on this. I will rather set the net around you and tie your feet and arms with my words and thus put you in the midst of the people there so that they may all see your lack of skill. But now we shall come to the business. Our hands are of course washed. Let us turn to prayers; do call on God. But wait a moment, tell me, you evil man, which God will you call on for help? For, otherwise, I am unable to have peace of mind.

O Lord, who have supreme authority over all, O Father of singular power, through this godless man your Church is receiving reproaches, bruises, and even wounds and pains. Arius is already preparing for you a well suited place and he persists in placing there for you, I believe, a Partner, but He is your Christ, who is from you, who is the author of our salvation, though he insists that He is your Son by adoption. Listen, I beg you, to his wonderful faith! Lord, he believes that you are moving in space. He dares to delimit you by fixing you within the circle of a seat. For where is the place where you are not present? Or where is it that all people do not realize your power on account of your laws that pervade the whole universe? For you surround everything yourself, and outside you one cannot imagine any space or anything else. Your power is so limitless in its operation.

Listen, O God, and all you people, pay attention. For this shameless and useless man, who has risen to the summit of depravity and lawlessness, puts on an appearance of piousness. "O no," he says, "I do not want God to appear to be involved in the suffering of acts of violence." Therefore, it seems to me, that you assume and fabricate things that are strange to believe, namely, that God created a newly-begotten and newly-built substance for Christ to provide a help for Himself. "For if you should take anything away from Him," he says, "you would by so much reduce Him." You corrupter and destroyer, this is, then, your faith? You suppose and believe that He who condemned the images of the pagans is Himself a created thing. Him, who, without any designing and calculating, accomplished everything through His external co-existence with the Father, Him you regard as one brought in to be a helper in certain tasks. Now, put into God — only of course if you dare — come, do put into Him the fear of and hope for the ftuture, again, the consideration and calculation involved in planning, the expression and clear distinction of His thought, and, in short, the actions of pleasure, laughing, and grieving. What do you say, now, you most wretched of all, you counsellor of evil? Admit, if you are able, that you are a miserable victim caught in your own evil-doing.

"Christ", he says, "has suffered for us." But, I have already said that He was sent down in the form of a body. "Indeed," he says, "but we must beware lest we appear to lessen Him." Is it not clear that, by saying this, you are raving mad, and belong to the society of wild animals? Look, the cosmos itself is a figure according to definite plan, and the stars have been arranged as images, and, generally, the spirit of this sphere-shaped vault is an image and a form of the things that actually exist. And God is, equally, present everywhere. How are in God acts of violence? How is God lessened? O you, murderous destroyer of right thinking, consider and conclude, by your own reflection, whether it is a fault that God is present in Christ. He saw the humiliation of the Logos, and without delay, meted out the punishment. There happen, besides, faults in the cosmos every day. Nevertheless, God is present, and tarries not with the punishments. How then is He lessened if the greatness of his power is perceived everywhere? In no way, I think. For the design of the cosmos is from God: all permanence is through Him, all justice is through Him. The faith in Christ is, without beginning, from Him. The whole law of God is Christ, and it is through Him that it is boundless and endless.

But you appear to be making inventions to suit your own thinking. What exceeding madness! Now, turn to your own destruction the sword of the Devil. Watch, all of you, what pitiful cries is he already emitting, stung by the bite of the viper. See, all, how, attacked by the poison, his blood vessels and his muscles are convulsed from pain; how far his whole body is wasted away: full of squalor, dirt, laments, shivering and thousands of miseries, he has become a horrible skeleton. How hateful is his thick and dirty hair; how deathly and utterly weak he looks, how bloodless his face is and how strained by anxiety; how all troubles attacking him at the same time — frenzy, madness and folly — have, through the long duration of his suffering, made him look like a wild animal. Suddenly, not even noticing his miserable condition, he says: "I am lifted up by pleasure, I leap up and dance with joy, I am on wings." And, again, he says with great vehemence: "Come, let us go to our ruin." This, at least, is true. For wickedness has abundantly supplied you with enthusiasm in its service, and what is normally bought at a high price, it has given to you most cheaply. Tell me now, where are your holy percepts? Wash yourself, if possible, with the Nile, you, man full of senseless madness. You have tried hard, with your godless arts, to throw the whole world into confusion. Do you not see that I, the man of God, already understand everything? But I am uncertain whether I should stay or go. For I cannot even look at such a man, and I am afraid of sinning by doing that, Arius, you son of Ares. You have placed us in light, but you have thrown yourself into darkness, unfortunate man. This is, apparently, the end of your labours.

But I come back to the place where you are saying that there are a great number of people who are won over to you. It is likely, I think, and take them, I say, take them. For they have surrendered themselves to be devoured by wolves and lions. Besides, however, every one of them will be compelled to pay, additionally, a tenfold head-tax, and will soon sweat very hard if he does not run, very quickly, to the Church with which there is Salvation, and does not return to the peace of Love by drinking the medicine of Unity. In the future, they will not be deceived by you, you who are convicted of wicked conscience, and they will not tolerate perishing by being entagled in your questionings. Your sophisms, for the future at least, will be clearly recognizable for all. And, you will not be able to accomplish anything; and, moreover, you will pretend, in vain, to reasonableness and mildness by your tricky phrases and by putting on, so to say, an external appearance of simplicity. In vain will be all your imposture. For the truth will immediately encircle you. The flood of its power will immediately extinguish your fires. The obligation of public services will fall upon your associates and fellow travellers, guilty of being involved in your scheme, unless they very quickly abandon your company in exchange for the incorruptible Faith. But you, man of iron heart, give me a proof of your purpose, if you are sure of yourself, and if you are safely anchored in the security of our Faith, and have an entirely pure conscience.

Come to me, I tell you, come to me, a man of God. Depend on it, with my inquiries I will penetrate the remotest parts of your heart. And, if it seemed that there is any symptom of madness there, I shall call on the grace of God and heal you so that you will be better than exemplary. But if your soul appears to be healthy, I will recognize the light of truth in you, thank God, and rejoice in your godliness.

And in another hand: May God watch over you, Beloved Brothers.

This, too, was delivered through Syncletius and Gaudentius, *commissarii*, when Paterius was the perfect of Egypt, and read aloud in the Imperial palace (there).

This letter, as Baynes says,[94] is so "improbable that for that very reason it is impossible to regard it as a forgery." One has to agree with this view.[95] However, Constantine clearly condemns in it Arius' heretical theology, and offers him to come into his presence to explain himself, to be healed by him, and to return to the true faith.

It may be, and it is even probable, that nothing came of Constantine's own personal plan to convert Arius. The next step, therefore, appears to have been an edict by Constantine ordering that all the works of the Arians, whom he calls Porphyrians, should be burnt, since they are dangerous to the Christian faith. Anyone concealing Arian literature was, on conviction, to suffer death. This edict[96] was issued to the bishops and the people and delivered by the same commissioners as the preceding letter to Arius and the Arians:

Constantine Victor Maximus Augustus to the Bishops and the People.

Since he imitated base and unfaithful men, Arius is worthy of suffering the same disgrace as is theirs. Just as, therefore, Porphyrius, the enemy of the

---

94. *Op. cit.* 361.

95. For the dating and some most useful notes, see H. Kraft, *op. cit.* 239-242; also, Dörries, *op. cit.* 103-112; Jones, *op. cit.* 189-190; Nordberg, *op. cit.* 23 f.; *et al.*

96. Athanasius, *De decretis Nic.* 39; Socrates, *H.E.* I, 9, 30-31; Sozomen, *H.E.* I, 21, 40; H. Kraft, *op. cit.* 230-233.

worship of God, composed some treatises against our religion and received an appropriate reward, so that consequently he was disgraced and filled with the worst reputation, and his writings, on the other hand, were destroyed, in similar fashion, it is, now, my decision that Arius and such as have opinions similar to his should be called Porphyrians in order that they may have the name of those whose way of life they imitate. In addition to this, if any treatise composed by Arius is found, let it be put into the fire, in order not only that his defective doctrinal works may be destroyed, but also that no reminder at all should remain of him. This, nevertheless, I order that if anyone is detected in concealing anything composed by Arius, and not giving it up instantly for feeding it to the fire, his penalty shall be death. For immediately after being convicted of this, he will suffer capital punishment. (In another hand: May God preserve you, beloved brothers.)

Thus Constantine continues the earlier actions he had taken by placing the writings of Porphyry and various Christian heretics on the list of forbidden books deemed dangerous to the Christian faith.[97] If we can believe a note at the end of the Athanasian edition of this edict, a copy of it was delivered again by the Imperial Commissars Syncletius and Gaudentius, and the edict should be dated to 333 A.D.[98]

Following the misbegotten efforts of his Arian enemies in 331 and 332 A.D., his full justification and the proof of his complete innocence on the Arian (and Melitian) charges against him, Athanasius was enjoying a really high regard in the eyes of the Emperor Constantine on account of the correctness of his position on the Arian question so much so that Constantine accepted Athanasius' stand that Arius ought not to be readmitted since Arius was equivocating and in fact was, in his heart, a heretic, unwilling, in truth, to accept the Creed of Nicaea.

The events that very soon followed and ended in the seeming triumph of the Arians over Athanasius and Nicaea should not make Constantine's strong stand, as expressed in the anti-Arian

97. See Baynes, *op. cit.* 367 f.; H. Kraft, *op. cit.* 230 ff.; Dörries, *op. cit.* 102-103; Jones, *op. cit.* 190; *et al.*
98. Cf. H. Kraft, *op. cit.* 231 ff., who disagrees. But Theodosius and Valentinian certainly refer to the Arius edict in *Cod. Theod.* XVI, 5, 6, (435 A.D., Aug. 5), making the genuineness of this edict look even more likely: See Dörries, *op. cit.* 112 f., who strongly defends the genuineness of the edict.

edict, for the year 333 A.D., the date of the edict, any less probable. In the following years, between 334 and 336 A.D., at councils, or rather quasi-councils, at Caesarea, Tyre, Jerusalem, and Constantinople, the Arian Eusebians resumed their efforts to remove Athanasius.

It may be that the Melitian bishop John Arcaph's visit to Constantine was a deciding factor in the Emperor's decision to call in early 334 A.D. a council of bishops to Caesarea, to investigate once more the earlier Melitian accusations against Athanasius.[99] It may also be that, planning his *tricennalia* of 335 A.D., the emperor wished it to coincide with a celebration of his completion of the unification of the Christian Church.[100]

Athanasius disobeyed the Imperial command to present himself at the Council of Caesarea.[101] The Bishop of Alexandria must have been aware that he would not have a chance before this council at Caesarea, presided over by Eusebius of Caesarea and under the baneful influence of bishops 'working for Arius' restoration' and regarding 'Athanasius as the chief obstacle to their designs'.[102] Indeed, there can be no doubt that the Council of Caesarea was composed of Athanasius' enemies and those under the influence of his enemies.

This is probably why Constantine did not take any action against Athanasius, and why he convoked a synod of bishops at Tyre for 335 A.D. in a letter that fairly well outlined, at least between the lines, the characteristics of the synod of Caesarea and, in particular, its futility in the absence of Athanasius, who had refused to present himself.[103] It is in this letter that certain bishops, undoubtedly specified by the leading Arian element of the Council of Caesarea, were ordered to appear at the Synod at Tyre under

99. Nordberg, *op. cit.* 26; Theodoretus, *H.E.* I, 27: a letter, perhaps to the bishops at Caesarea, to plead for unity, with references to refusals to come to the current synod; for the same letter of Constantine to the bishops, see Eusebius, *Vita Constant.* IV, 42.

100. See Jones, *op. cit.* 191.

101. Sozomen, *H.E.* II, 25; Theodoretus, *H.E.* I, 27: a reference very likely to Athanasius' refusal to appear at the synod of Caesarea.

102. Jones, *op. cit.* 191 f.

103. Eusebius, *Vita Constant.* IV, 42; Theodoretus, *H.E.* I, 27; H. Kraft, *op. cit.* 257 f.; Dörries, *op. cit.* 114-117.

threat of banishment should any bishop disobey the Emperor's command:[104]

It would be proper and most appropriate to the happiness of the times that the Catholic Church should be without factions, and the servants of Christ, now, be freed from all reproach. Since, however, some, driven by a mad desire for sickly dissension — for I would not say that they are living as they should — some are trying to create general confusion, a situation that appears to have become the greatest of all misfortunes, therefore, I command that you come, so to say, with all haste and without any delay, to form the synod which is to give aid to those in need of help; to heal the brothers who are in dire peril; to bring back to unity the members which are separated; to rectify the mistakes while there is opportunity; in order to give back to so many provinces the harmony they should have, which — what madness! — the arrogance of a very few persons has destroyed. I believe that all people agree that, if you should restore the peace, it would be pleasing to God, the Lord of the universe, surpass all my desires as well as yours, and bring no ordinary honour to you. Do not delay, therefore, but hasten, with a strenuous effort, to put an end to these dissensions in the fitting manner, by coming together in all that sincerity and faith that our Saviour, whose servants we are, demands, although without words, especially from us on all occasions. As far as it is in my power, I will see that nothing will be lacking for you. All things that you indicated in your letters have been done by me. I have summoned the bishops specified by you, ordering that they come and share their thoughts with you. I have dispatched Dionysius, a man of consular rank, who will remind those obligated to come with you to the synod. He will also be present to supervise the proceedings, and, especially, the orderly conduct. For should anyone dare, — though I do not think any one will — even now, to frustrate our command by refusing to attend, somebody will be sent from here and, by banishing him in virtue of an imperial decree, he will teach him that it is not proper to resist an emperor's measures enacted in the interest of truth. For the rest, it will be your Holinesses's task, influenced by feelings neither of hostility nor favouritism, but in strict obedience to ecclesiastical and apostolic rule, to conceive a suitable therapy for trespasses or even mistakes accidentally made in order that you may free the Church from all blame, and lighten my worries, and that, by restoring the blessing of peace to those who are now standing apart, you may procure for yourselves very great glory. May God watch over you, Beloved Brothers.

In threatening banishment against those refusing to answer the call to Tyre, Constantine probably had Athanasius in mind. He

104. Eusebius, *Vita Constant.* IV, 42, and as in note 103, *above.*

sent a command to Athanasius to appear.[105] Finally, Athanasius did appear at Tyre, but only after a long hesitation, which was also the reason for the Emperor's special summons to him.[106] Nevertheless, on July 11, 335 A.D., Athanasius, "under strong compulsion," left for Tyre, accompanied by forty-eight bishops supporting him.[107] But these and the other anti-Arian bishops were outnumbered by the pro-Arians by nearly two to one.[108]

The proceedings, or at least the major events of the Council of Tyre were reported by Athanasius and later Church historians.[109] It was clear from the beginning, and even well before, that the main if not only purpose of the Council of Tyre was to condemn Athanasius. In any case, the Council was packed with pro-Arian, or at least with anti-Athanasian bishops. Most of the old charges such as "the case of the broken Chalice," the "affair Arsenius and Arcaph" were again brought up and again refuted. It was the old Arian and Melitian plot to destroy Athanasius, their staunchest enemy,[110] all over again. New charges were made as well as old ones. The new charges alleged 'episcopal autocracy mixed with violence'; that the "people of Alexandria" could not continue attendance at church because of Athanasius, and that Athanasius was himself not validly elected as Bishop of Alexandria. This is not to mention some other charges, of moral turpitude, for example, which were false and ridiculous. Athanasius[111] successfully repelled some of the allegations, but requested, in fairness, delay to enable him to investigate the other charges. Since Athanasius does not mention some of the new charges, it is assumed by some modern historians[112] that he was guilty.

Finally, the 'Council of Tyre' appointed the 'the Mareotic Commission' to investigate on the spot the old charges concerning

105. Athanasius, *Apol. c. Arian.* 71.
106. See Jones, *op. cit.* 193 ff.; Baynes, *op. cit.* 362, n. 68; Nordberg, *op. cit.* 27; H.I. Bell, *Jews and Christians etc. op. cit.* 45-71; "Athanasius: a Chapter in Church History," *The Congregational Quarterly* 3 (1925) 158-176.
107. Bell, "Athanasius etc." *op. cit.* 167.
108. Kidd, *op. cit.* V. ii, 60.
109. Athanasius, *Apol. c. Arian.* 71-83; Sozomen, *H.E.* II, 25; Socrates, *H.E.* I, 28-31; *etc.*
110. E.g. Sozomen, *H.E.* II, 25.
111. *Ibid.*
112. E.g. by Jones, *op. cit.* 193-198.

Macarius, Ischyras, and 'the broken chalice'. It was composed of well known Arian bishops such as Theognius and others. Athanasius' detailed documentation of these proceedings shows the Arian spirit of the commission, and that it was not interested in truth but only in the destruction of their enemy. However, even witnesses for the prosecution came forward with evidence favouring Athanasius. Protests against the unfairness of the proceedings were all in vain, and the presence of Dionysius, the Imperial representative, did not help to assure fair process.[113] Thus it can be no surprise at all that in the end the Council accomplished what it had set out to do: it deposed Athanasius from the see of Alexandria.[114] The Council had to condemn Athanasius in his absence since he and his followers had withdrawn, or perhaps escaped, from the Council, to appeal at Constantinople to the Emperor himself personally asking him to call the bishops assembled at Tyre into his presence so that Athanasius might face his accusers before the Emperor.

But just before this new 'council' at Constantinople could take place, Constantine invited the Council Fathers to attend the dedication of the great church of the Holy Sepulchre in Jerusalem. This 'Council of Jerusalem' apart from attending the dedication ceremonies,[115] did accomplish some very surprising business — if anything accomplished by these 'Council Fathers' can still be surprising: it readmitted Arius,[116] and then instructed the Church of Alexandria to receive Arius and his fellowers, who had been excluded from the Church by "the enemy of all goodness."[117]

Athanasius arrived at Constantinople on October 5, 335 A.D. and the Council Fathers must have been celebrating the dedication of the Church of the Holy Sepulchre and the reception of Arius when they received a new order from the Emperor: they were to come to him in Constantinople to account for their treatment of Athanasius:[118]

113. Athanasius, *Apol. c. Arian.* 71-83.
114. Socrates, *H.E.* I, 32; Sozomen, *H.E.* II, 25.
115. Described in lavish terms by Eusebius, *Vita Constant.* IV, 43-47.
116. Athanasius, *Apol. c. Arian.* 84; *De synodis* 21.
117. See Baynes, *op. cit.* 362 f.; Jones, *op. cit.* 198 f.; Dörries, *op. cit.* 117 ff.; H. Kraft, *op. cit.* 149 f.
118. Athanasius, *Apol. c. Arian.* 86; Sozomen, *H.E.* II, 28; Socrates,

Constantine Victor Maximus Augustus to the Bishops assembled at Tyre.

I do not know what your synod, with noise and tumult, has decided, but it seems that somehow the truth has been perverted through confusions and disorders, since, in your love of contentiousness, which you seem to be determined to keep up, you have failed to notice what is pleasing to God. But it will be the task of Divine Providence to make manifest and dissipate the evil that has resulted from such contentiousness, and to show to us plainly, whether you, in your assembly there, have any concern for the truth, and whether you made your decisions without being influenced by feelings of favouritism and hostility. Therefore, I want you all to assemble before my Piety, so that you may yourselves give me an exact account of proceedings.

The reason why I have decided to write to you, and why I, through (this) my letter, summon you before me, you will learn from the following. As I was entering Constantinople, our most happy city that is named after me, — I happened to be riding on horseback at that time — the Bishop Athanasius, with some of his followers, came up to me in the middle of the road, so suddenly that it produced in me great consternation. God, who knows everything, is my witness that, at first sight, I could not recognize who it was, until some of my attendants, — since, of course, I inquired of them — informed me who he was and what injustice he was suffering. I did not, on this occasion, enter into conversation with him, nor did I give him a hearing. But, though he asked me for an audience, I refused it and almost ordered him to be removed. But when he only demanded with great boldness that you ought to be summoned to appear that he might before me, in your own presence, complain of the ill-treatment which he has received, this seemed to me to be reasonable and, in accordance with the spirit of our times, I willingly ordered this letter to be written to you, so that all of you who constituted the synod of Tyre, might, without delay, hasten to the court of my Clemency, and that you might prove by facts that your judgement was unbiassed and just, right before me, since not even you will deny that I am a true servant of God.

For it is through my service to God that peace prevails everywhere, and that even the barbarians truly praise the Name of God — people, who until now have not known the truth — and it is evident that he who does not know the truth does not know God either. Nevertheless, as I have said above, the barbarians have, through me, the true servant of God, come to the knowledge of God, and learned to fear Him, since they experienced through actual events that He shields and protects me all the time. For this reason especially they know God, and they now fear Him because of the dread they have of me. But we who have to announce the mysteries of His Mercy (for I can hardly say that we keep them) we, I say, do nothing but what leads to dissension and hatred, and what, in one word, brings mankind to destruction.

But, as I have said, come to me, all of you, with the greatest speed, and you may be convinced that I will attempt, with all my power, to bring about that in the Law of God especially those things will be preserved intact, to which no reproach nor incorrect interpretation can attach, and that the enemies of the Law, who, under the pretext of the Holy Name, cause all maner of blasphemies, will be scattered, completely destroyed, and annihilated.

The reaction of the good Council Fathers of Tyre[119] was at first perhaps a little panicky, but then they quickly recollected themselves. "Conscious of what they had done," Eusebius of Nicomedia and his pro-Arian followers sent most of the other bishops home, and only then, namely, the two Eusebiuses, Theognius, Maris, Patrophilus, Ursacius, and Valens went to Constantinople. Thus the Council of Tyre was reduced to a mere clique of bishops who were coming to the Emperor to tell not the truth, as the Emperor had hoped, but untruth, to destroy Athanasius. 'The broken chalice,' 'Arsenius' and the other previous charges were no longer brought up by the Eusebians, but they invented another accusation, a truly deadly one,[120] namely, that Athanasius had threatened somehow to stop the transportation of corn from Alexandria to Constantinople. The accusers produced a number of bishops who supposedly had heard this threat. It was thus that Athanasius stood convicted of treason. The Emperor was once more deceived by these bishops he so naively trusted, and immediately exiled Athanasius to Trèves in Gaul. Or,[121] is it possible that Constantine's real reason for banishing Athanasius was the bishop's unbending stand against admitting Arius into the Church in Alexandria? If this is so the pro-Arian bishops possibly only provided the Emperor with the pretext for getting rid of Athanasius, in order finally to bring about a semblance of unity, though not quite what Constantine had wished for. This, however, must remain what it is — a speculation.

But the admission of Arius into the Church in Alexandria never

H.E. I, 34; Jones, op. cit. 200 f.; H. Kraft, op. cit. 258 f.; Dörries, op. cit. 119-124.

119. Athanasius, Apol. c. Arian. 87; Socrates, H.E. I, 28; 35; Sozomen, H.E. II, 28; etc.

120. Socrates, H.E. I, 35; Athanasius, Apol. c. Arian. 87.

121. E.g. Socrates, H.E. I, 35.

took place, for,[122] returning with his associates once more to Egypt, he was once more refused communion there, and then going to Constantinople to ask for admission there, he was refused even by Alexander, the Bishop of Constantinople. Arius had perhaps been called by Constantine himself to Constantinople to be received there. However, despite the Imperial will, Arius was once more refused admission, because, it appears, of the opposition and desperate prayers of Bishop Alexander, who begged God for His intervention in the matter.

On the Saturday before the Sunday appointed for his admission into the Church in Constantinople, according to a letter of Athanasius,[123] Arius, a "little before sunset," was compelled by a call of nature to enter a place appointed for such emergencies. His companions, waiting in vain outside for Arius to emerge from the public convenience, finally, broke into the place and found him dead upon the seat.

Shortly before this, Arius had sworn that he accepted the Catholic truth even if he had ever stated it otherwise. Thus Athanasius and others, not excluding the Emperor Constantine, were convinced that Arius had committed perjury, and that thus the expectations of Arius were rendered futile by the judgement of God, who saw through the hearts of the pro-Arian bishops as well as that of Arius. This was something the pro-Arian bishops, wolves in sheep's clothing, could not by any amount of deceit circumvent.

Nonetheless, the see of Athanasius was never filled by the election of a new Bishop of Alexandria. Athanasius was never recalled by Constantine, who to repeated appeals only answered that he had to accept the decision of the Council of Tyre that had deposed Athanasius.[124]

It seems that already perhaps on June 17, 337 A.D., soon, *i.e.* only a few weeks, but possibly not quite that soon, after the passing of the Great Emperor, Athanasius was definitely recalled from exile by a letter of Constantine the Second, the son of Constantine the Great.[125]

---

122. *Ibid.* 37; Sozomen, *H.E.* II, 29.
123. See *Epist. ad Episc. Egypt. et Lib.* 18, 19; *idem, Epist. ad Serapion.*; see also Theodoretus, *H.E.* I, 13; Socrates, *H.E.* I, 38; Sozomen, *H.E.* II, 30.
124. Sozomen, *H.E.* II, 31.
125. Athanasius, *Apol. c. Arian.* 87; cf. Nordberg, *op. cit.* 32-35.

CONSTANTINE: A CHRISTIAN MONARCH AND TRUE APOSTLE

The death of the Great Monarch took place on May 22, 337 A.D., at the feast of Pentecost, and he was then buried in the Church of the Apostles in his own city.[1]

A few days before his death he was baptized, and there are several unanswered questions about this baptism. It may fairly be assumed that it was Eusebius, Bishop of Nicomedia, who baptized Constantine.[2] It is now beyond question that he was not baptized by Pope Sylvester, as is claimed in an inscription on an Egyptian obelisk set up on the piazza of the Lateran Basilica by Pope Sixtus V.[3]

The surprising matter about Constantine's death, however, is not that he was baptized, but that he left his baptism to almost the last moment of his life. Indeed, the lateness of Constantine's baptism is not simply puzzling but has also made it difficult for us to recognize the true nature of his Christianity, since it has often been cited in arguments that doubt the sincerity of his Christian faith. Although he may have intended to be baptized, in imitation of Christ, in the river Jordan, it is most unlikely that[4] Constantine deferred his baptism "until he could be baptized" in this river. Modern authors[5] advance the farfetched belief that Constantine

1. For a most detailed description of his baptism, death, and burial, see Eusebius, *Vita Constant.* IV, 60-73; see also brief reports in Theodoretus, *H.E.* I, 30-32; Socrates, *H.E.* I, 39-40; Sozomen, *H.E.* II, 34.
2. Jerome, *Chron. ad ann.* 2353, states this.
3. This claim has been proved legendary; see e.g. F.J. Dölger, "Die Taufe Konstantins und ihre Probleme," *Konstantin d. Gr. und seine Zeit* (Freiburg, 1913) 377-447; esp. 389; also, N.H. Baynes, "Constantine the Great and the Christian Church," *Proceedings of the Brit. Acad.* 15 (1929) n. 78; *et al.*
4. Eusebius, *Vita Constant.* IV, 62, and as claimed by Theodoretus, *H.E.* I, 30.
5. Not to mention Gibbon and others, as e.g. J.R. Palanque, *The Church in the Roman Empire* (London, 1949) 12-24.

postponed his formal entry — his baptism — into the Church only to retain a footing in both the Christian and the pagan camps. Some[6] suggest that Constantine, regarding himself as the 'Servant of God', may have felt himself to have such a special relation with God that he did not need the baptism, or that,[7] in a similar vein, he, wishing at a much earlier time to enter the Church, was told by Eusebius[8] and other bishops that he, like Saint Paul, though unbaptized, was directly initiated by God by his visions. The question can, of course, be asked whether anyone may blame Constantine for not "missing" the baptism when leaders of the Church declared it to be unnecessary for him? Perhaps nobody can blame Constantine except the bishops even if the story is true. But, of course, it is most regrettably true that many of the bishops surrounding Constantine were only too eager to flatter the first Christian Emperor and even to encumber him with subservient and flattering praise, in their own interests, but against his.[9]

The key must be in what Constantine himself said on the very occasion to explain why he decided finally to have himself baptized. We may be able to understand Constantine's real reasons for the postponement of his baptism till almost the last moment of his life if we listen to what he said at this moment of truth, when he would probably not be eager to listen to empty flattery, and when the churchmen were perhaps finding that flattery would no longer be useful.

Saying that this was the time he had long been hoping for in order to gain Salvation in God by receiving the seal of Salvation, the baptism, Constantine, then, expresses the key words: μὴ δὴ οὖν ἀμφιβολία τις γιγνέσθω, i.e. "let there be then no more ἀμφιβολία". The meaning of the word ἀμφιβολία is disputed. If this word means 'doubt' or 'hesitation,' it is not likely at all to mean, in its context, doubt[10] about the Christian faith, of which

6. E.g. A.H.M. Jones, *Constantine the Great and the Conversion of Europe* (London, 1968) 240 f.; H. Kraft, "Zur Taufe Kaiser Konstantins," *Studia Patristica* 1 (1957) 647; *et al.*
7. H. Kraft, *ibid.* 646 f., *et al.*
8. E.g. *De laud. Const.* XI. 1.
9. See e.g. the judgment of Jones, *op. cit.* 241.
10. H. Kraft, *op. cit.* 646 f., though leaving the object of this 'doubt' unanswered, indirectly suggests, with the text from Gelasius Cyz., *H.E.* II, 7, 1-7 (*Oratio ad Sanctum coetum* 7), that the object of this 'doubt' was 'faith'

Constantine had been a fervent champion ever since 312 A.D. Nor is it likely to mean hesitation in the sense[11] that Constantine had been hedging all his life by trying to be Christian to the Christians and heathen to the heathens. The context of the word ἀμφιβολία should indicate the true meaning of Constantine. By saying that if God would prolong his life, he would follow a life that befitted a Christian, Constantine all but explicitly says that he has so far postponed his baptism because he was not sure whether, or rather that he was sure that he could not live up to the rules of a Christian life.[12] Thus the postponement. Fully aware of his weaknesses, about which there are enough historical facts preserved — some of them may be found in his treatment of his most loyal son Crispus and of his wife Fausta — Constantine had good reasons for doubting his capacity to keep the Divine Law. At the same time, knowing also that the forgiveness of sins was more difficult after baptism, and that baptism, the seal of immortality, washed away all sins, including the kind of sins he must have been aware of in his own stormy life, Constantine was doing exactly what many Christians of his age were doing: postponing this all important means of purification till the time when they were not even able, or much less inclined, to sin any more.[13]

Since the postponement of baptism could and very often did make a license for sins out of forgiveness of sins, but also for other reasons, the Church disapproved of the practice of this deliberate postponement of the baptism.[14] In postponing his baptism to the very end of his life, then, Constantine followed a very human practice probably quite widespread in the fourth century probably

(πίστις); also, id., Kaiser Konstantins religiöse Entwicklung (Tübingen, 1955) 152 f.

11. Th. Keim, Der Ubertritt Constantins des Grossen zum Christentum (Zürich, 1862); cf. Kraft, "Zur Taufe etc." op. cit. 643.

12. Also, F.J. Dölger, "Die Taufe Konstantins und ihre Probleme," op. cit. 377-472; Jones, op. cit. 243.

13. Dölger, "Die Taufe K. etc."; op. cit. 429 ff.; H. Kraft, Kaiser Konstantins rel. Entw., op. cit., 151 ff.; Jones, op. cit. 246 f.; et al. Concerning the reports on the "murder" of Fausta and the execution of Crispus, see H. Kraft, Kaiser Konstantins rel. Entw., op. cit. 129 ff.; Otto Seeck, "Die Verwandtenmorde Konstantins des G.," Zschr. f. Wiss. Theol. 33 (1890) 63-77.

14. Synod of Neocaesarea, canon 12; also Basil, Hom. 13, 5; Greg. Naz., Or. 40, 11; Chrysost., In Acta Apost. hom. 1, 8; etc.

for the very same reasons as many Christians kept postponing the Sacrament that guaranteed them eternal salvation provided, of course, that they had the Christian faith in their hearts. And there can be no doubt that Constantine had had true, though not perfect, faith for a long time, probably since 312 A.D.

All this, of course, did not mean that Constantine was a perfect Christian, but rather, on the contrary, that he was really a very weak Christian, finding it − like most Christians − difficult to live up to the standards of Christianity. That Constantine was a Christian at least at the end of his life cannot be doubted, provided that one does not judge the question by the quality of his Christianity.

That Constantine was baptized, and that well before his baptism in 337 A.D. he had been a Christian, is, without doubt or hesitation, admitted by ancient historians such as Socrates, Sozomen, Theodoretus, and others.[15] Other ancient historians, who did not belong to the same fold, though not denying the Christianity and baptism of Constantine, put the whole matter in an entirely different light. For Libanius, Julian the Apostate, and Zosimus, Constantine was a renegade and an outcast. Accordingly,[16] it was only when, after the 'murders of his son Crispus and his wife Fausta,' he was looking for purification and had been resfused it by the pagan priests that he joined Christianity. Curiously, however, while he naturally blames Constantine for the 'disintegration' of the Roman Empire and puts the beginning of this process at the year 313 A.D., the hostile ancient historian connects Constantine's conversion with the events of 312-313 A.D., though according to this historian, he was keeping his Christianity a secret until he became the sole Emperor in 324 A.D.[17] after his defeat of Licinius. Julian expresses very similar views about Constantine's

15. *Passim.* Also, Ambrosius, *De obitu Theodosii* 40; Orosius, *Historia adv. pag.* VII, 28; for stories on his conversion and baptism, see e.g. F. Halkin, "L'empereur Constantin converti par Euphratas," *Anal. Boll.* 78 (1960) 5-17; "Le règne de Constantin d'après la Chronique inedite du Pseudo-Symeon," *Byzantion* 29-30 (1959-1960) 7-27; the inscription on Constantine's baptism by Pope Sylvester; etc.

16. Zosimus, II, 29.

17. J. Straub, "Konstantins Verzicht auf dem Gang zum Kapitol," *Historia* 4 (1955) 302 ff.; K. Aland, "Die religiöse Haltung Kaiser Konstantins," *Studia Patristica* 1 (1957) 595 f.; *et al.*

baptism.[18] Libanius,[19] though placing the conversion of Constantine in the year 325 A.D., perhaps only to *prove* that the God of the Christians had had nothing to do with Constantine's victories over the pagan Maxentius (312) and Licinius (324 A.D.), nevertheless recognizes that the battle at the Milvian Bridge was one of religion, in which paganism was conquered by Christianity, thus in fact dating the beginning of the Christian Empire to 312 A.D.[20] The Christian historian,[21] in answer to pagan distortions that Constantine's conversion was associated with the 'murder of his son' Crispus, makes a valiant effort to demonstrate that Constantine had been a Christian and favourable to Christians well before 326 A.D., in fact way back in his campaign and his vision of the Cross in the skies in 312 A.D.[22] Thus *both* Christian and pagan writers believed that Constantine had indeed been baptized, and regarded him, though with vastly different feelings, as undoubtedly a Christian, good or bad, but a Christian.

Libanius, Julian the Apostate, Zosimus, and others have their modern counterparts in those who deny that Constantine sincerely and genuinely became a Christian. There follow in the footsteps of the ancient scoffers or deniers the Gibbons, the Burckhardts, the Henri Grégoires, the Jaques Moreaus, and others akin to these,[23] who deny that Constantine ever was a Christian, or a genuine one, though they 'admit' that Constantine's religion was mixture of paganism and some sort of Christianity — half-pagan and half-Christian at best. But one should not really go to any trouble in trying to refute Gibbon's and Burckhardt's 'arguments' against Constantine's Christianity, in which they point at some of

18. *Convivium Caesarum, Opera* (ed. Hertlein) 336 A-B.
19. *Or.* XXX.
20. See W. Seston, "L'opinion païenne et la conversion de Constantin," *Rev. Hist. Phil. Rélig.* 16 (1936) 257 ff.
21. Sozomen, *H.E.* I, 3-5.
22. Cf. Seston, *op. cit.* 260.
23. E. Gibbon, *The History of the Decline and Fall of the Roman Empire*, ed. J.B. Bury, vol. 2 (1896) c. 20, esp. 295-307; Jacob Burckhardt, *The Age of Constantine the Great* (New York, 1949) esp. 292-306; H. Grégoire, "La 'conversion' de Constantin," *Rev. Univ. Brux.* 36 (1930-31) 231-272; J. Moreau, "Sur la vision de Constantin (312)," *Rev. d. Etud. Anc.* 55 (1953) 307 ff.; "Zur Religionspolitik Konstantins des Grossen," *Ann. Univ. Sarav.* 1 (1952) 160 ff.; *et al.*

171

Constantine's acts of violence and cruelty — acts which are obviously unworthy of a "good Christian." Insistence on such arguments as these is ridiculous.[24] The question is not whether Constantine was a "good Christian".

Nor should one bother too much with arguments accusing Eusebius of deliberate fraud by inventing stories to paint Constantine as a Christian and, moreover, as God's personal choice and representative. While the Church Historian, according to the literary custom and indeed the expectation of the age, used very generous rhetoric in describing Constantine's achievements, and while he was quite capable of 'suppressing' or rather being intentionally 'silent' on events that could not and would not support the picture of the Emperor he had in mind, Eusebius on the other hand — although he may have at times been honestly mistaken or naive — never committed fraud or the sin of lying in presenting what he stated as facts, or what had, according to his testimony, been related to him as facts.[25]

It must be on the basis of what Constantine did and said for Christianity that his Christianity (i.e. whether he was in fact a Christian or not) must be decided. Once more, the 'judgement' that Constantine was a man without religion and that the utilized religion in the interest of his policy,[26] must be rejected; to make him out a free thinker of this type would indeed have made him a *rara avis*[27] in the 4th century. Others, indeed, thinking of Constantine's achievements, acts and legislative acts, believe that he was, with respect to religion, between paganism and Christianity. According to this thinking, Constanine had to act cautiously, had to please both sides of the Roman Empire, the Christians with their bishops and their powerful God and the pagans with their past and their terrifying magic.[28] In other words, Constantine, as

24. See R. MacMullen, *Constantine* (London, 1970) 109.
25. F. Winkelmann, *Die Vita Constantini des Eusebius* etc. (Halle, 1959); *Die Textbezeugung der Vita Constantini des Eusebius von Caesarea* (Berlin, 1962); "Zur Geschichte des Authentizitätsproblems der Vita Constantini," *Klio* 40 (1962) 187-243; "Die Beurteilung des Eusebius von Caesarea und seiner Vita Constantini im Griechischen Osten," *Byzantinische Beiträge* (Berlin, 1964) 91-119.
26. The opinion of Gibbon, *above*, and of others after him.
27. Palanque, *op. cit.* 12 ff.
28. H.M. Gwatkin, "Constantine and his City," *Cambridge Med. Hist.* vol. i (Cambridge U.P., 1957) 9 f.

some[29] would put it, was in an ambiguous position and it is thus that there was a "conscious ambiguity in his acts and government in general: he was a Christian emperor ruling a pagan empire and bound to a pagan past."

It was only in his secular policies, but particularly in his secular legislation that Constantine may have the *appearance* of being ambiguous, in the sense that he may have assumed a compromising stand by taking up his position between Paganism and Christianity. The influence of Christianity is obviously visible in several of Constantine's laws;[30] however it seems that it is not regarded by modern critics as very considerable, but rather as weak and rare.[31]

It is perhaps in his laws concerning the family that we find a very pleasing influence of Christianity. The fact that Constantine prohibited the husband from keeping a concubine while the marriage lasted[32] was most likely due to the influence of Christianity. This measure clearly belongs to the idea of genuinely Christian marriage. Similarly significant were Constantine's measures to make divorce, either for the husband or for the wife, more difficult. Even though *adultery* was one of the *public crimes*, the right of accusation was limited by Constantine only to the husband and the adulterous wife's closest kin.[33] Another law of Constantine[34] limited the legal reasons that permitted a wife and a husband to send notice of divorce to her or his spouse. Accordingly, wives were permitted to repudiate their husbands only for murder, poisoning, or grave-robbery, but not any longer for drunkenness, gambling or running after other women. Husbands, on the other hand, were limited in seeking divorce to reasons such as adultery, poisoning, or procuring. In these and some other laws governing family life Constantine certainly displayed his belief in or at least approval of the Christian idea of the sanctity of marriage.

29. Such as N.H. Baynes, "Constantine", *Cambridge Anc. Hist.* vol. 12 (Cambridge U.P., 1956) 685.
30. For a good study of this influence, see J. Vogt, "Zur Frage des Christlichen Einflusses auf die Gesetzgebung Konstantins d. G." *Festschrift L. Wenger* 2 (1945) 118-148.
31. Jones, *op. cit.* 231; H. Dörries, *Das Selbstzeugnis Kaiser Konstantins* (Göttingen, 1954) 274; *et al.*
32. *nemini licentia concedatur constante matromonio concubinam penes se habere*, Just. V, 26, 1 (326 A.D., June 14); Dörries, *op. cit.* 192; 273.
33. *C. Th.* IX, 7, 2; Dörries, *op. cit.* 190; 273; (326 A.D., Apr. 25).
34. *C. Th.* III, 16, 1; Dörries, *op. cit.* 196; 273; (331 A.D.).

In some of his constitutions,[35] Constantine ordered grants of money, food, and clothing to indigent parents who might otherwise be tempted to sell or even expose their children. Although there had been pagan examples of similar measures, particularly under some of the high-thinking emperors, it is very possible that Constantine received his inspiration in this matter from the ideas of the Christian Church[36] on the practice of the acts of mercy towards the poor and helpless.

Very moving is Constantine's solicitude[37] in ordering that whenever Imperial estates were being broken up among several lessees, slave families were not to be broken up by the separation of children from their parents and husbands from their wives. Since Constantine otherwise betrayed very little sympathy for slaves, it might be that in this most humane measure he was inspired by the Church, which was concerned about the family, but particularly about the stability and sanctity of marriage. What else the Emperor did for slaves was to make their *manumission* valid also when it was done *religiosa mente*, meaning probably "with religious motivation" in a church and under the eyes of the bishop, or even only in the presence of priests; according to this same law, priests were permitted to manumit validly their own slaves, even out of the sight of a priest, and even only orally, without any written documentation.[38] This law certainly made manumission much easier and may have served as an exhortation to Christians, and especially priests, to free their slaves in the true spirit of brotherly love.

Another area in which Christianity showed some (though far from enough) influence in bringing about improvement was the gladiatorial games. In one constitution,[39] Constantine ordered that if any person should be condemned to the arena or to the mines, he was to be branded on his hands or on the calves of his legs, "so

35. *C. Th.* XI, 27, 1 (315 A.D.) and XI, 27, 2 (322 A.D.); C. Pharr, *The Theodosian Code etc.* (New York, 1969) *ad loc.*
36. Jones, *op. cit.* 231.
37. *C. Th.* II, 25, 1 (334 A.D. (?) Apr. 29); Dörries, *op. cit.* 200; 276; Pharr, *op. cit. ad loc.*
38. *C.Th.* IV, 7, 1; 321 A.D., April 18; Pharr, *op. cit. ad loc.*; also, Dörries, *op. cit.* 182.
39. *C. Th.* IX, 40, 2; 315 or 316 A.D., March 21; Pharr, *op. cit. ad loc.*; Dörries, *op. cit.* 168; 276.

that the face, which has been made in the likeness of celestial beauty may not be disfigured." One may only hope that branding on the hands or legs became less painful, though reference to 'heavenly beauty' makes the influence of the Church obvious. In 325 A.D. Constantine put a complete ban on gladiatorial shows[40] and ordered that convicted criminals formerly condemned to gladiatorial games should now be sent to the mines instead. Although this may have considerably extended the agony and increased the suffering of the condemned criminal, it nevertheless eliminated institutionalized shedding of blood, again probably through the influence of the Church. It was unfortunate that this law soon became unenforceable and gladiatorial games were in fact abolished only in the early 5th century.[41] Even forty years later, a law of Emperors Valentinian and Valens laid down that Christians convicted of any crime at all should not be sentenced to the arena.[42] Clearly, Constantine and some other Emperors were quite impotent in the face of some long-established and deep-rooted traditions of the Roman Empire.

There are other examples of legislation by Constantine that, in contrast to some of the above mentioned constitutions, show a great measure of what we may regard as shocking brutality — nothing new, since all legislation of this type was based on Roman traditional discipline — and it cannot even be said that Constantine did not agree with this 'cruel' legislation, or that he had no knowledge of it. If e.g., according to a piece of legislation[43] of the young Constantine, any free woman, "unmindful of her honourable status" (*immemor honestatis*) was united to a slave, she was to lose her freedom and her children were to be slaves of the master of the slave to whom she united herself in cohabitation. At a later date, all this became much stricter, and indeed quite brutal, when Constantine ordered[44] that if any woman had a clandestine love

---

40. *C. Th.* XV, 12, 1; 325 A.D., Oct. 1; Pharr, *op. cit. ad loc.*; Dörries, *op. cit.* 188; 276.

41. See Jones *op. cit.* 231; Eusebius, *Vita Constant.* IV, 25.

42. *C. Th.* IX, 40, 8; 365 A.D., Jan. 15; Pharr, *op. cit. ad loc.*; Dörries, *op. cit.* 170.

43. *C. Th.* IV, 12, 1; 314 A.D., April 1; Pharr, *op. cit. ad loc.*; Dörries, *op. cit.* 166; IV (13), 1.

44. *C. Th.* IX, 9, 1; 326 A.D., May 29; Pharr, *op. cit. ad loc.*; Dörries, *op. cit.* 191; 275.

affair with a slave, she was subject to capital punishment, and the "rascally slave was to be delivered to the flames."

Is it correct to say that Constantine, because of this sort of legislation, stood somewhere between Paganism and Christianity? Hardly, because, in some instances, when he tried to change cruel law or tradition, he was powerless, and in other cases he left cruel laws and traditions essentially unchanged, or else he made them even more strict, because he believed that they were just. How was Constantine to know that some of the laws were wrong from the point of view of Christian brotherly love? Was his occasional Draconic severity *wrong*? One might argue[45] that Constantine was not a social revolutionary, and that he left the Social Order of the Empire as he had found it in the beginning of his rule. The Emperor simply wanted to preserve the essential social structure of the Empire. If the laws were in many instances harsh, they were nevertheless to be obeyed by all concerned, and people, in any age and probably in most situations, knowingly and at their own risks, break the laws. Did not holy kings — not to mention unholy ones who were nevertheless known as Christian rulers — acting like Constantine, enact and carry out often Draconically severe laws to preserve the social order which they believed was good, often only to extirpate some serious social disorder?[46] Does not Holy Scripture unequivocally tells slaves that they are to obey their masters and keep their places? The classical passages of the New Testament from Saint Paul[47] and the first Pope, Saint Peter,[48] instruct Christian slaves that they should obey their masters in fear and trembling, doing the will of God, since when they suffer patiently it is acceptable to God, and that in doing this they follow, as they always should, the example of Christ. It is important that Christ, the founder of the Christian religion, gave this very example to be followed, and His own mission, — in contrast to the avowed mission of many churchmen of our own days — to be followed by Christians, was not to change the social order but

45. As Dörries, *op. cit.* 274 f., does.
46. See the lives of saintly kings of Europe, such as the life of St. Stephen of Hungary (*Vita Maior* and *Vita Minor*, ed. W. Wattenbach in *Monumenta Germaniae Historica, Scriptores* XI (1854) 224-42, etc.
47. *Ephesians* 6, 5.
48. *I Peter* 2, 18-25.

to lead people to the performance of the will of God, namely that they be holy. If he was supposed to change the social order, then Constantine could not learn it from the Holy Scriptures, and still less from the leaders of the Christian Church, the bishops and priests. If anybody committed a sin of omission to use this favourite and trite term of Christian ministers of the last 10-15 years with regard to OUR failure to bring about a 'just' social structure, even without God and Christianity – this sin of omission was committed by the bishops and priests; but they were probably satisfied with the existing social order, or if they were not, we do not know of it. They would not, in any case, have dared to tell Constantine that he was to turn the social structure upside down. The Roman Empire was certainly not ready for any serious social change.

If the true spirit of Christian brotherly love is, with some obvious exceptions, not very evident in Constantine's social legislation, his Faith in Christianity shone brilliantly in the generosity of his material and moral support for the Holy Church of God.

Giving the Christian Church religious freedom of worship and returning to it all corporate property confiscated during the past persecutions,[49] Constantine heaped on the Church privilege after privilege with the single purpose of making it possible for the Church and its representatives, the clergy, to dedicate themselves completely to its mission of spreading the true teachings of Christ.

Ever since what appears to be his initial gesture of the kind by which he granted immunity to all clerics,[50] Constantine never seemed to have tired of granting new privileges to the Church and making them safer. Whenever he noticed that the privilege he had granted was being circumvented by pagans or heretics, and that Catholic clerics were being required to perform public works, Constantine hastened to remedy the situation by ordering substitutes for them.[51] When he heard that Catholic clerics were forced by "men of different superstitions" to perform lustral sacrifices, he ordered that any person presuming thus to force people devoted

49. See Edict of Milan, Eusebius, *H.E.* X, v, 1-14; and the first of the 'African letters' to Anullinus, *ibid.* 15-17.
50. *Ibid.* X, vii, 1-2.
51. *C. Th.* XVI, 2, 1; 313 A.D. (?); Pharr, *op. cit. ad loc.*; *C. Th.* XVI, 2, 2; 319 A.D.; Pharr, *op. cit. ad loc.*; Dörries, *op. cit.* 165; 278; 176 f.

to the service of the Most Holy Law, should be publicly beaten with clubs, provided that his legal status so permitted it; otherwise he was to pay a very heavy fine to the municipality.[52] Privileges exempting clerics from the performance of public duties made it tempting for many wealthy individuals to enter the clergy to evade their public duties. Constantine therefore regulated by laws the eligibility for becoming clerics and thus the coveted immunity from public works: "The wealthy must assume secular obligations, and the poor must be supported by the wealth of the Church".[53]

To make the service of the priests of the Catholic Church all the better and more free of other concerns, he made ever since the appearance of his first documented act of doing this[54] unlimited amounts of money available to the Catholic Church. He made generous gifts of corn to churches for distribution by the bishop to the clergy and the poor.[55]

The funds and resources he made available for the repair and enlargement of churches and the erection of new churches were apparently unlimited.[56] He erected magnificent churches in Constantinople[57] and Nicomedia,[58] ordered the building of the Golden Church in Antioch, built the basilicas of Saint Peter and Saint Paul, endowing them with extensive landed estates to provide a generous income for them. The Emperor Constantine also of course left some monuments of his faith on the Holy Land by building the most magnificent Church of the Holy Sepulchre. A letter written by him to Macarius, the Bishop of Jerusalem, testifies to his zeal and munificence in building this church on the site of the Resurrection.[59] It was by his generosity to the Church and also by the piety of his old mother, Helena, that he built two churches, one at the grotto of the Nativity of Christ, and the other

52. C. Th. XVI, 2, 5; 323 A.D., May 25; Pharr, op. cit. ad loc.; Dörries 186.
53. C. Th. XVI, 2, 3; 320 A.D. (?) July 18; or 329 A.D. (?). Pharr, op. cit. ad loc.; Dörries, op. cit. 179; 279; Jones, op. cit. 216.
54. Eusebius, H.E. X, vi, 1-5.
55. Jones, op. cit. 214.
56. Eusebius, Vita Constant. II, 46; Optatus, App. X.
57. Socrates, H.E. I, 16.
58. Eusebius, Vita Constant. III, 50.
59. Ibid. 25-40.

on the Mount of Olives at the place of Christ's Ascension.[60]

By building all these and many other churches, Constantine expressed his truly great faith in the Christian religion, and at the same time vastly increased the glory of the Holy Church, which was proclaimed in the magnificence of these buildings.

One who spent an unlimited amount of the Empire's resources on building, rebuilding and repairing Christian churches naturally wished to have the Lord's Day spent properly. Constitutions[61] were legislated by Constantine prohibiting court sessions on the "venerable day of the sun" (venerabilis dies solis), yet permitting the legal manumission of slaves, and also countryfolks to collect, if necessary, the harvest and the vintage. Despite some scholars,[62] it is quite clear from these constitutions that notwithstanding the seemingly pagan title (dies solis) used by the Emperor, it was the Lord's Day, the Christian Sabbath, for which he held certain works most unfitting (indignissimum).[63]

Though he at times banished bishops and priests, for non-compliance with the Creed of the Church, or perhaps for apparent 'treason', or only for insubordination to the Imperial Will, Constantine showed his unlimited respect for the office of the bishops. It must have been because of this most religious respect that he repeatedly[64] confirmed the bishops' judicial authority in that he enacted that either party in a civil suit was free, despite the other party's objection, to demand the jurisdiction of the bishop of the place, the bishop's verdict being final and not subject to review.

Constantine's involvements in handling the Donatist schism[65] and Arian and other heresies[66] show clearly that he was with all his heart and mind with what he firmly believed to be the true Church of Christ, whose servant he believed himself to be.

60. *Ibid.* 41-43.
61. *C. Theod.* II, 8, 1a (321 A.D., March 3); *C. Theod.* II, 8, 1 (321 A.D., July 3); Dörries, *op. cit.* 181; 276; J. Gaudemet, "La législation religieuse de Constantin," *Rev. d'hist. de l'église de France* 33 (1947) 43 ff.
62. Pharr, *op. cit.* note to *C. Th.* II, 8, 1.
63. Baynes, "Constantine," *C.A.H. op. cit.* 694.
64. *Sirm.* I; (333 A.D., May 5); also, *C. Th.* I, 27, 1; 318 A.D., Jan. 23 (O. Seeck, *Regesten etc.* (Stuttgart, 1919) 57; Gaudemet, *op. cit.* 37 ff.), or 321 A.D. (A. Piganiol, *L'Empereur Constantin* (Paris, 1932) 138, n. 1; Gaudemet, *op. cit.* 32 ff.).
65. Chapter on "The Donatist Schism," *above.*
66. Chapter on "Arianism and Constantine," *above.*

Had Constantine remained a pagan like his predecessors ever since Julius Caesar and Augustus, he would in all probability have acted as they had done in respecting all the religious scruples and privileges of the Jews. Exceptions such as Hadrian and Septimius Severus and a few others acted very much against the traditional Roman respect for the privileged status of Judaism,[67] because, whether on account of antipathy or Jewish rebellions, they wanted to punish the Jews, or even to end their religion. Although he often expressed his detestation of Judaism, Constantine nevertheless did not oppress its followers. Under Constantine, the Jews certainly lost some of their ancient and honoured privileges, such as immunity from membership of municipal councils, but, as Jones[68] points out, Jews could hardly expect to retain their exemption when Christians were obliged to fulfil such duties. But Constantine[69] later allowed the immunity of two or three persons from municipal councils in each city, and, still later[70] he extended this privilege to all officials of the synagogue, who thus achieved, in this respect, equal status with the Christian clerics.

Constantine's constitutions against Jewish proselytism recall the thoughest measures of some earlier Emperors. According to some constitutions,[71] if any Jew purchased a Christian slave or a slave of any other sect and then had him circumcised, the slave was to receive his freedom. At the same time, Constantine encouraged Jews to turn to Christianity,[72] promising them protection against the molestations of Jewish assailants and threatening their Jewish molesters with death by fire.[73]

If several of these Jewish-related laws of Constantine were not — though they probably were — the result of his convinced Christianity, then some of his public statements on Judaism certainly were. He made his most characteristic reference to Judaism in his

67. Paul Keresztes, "The Emperor Septimius Severus: A Precursor of Decius," *Historia* 19 (1970) 565-578.

68. *Op. cit.* 220.

69. *C. Th.* XVI, 8, 3; 321 A.D., Dec. 11.

70. *C. Th.* XVI, 8, 2; 330 A.D., Nov. 29.

71. E.g. *Sirm.* 4, perhaps of 336 A.D.; Pharr, *op. cit. ad loc.* and an earlier but not extant constitution.

72. *Sirm.* 4.

73. *C. Th.* XVI, 8, 1; perhaps of 315 A.D.; Pharr, *op. cit. ad loc.*; Gaudemet, *op. cit.* 54 ff.; Dörries, *op. cit.* 170; 203; 277.

perhaps notorious letter to the Christian Church throughout the Roman Empire after the Nicaean Council's decision on effecting a uniform date for the celebration of Easter.[74] It is not his detestation of Judaism and the abusive language he used in this letter that is significant from our point of view — since he used probably much stronger language in some of his other letters — but *the fact* that he was using terminology expressing deep-rooted and traditional Christian belief about the Divinity of Christ, his Master, and that the Jews were described as 'deicides' and a 'perfidious race,' and that he used other derogatory adjectives for describing Judaism, forgetting that Christianity was an off-shoot of Judaism, though with significant differences. No pagan Emperor, or one merely friendly to Christianity, would have written in this manner, only one who was a convinced and devoted Christian.

Accusations by Julian the Apostate, Libanius, Zosimus, and others that Constantine had deserted and destroyed paganism are, more or less, given substance by his legislation against the various practices of paganism. That these ancient witnesses were hostile towards Constantine cannot be doubted, but it is equally clear that, on the other side, Eusebius was often too flattering to the Emperor; however, despite the historian's omissions of 'unfavourable' facts, it seems he never falsified facts. This is why Jones says[75] it is difficult to know how far Constantine went in direct attack on pagan worship.

Some constitutions[76] prohibit "soothsayers, priests and all persons who are accustomed to minister such ceremonies" from approaching the home of another even under the protestation of friendship; those who had disregarded this prohibition were to be burnt alive, and those who had invited them were to be exiled after the confiscation of their property. However, the same constitutions permitted the practice of divination and sacrifices in public. A third constitution[77] permitted the above practices if they were for therapeutic purposes and to keep away ruinous rain and hail at the time of harvest, since they were not performed to injure anyone's person.[78]

74. Eusebius, *Vita Constant.* III, 17-20.
75. *Op. cit.* 211.
76. *C. Th.* IX, 16, 1-2.
77. *C. Th.* IX, 16, 3; Pharr, *op. cit. ad loc.*
78. Also, Gaudemet, *op. cit.* 48 ff.

There can be no doubt about Eusebius' report that Constantine suppressed some famous pagan temples such as that of Asclepius at Aegae in Cilicia[79] and others at Apheca and Heliopolis in Phoenicia,[80] centres of ritual prostitution, which must have been most offensive to Christianity and therefore a good reason for a Christian Emperor to suppress them.

Like some of his predecessors, he undoubtedly removed[81] certain works of art from pagan temples for the decoration of Constantinople, and fixtures such as bronze doors for use here and there. Sometimes pagan cult images were stripped of their gold plating. Although Eusebius attributes some of these acts to religious motives on Constantine's part, Constantine's lack of feeling for, not to mention disbelief in, pagan cults is truly significant in these actions of one to be regarded as the first Christian Emperor. Constantine's measures in closing down temples and prohibiting private cult ceremonies may have started some rumours that he was going to prohibit all practice of pagan religion, even in public. In a letter that he wrote after his defeat of Licinius in 324 A.D., Constantine squashes these rumours and scornfully assures the pagans of his Empire of their freedom[82] to continue in their error and to offer their sacrifices of superstition.

Similar confessions of Faith occur in many of Constantine's numerous letters and other documents,[83] where the Emperor does not simply express friendly and sympathetic sentiments and declare great decisions to benefit a religion, but speaks of the Christian religion as "my faith," and "our Mother," the Church of God, the Holy Catholic Church. It is because of these open confessions of the Christian faith, its defence against schisms and heresies, and his many deeds on behalf of Christianity after 312/313 A.D. that there can be no reasonable doubt that Constantine left paganism and embraced Christianity very early, soon or even perhaps immediately after his heavenly vision of the Cross and his victory over Maxentius. Many scholars accept this early conversion to the

79. *Vita Constant.* III, 56.
80. *Ibid.* 55; 58.
81. *Ibid.* 54.
82. *Ibid.* II, 48-60.
83. Most revealing and openly confessional are his letters to the Council of Arles in 314 A.D.

Christian Church as a historical fact.[84] The only question remaining is: how early after the great events of 312 A.D. did this conversion take place? Certainly a convinced Christian from the very early part of his rule, Constantine was much more than that; he was a true Christian Confessor and Apostle. Time and again, in season and out of season, he confessed and, indeed, as is clear from his numerous letters, preached the Christian Faith to his Christian (and non-Christian) subjects from the Western boundaries of the Empire to those in the East. He often found it necessary and, indeed, imperative to preach to and even reprove, entreat and rebuke, patiently – but often losing his patience – priests and bishops of the Christian Church, but especially those priests and bishops who had been guilty of schism and heresy.

But Constantine's attention went well beyond the Christian Church and even the boundaries of the Roman Empire. His letter to King Sapor of Persia[85] anticipated by many a year the zealous activities of later ages for the propagation of the Faith:

By keeping the faith of God, I share in the true light. Since I am guided in my way by the light of truth, I acknowledge the faith of God. Consequently, as my actions confirm it, I profess the most holy religion. I confess that as a disciple of the Holy God I observe this worship. With the power of this God on my side to help me, beginning at the boundaries of the Ocean, I have gathered every nation, one after another, throughout the world, to the certain hope of salvation, so that all those who, enslaved by so many tyrants and overcome by their daily sufferings, had been on the brink of extinction, received the protection of the commonwealth and, through, as it were, some service of mine, were brought back to a new life. This God I worship and my army is dedicated to Him and wears His sign on their shoulders, marching directly wherever the cause of justice summons them, and I receive from these without delay the reward of splendid trophies. I confess that I honour this God with never-dying remembrance, this God in the highest I contemplate with a pure and simple mind.

84. Baynes, "Constantin the Great and the Christian Church," *op. cit.* 367 f.; A. Alföldi, "Hoc signo victor eris," *Pisciculi* (Festschrift F.J. Dölger, 1939) 1-18; *The Conversion of Constantin and Pagan Rome* (Oxford U.P., 1969); K. Aland, *op. cit.* 574 ff.; H. Dörries, *Constantine the Great* (New York, 1972) 38; 46 f.; K. Müller, "Konstantin d. Gr. und die christliche Kirche," *Hist. Zschr.* 140 (1929) 261; 264-70; H. Lietzmann, "Der Glaube Konstantins des Grossen," *SB. Preuss. Akad. Wiss. Phil.-hist. Kl.* (1937) 263 ff.; *et al.*
85. Eusebius, *Vita Constant.* IV, 9-13.

I call on this God upon my bended knees, while I dissociate myself from all blood offered to the abominable idols; I shun all their odious and ill-omened odours, and I avoid all magic fire – by the means of all these, unlawful and horrible errors defiled many of the nations and hurled down and consigned whole families to the bottom of the world below. For the God of the universe does not tolerate that those things which He in His providence for men and through His love for men revealed to us to satisfy our needs should be diverted to the greed of any man. On the other hand, He only demands of men a pure mind and an unsoiled soul, and weighs their deeds of virtue and piety. For He is pleased with works of kindness and tenderness; He loves the meek, hates the rebellious; He loves faith, chastizes unbelief; He breaks the power of presumption, and punishes the pride of the arrogant. He utterly destroys those who are exalted by pride, He duly rewards the humble and the long-suffering. Since he regards a just kingship very highly, He strengthens it by His own assistance, and maintains the understanding of the King with the serenity of peace.

I do not believe, my Brother, that I am in error when I confess that this God is the Creator and Father of all, whom many of my Imperial predecessors, led astray by (the) madness of errors, attempted to deny. But, in the end, they all had such terrible punishment that all generations of men who succeeded them put their misfortunes as another warning before those who were emulating their examples. One of these, I believe, has become he, whom Divine vengeance, like a thunder-bolt, drove away from here and handed over to your country, and who, becoming notorius on account of his shame, was displayed as a trophy before your people.

It seems, indeed, to have happened well that the punishment of such people as these has become manifest in our own time. For I myself witnessed the end of those who with unlawful edicts were lately exterminating the people devoted to God. Therefore let there be much thanksgiving to God, because all men who observe the Divine law exult and rejoice, since, thanks to His unfailing providence, peace has again been restored to them. Consequently, I am convinced that everything is as auspicious and safe for us as possible, since, as a result of their pure and true religious service on account of their agreement on His Divine nature, He might gather all people to Himself.

Think with what pleasure I heard that the strongest provinces of Persia are, so agreeably with my desire, to a very large extent inhabited by people of this type, I mean by Christians, and it is only on their behalf that I am speaking. May it be as prosperous as possible both for you and them in equal measure. For thus you will have the mercy and goodwill of God, the Lord and Father of all. Therefore, I hand these people over to your safekeeping because you are so powerful; I entrust them to you because you are known for your piety. Treat them with affection in accordance with your humanity. By your faithfulness, you will confer both on yourself and us an immeasurable benefit.

This letter may sound to some[86] no more than a remarkable or even important letter, but this is a *truly Constantinian* letter in that it shows Constantine as an unrestrained Confessor of Christianity and a true protector of Christians everywhere. Looking at the letter with the eyes of a pragmatist,[87] one may surmise that it may have done "more harm than good" to Christians in Persia and elsewhere, but what is really relevant here is Constantine's confession of Christianity to a powerful king of Rome's traditional enemy, Persia, and his zeal for the protection of the Christian Church and its followers. And what a confession of Faith this letter is! It is a sparkling jewel in Constantine's Confessor's crown made of his numerous letters and documents:[88] "I profess the most Holy Religion, I confess that I am a disciple of the Holy God; this God I worship and my army is dedicated to Him and wears His sign on their shoulders, marching wherever the cause of justice summons them; I honour this God with a never-dying remembrance, this God in the highest I contemplate with a pure and simple heart ..." This is truly Constantine!

Whatever may be the meaning of Constantine's reported statement[89] that he was "the bishop (ἐπίσκοπος) of those outside, appointed by God," Constantine was vastly more than a bishop, though unconsecrated and lacking a bishop's spiritual powers, for he *watched over* his subjects and the Christian Church, and even over the bishops themselves with a close and careful 'supervision,' genuine 'episcopal concern,' for the welfare of the Church and the whole Roman Empire and, indeed, of the world.

Apart from Eusebius of Caesarea and, indeed, apart from Constantine himself, there are many others who believe that the Emperor Constantine was Providential for the Christian Church.

86. Baynes, "Constantine the Great and the Christian Church," *op. cit.* 364 f.

87. As e.g. Jones, *op. cit.* 207 f., did.

88. The authenticity of this letter has, of course, been questioned. But see H. Kraft, *Kaiser Konstantins religiöse Entwicklung, op. cit.* 262; Dörries, *Das Selbstzeugnis etc. op. cit.* 333 f.; esp. 48 f.

89. Eusebius, *Vita Constant.* IV, 24: ἐγὼ δὲ τῶν ἐκτὸς ὑπὸ θεοῦ καθεστάμενος ἐπίσκοπος ...; Baynes, "Constantine the Great and the Christian Church," *op. cit.* 363 f., n. 70; Jones, *op. cit.* 204 ff.

This must of course be true with regard to Constantine's ending the persecutions of the Church, of his giving it complete freedom of worship and, moreover, of his placing all his material and moral wealth and power at the disposal and for the well-being of his Holy and Catholic Church. Protecting the Church from its external enemies was not enough. The first Christian Emperor had to protect it from even more dangerous enemies – those within, "wolves in sheep's clothing," the Donatist schismatics, the pro-Arian bishops and priests and other schismatics and heretics who were destroying the Church from within. That despite many synods of bishops and, particularly, the Council of Nicaea, the very symbol of orthodoxy and unity, and despite several most faithful and truly Christian bishops such as the great Athanasius, the very embodiment of orthodoxy, Constantine's fight to ensure the unity of the Church by the universal acceptance of truly Christian Faith was not a complete success, must be blamed on many bishops who were unfaithful to their vocation and their duty to preserve the true Christian Faith.

Ever since Constantine's death – even as early as in the rule of his sons – unscrupulous rulers on the one hand, and weak, selfish and unfaithful priests, theologians, and even bishops on the other, have split up the Christian Church into hundreds of sections with schisms and heresies. It seems obvious that unless the representatives of the Church, the priests, bishops, and, of course, the so-called theologians were faithful and holy servants of Christianity, faithful servants, first, of God and, then, of kings, they, willingly or unwillingly, became useful tools of unscrupulous rulers, and thus the unity of the Christian Church has ever remained a vain and elusive goal and the effort to achieve unity doomed to failure from the outset. Will there come some new Athanasiuses, holy and incorruptible priests and bishops of the Church, and, also, a new Constantine, a great and truly Christian Monarch, to bring about with their orthodoxy and firmness this elusive unity throughout a new and Holy Roman Empire?

GENERAL BIBLIOGRAPHY

Adriani, M., "La Storicità dell' editto di Milano," *Studi Rom.* 2 (1954) 18-32.

Agnes, Mario, "Alcune considerazioni sul cosidetto 'Editto' di Milano," *Studi Rom.* 13 (1965) 424-432.

Aland, K., "Die religiöse Haltung Kaiser Konstantins," *Studia Patrist.* 1 (1957) 549-600.

Albertario, E., "Alcune osservazioni sulla legislazione di Costantino," *Acta Congressus Iuridici Internationalis 1934* i (Rome, 1935).

Alföldi, A., "The Helmet of Constantine with the Christian Monogram," *J. of Roman Stud.* 22 (1932) 9-23.

Alföldi, A., *A Festival of Isis in Rome under the Christian Emperors of the IVth Century* (Dissert. Pannonicae II 7, 1937).

Alföldi, A., "Hoc signo victor eris. Beiträge zur Geschichte der Bekehrung Konstantins des Grossen," *Pisciculi* (Festschrift F.J. Dölger, 1939) 1-18.

Alföldi, A., "La conversione di Costantino e Roma pagana," *Corvina-rassegna italo-ungherese* 6 (1934) 529-544.

Alföldi, A., *The Conversion of Constantine and Pagan Rome*, transl. by Harold Mattingly (Oxford U.P., 1948 and 1969).

Alföldi, A., "The Initials of Christ on the Helmet of Constantine," *Studies in Roman Economic and Social History* (Princeton, 1951) 303-311.

Alföldi, A., "Cornuti. A Teutonic Contingent in the Service of Constantine the Great and its Decisive Role in the Battle at the Milvian Bridge," *Dumbarton Oaks Papers* 13 (1959) 169-183.

Alföldi, Maria R., "Die Sol-Comes-Münze vom Jahre 325. Neues zur Bekehrung Constantins," *Jahrbuch für Antike und Christentum*, Ergänzungsband I (Münster, 1964) 10-16.

Alföldi, Maria R., *Die constantinische Goldprägung* (Mainz, 1963).

Alföldi, Maria R., Dietmar Kienast, "Zu P. Bruuns Datierung der Schlacht an der Milvischen Brücke," *Jahrbuch für Numismatik und Geldgeschichte* (1961) 33-44.

Allard, Paul, *La persécution de Dioclétien et le triomphe de l'église* (Paris, 1890).

Altheim, F., "Runen als Schildzeichen," *Klio* 31 (1938) 51-59.

Altheim, F., "Konstantins Triumph von 312," *Zeitschrift für Religions- und Geistgeschichte* 9 (1957) 221-231.

187

Amelotti, Mario, "Da Diocleziano a Costantino, note in tema di costituzioni imperiali," *Studia et documenta historiae et iuris* 27 (1961) 241-323.

Anastos, M.V., "The Edict of Milan 313. A Defence of its Traditional Authorship and Designation," *Revue des Etudes Byzantines* 25 (1967) 13-41.

André, J., *La conversion de Constantin* (Lille, 1954).

Andreotti, Roberto, "L'imperatore Licinio ed alcuni problemi della legislazione costantiniana," *Studi in onore di Emilio Betti* 3 (Milan, 1962) 41-63.

Artner, E., "A propos du christianisme de Constantin" (in Hungarian), *Theologia* (1940) 130-142; 191-192.

Aufhauser, J.B., *Konstantins Kreuzvision* (Bonn, 1912).

Babut, E.-Ch., "Evêque du dehors," *Revue critique d'histoire et de littérature* 68 (1909) 362-364.

Badcock, F.J., "Christianity to the Edict of Milan," *Church Quart. Rev.* 122 (1936) 19-31.

Baker, G.P., *Constantine the Great and the Christian Revolution* (London, 1931).

Bardy, G., "L'église d'Antioche au temps de la crise arienne (312-330)," *Bulletin d'Ancienne Lit. et d'Archéol. Chrétiennes* 4 (1914) 241-261.

Bardy, G., "La politique réligieuse de Constantin après le concile de Nicée," *Revue Sc. rélig.* 8 (1928) 516-551.

Bardy, G., "Sur la réiteration du concile de Nicée (327)," *Recherches de Science Relig.* 23 (1933) 430-450.

Barini, J., "La politica religiosa di Massimino Daza," *Historia* 2 (1928) 716-730.

Batiffol, P., "Les étapes de la conversion de Constantin," *Bulletin d'ancienne litt. et d'arch. chrét.* 3 (1913) 178-188; 241-264.

Batiffol, P., ("Interpretation des descriptions du chrismon Constantinien") *Bull. Soc. nat. Antiqu. de France* (1913) 211-216.

Batiffol, P., "Les documents de la Vita Constantini," *Bulletin d'ancienne litterature et d'arch. chrét.* 4 (1914) 81-95.

Batiffol, P., *La paix constantinienne et le catholicisme* (Paris, 1914).

Baudoin, F., *Constantinus Magnus, sive Commentariorum de Constantini imp. legibus ecclesiasticis et civilibus libri duo* (Lipsiae, 1727).

Baynes, N.H., "Rome and Armenia in the Fourth Century," *English Historical Review* 15 (1910) 625-643.

Baynes, N.H., "Optatus," *J. of Theol. Studies* 28 (1924) 37-44.

Baynes, N.H., Optatus: an Addendum," *J. of Theol. Studies* (1925) 404-406.

Baynes, N.H., "Athanasiana," *J. of Egyptian Archeology* (1925) 58-69.

Baynes, N.H., "The Chronology of Eusebius,"*Class. Quart.* 19 (1925) 94-100.

Baynes, N.H., "Alexandria and Constantinople: a Study of Ecclesiastical Diplomacy," *J. of Egyptian Archeology* 12 (1926) 145-156.

Baynes, N.H., *The Historia Augusta; its date & purpose* (Oxford U.P., 1926).

Baynes, N.H., "Constantine the Great and the Christian Church," *Proceedings of the Brit. Acad.* 15 (1929) 341-442.

Baynes, N.H., "Rome and the Early Middle Age," *History* 14 (1930) 289-298.

Baynes. N.H., "Some Aspects of Byzantine Civilization," *J. of Roman Studies* 20 (1930) 1-13.

Baynes, N.H., "Constantine," *Cambridge Ancient History* (Cambridge U.P., 1956) vol. 12, 678-709.

Baynes, N.H., "Eusebius and the Christian Empire," *Byzantine Studies and Other Essays* (London, 1955) 168-172; and in the *Annuaire de l'institut de Philologie et d'histoire orientales* 2 (1933-34); *Mélanges Bidez* (Brussels, 1933) 13-18.

Baynes, N.H.; G.W. Richardson, "The Chronology of Eusebius," *Class. Quart.* 19 (1925) 94-100.

Beck, H.G., "Konstantinopel – das neue Rom," *Gymnasium* 71 (1964) 166-174.

Becker, E., "Konstantin der Grosse, der neue Moses – Die Schlacht am Pons Milvius und die Katastrophe am Schilfmeer," *Zeitschr. für Kircheng.* 31 (1910) 161-171.

Bell, H.I., *Jews and Christians in Egypt* (British Museum, 1924) esp. 38-71.

Bell, H.I., "Athanasius: a Chapter in Church History," *The Congregational Quarterly* 3 (1925) 158-176.

Bernareggi, A., "Costantino imperatore et pontifice massimo," *La Scuola Cattolica* 41 (1913) 237-253.

Biasotti, G., *La grande battaglia di Costantino contra Massenzio da Saxa Rubra al Pons Milvius 28. Ottobre 312* (Rome, 1912).

Bihlmeyer, Karl, "Das angebliche Toleranzedikt Konstantins von 312," *Theolog. Quartalschrift* 96 (1914) 65-100; 198-224.

Blant, E. le, *Les persécutions et les martyrs* (Paris, 1893).

Boak, A.E.R., "Constantine and Rome," *Queens Quarterly* 57 (1950) 182-196.

Boissier, Gaston, *La fin du paganasme* (Paris, 1891).

Brasseur, André, "Les deux visions de Constantin," *Latomus* (1946) 35-40.

Bratke, E., "Das Monogram Christi auf dem Labarum Constantins des Grossen," *Festschr. z. Feier des 25-jährigen Bestehens des Gymnasiums zu Jauer* (Jauer, 1890) 71-85.

Brezzi, P., *Dalle persecuzioni alle pace di Costantino* (Rome, 1960).

Brezzi, P., *La politica religiosa di Costantino* (Naples, 1965).

Brieger, Theodor, "Constantin der Grosse als Religionspolitiker," *Zeitschr. f. Kircheng.* 4 (1881) 163-203.

Brilliantov, A.J., *Kaiser Konstantin der Grosse und das Mailänder Edikt von 313* (Petrograd, 1916).

Bruck, G., "Die Verwendung christlicher Symbole auf Münzen von Constantin I bis Magnentius," *Numismatische Zeitschrift* 76 (1955) 26-32.

Bruun, P., *The Constantinian Coinage of Arelate* (Helsinki, 1953).
Bruun, P., "The Battle of the Milvian Bridge. The Date Reconsidered," *Hermes* 88 (1960) 361-370.
Bruun, P., "The Consecration Coins of Constantine the Great," *Arctos* 1 (1954) 19-31.
Bruun, P., "Studies in Constantinian Chronology," *Numismatic Notes and Monographs* 146 (New York, 1961).
Bruun, P., "Constantine and Licinius A.D. 313-337," *The Roman Imperial Coinage* vol. VII (London, 1966).
Burch, Vacher, *Myth and Constantine* (London, 1927).
Burckhardt, Jacob, *The Age of Constantine the Great*, Transl. Moses Hadas (New York, 1949).
Burn, A.E., *The Council of Nicaea* (1925).
Calderone, S., *Costantino e il cattolicesimo* (Florence, 1962).
Carassai, C., "La politica religiosa di Costantino e la proprietà della chiesa," *Archivio della R. Società Romana di Storia Patria* 24 (1901) 95-157.
Carson, R.A.G., "The Emperor Constantine and Christianity," *History Today* 6 (1956) 12-20.
Castritius, H., *Studien zur Maximinus Daia* (Frankfurt, 1969).
Cataudella, M.R., "Per la cronologia dei rapporti fra christianesimo e impero agli inizi del iv sec.," *Siculorum Gymnasium* 20 (1967) 83-110.
Cataudella, M.R., "La data della editto di Serdica e i vicennalia di Galerio," *Riv. di Cultura classica e medioevale* 10 (1968) 269-286.
Centonze, L., *L'imperatore Costantino e la chiesa cattolica* (Bari, 1912).
Chadwick, H., "The Fall of Eustathius of Antioch," *J. of Theological Studies* 49 (1948) 27-35.
Chadwick, H., "Ossius of Cordova and the Presidency of the Council of Antioch," *J. of Theological Studies* 9 (1958) 292-304.
Chénon, Emile, "Les conséquences juridiques de l'Edit de Milan," *Nouvelle Revue historique de droit français et étranger* 38 (1914-15) 255-263.
Clerq, V.C. de, "Ossius of Cordova; a Contribution to the History of the Constantinian Period," *Stud. in Christian Antiquity* 13 (1954).
Coleman, C.B., *Constantine the Great and Christianity* (Columbia U.P., New York, 1914).
Correa d'Oliveira, E., *L'imperatore Costantino* (Milan, 1942).
Costa, G., "La politica religiosa di Costantino il Grande," *Rassegna contemporanea* 6 (1913) 903-925.
Costa, G., "La battaglia di Costantino a Ponte Milvio," *Bilychnis* 2 (1913) 197-208.
Costa, G., "Critica e tradizione. Osservazioni sulla politica e sulla religione di Costantino," *Bilychnis* 3 (1914) 85-105.
Crivelucci, A., "L'Editto di Milano," *Studi Storici* 1 (1892) 239-250.
Crivelucci, A., "L'origine della leggenda del monogramma e del labaro," *Studi*

Storici 2 (1893) 88-104; 222-260.

Crivelucci, A., "Gli editti di Costantino ai provinciali della Palestina e agli Orientali," *Studi Storici* 3 (1894) 369-384; 415-422.

Crivelucci, A., "Intorno all'Editto di Milano," *Studi Storici* 4 (1895) 267-273.

Crivelucci, A., "I documenti della 'Vita Constantini'," *Studi Storici* 7 (1898) 411-429; 453-459.

Cross, F.L., "The Council of Antioch in 325 A.D.," *Church Quarterly Review* 128 (1939) 49-76.

Cross, F.L., *The Study of Athanasius* (Oxford, 1945).

Cutts, E.L., *Constantine the Great. The Union of the State and Church* (London, 1881).

Daniele, J., *I documenti constantiniani della 'Vita Constantini' di Eusebio di Cesarea, Analecta Gregoriana* 1 (Rome, 1938).

Decker, D. de, "La politique religieuse de Maxence," *Byzantion* 38 (1968) 472-562.

Delaruelle, E., "La conversion de Constantine, état actuel de la question," *Bulletin de litt. ecclesiastique* 54 (1953) 37-54; 84-100.

D'Elbée, H., *Constantine le Grand* (Paris, 1947).

Delehaye, H., "Eusebii Caesariensis de Martyribus Palaestinae longioris libelli fragmenta," *Anal. Bolland.* 16 (1897) 113-139.

Delehaye, H., "Les martyrs d'Egypte," *Anal. Bolland.* 40 (1922) 5-154; 299-364.

Desroches, H.P., *Le labarum* (Paris, 1894).

Dölger, F.J., *Konstantin der Grosse und seine Seit. Gesammelte Studien. Festgabe zum Konstantins – Jubiläum 1913.* Edit. by F.J. Dölger (Freiburg, 1913).

Dölger, F.J., "Die Taufe Konstantins und ihre Probleme," *Konstantin der Grosse u. s. Zeit, etc.*, ed. F.J. Dölger (Freiburg, 1913) 377-472.

Dörries, Hermann, *Das Selbstzeugnis Kaiser Konstantins* (Göttingen, 1954).

Dörries, Hermann, *Konstantin der Grosse* (Stuttgart, 1958).

Dörries, Hermann, *Constantine and Religious Liberty* (Yale U.P., 1960).

Dörries, Hermann, *Constantine the Great* (New York, 1972).

Duchesne, L., "Constantine et Maxence," *Nuovo Bullettino di Archeologia Cristiana* 19 (1913) 29-35.

Egger, R., "Das Labarum, die Kaiserstandarte der Spätantike," *Wiener Akad. d. Wiss., Phil.-hist. Kl.*, Sb. 234, I (Wien, 1960).

Ehrhardt, A., "Constantin der Grosse, Religionspolitik und Gesetzgebung," *Zeitschrift der Savigny-Stiftung für Rechtsgeschichte* 72 (1955) 154-190.

Ehrhardt, A., "The Adoption of Christianity in the Roman Empire," *Bulletin of the John Rylands Library* (1962) 97-114.

Elbée, H. d', *Constantin le Grand* (Paris, 1947).

Ensslin, W., "Gottkaiser und Kaiser von Gottes Gnaden," *Sb. d. Bayer Akad.*

d. Wiss. Phil.-hist. Kl. (1943).

Ensslin, W., "Staat und Kirche von Konstantin dem Grossen bis Theodosius dem Grossen," *Akten des IX Internat. Kongresses f. byz. Studien* 2 (Athens, 1956) 405-415.

Feder, A., "Konstantins des Grossen Verdienste um das Christum", *Stimmen aus Maria Laach* 84 (1913) 28-43.

Fera, G., *Costantino e il cristianesimo* (Milan, 1964).

Ferrura, A., "Per il centenario della morte di Costantino," *La Civiltà Cattolica* 88 (1937) 385-394.

Firth, J.B., *Constantine the Great* (London, 1905).

Flasch, F.M., *Constantin der Grosse als erster Christlicher Kaiser* (Würzburg, 1891).

Flores, A., *La conversion de Constantin le Grand* (Paris, 1949).

Fortina, M., "La politica religiosa dell'imperatore Licinio," *Rivista di Studi Classici* 7 (1959) 245-265; 8 (1960) 3-23.

Franchi de' Cavalieri, Pio, *Constantiniana* (Rome, 1953).

Frend, W.H.C., *The Donatist Church* (Oxford U.P., 1952).

Frend, W.H.C., *Martyrdom and Persecution in the Early Church* (New York U.P., 1967).

Funk, F.X., *Konstantin der Grosse und das Christentum* (Paderborn, 1899).

Gagé, J., "La 'virtus' de Constantin," *Rev. Etudes Lat.* 12 (1934) 398-405.

Gagé, J., "Le signum astrologique de Constantin et le millenarisme de Roma Aeterna," *Revue d'histoire et de philosophie religieuses* 31 (1951) 181-223.

Gaggia, G., "La conversione e religione di Costantino," *La Scuola Cattolica* 41 (1913) 74-117.

Galletier, M.E., "La mort de Maximien d'après la panégyric de 310 et la vision de Constantin au temple d'Apollon," *Rev. des Etudes Anciennes* 52 (1950) 288-299.

Galli, E., "L'editto di Milano del 313," *La Scuola Cattolica* 41 (1913) 39-73.

Gardthausen, V., *Das alte Monogramm* (Leipzig, 1924).

Gascou, J., "Le rescrit d'Hispellum," *Mélanges d'Archéologie et d'Histoire* 79 (1967) 609-659.

Gaudemet, J., "La législation religieuse de Constantin", *Revue d'Hist. de l'Eglise de France* 33 (1947) 25-61.

Gaudemet, J., "Constantin restaurateur de l'ordre," *Studi in onore di Siro Solazzi etc. (1899-1948)* (Naples, 1948) 652-674.

Gerland, E., "In welchem Jahre gelangte Konstantin der Grosse zur Alleinherrschaft?" *Byzantinische Zeitschrift* 30 (1929/30) 364-373.

Gerland, E., "Konstantin der Grosse in Geschichte und Sage," *Texte und Forschungen zur byz.-neugr. Philol.* 23 (Athens, 1937).

Gibbon, E., *The History of the Decline and Fall of the Roman Empire*, edit. by J.B. Bury, vol. 2 (1896) ch. 20.

Gillman, I., "Constantine the Great in the Light of Christus Victor Concept," *J. of Religious History* 1 (1961) 197-205.

Görres, F., "Eine Bestreitung des Edicts von Mailand durch O. Seeck," *Zsch. f. Wiss. Theol.* 35 (1892) 285-295.

Görres, Franz, "Die Religionspolitik des Kaisers Licinius," *Philologus* 72 (1913) 250-262.

Greenslade, S.L., *Church and State from Constantine to Theodosius* (London, 1954).

Grégoire, Henri, "L'étymologie de 'labarum'," *Byzantion* 4 (1927-28) 477-482.

Grégoire, Henri, "La 'conversion' de Constantin," *Revue de l'Univ. de Bruxelles* 36 (1930/31) 231-272.

Grégoire, Henri, "La statue de Constantin et le signe de la croix," *L'Antiquité Classique* 1 (1932) 135-143.

Grégoire, H., on A. Piganiol, *L'Empereur Constantin* (Paris, 1932) *Byzantion* 7 (1932) 645-652.

Grégoire, Henri, on A. Alföldi, "The Helmet of Constantine etc." (*above*) *Byzantion* 7 (1932) 652-655.

Grégoire, Henri, "Encore l'étymologie de 'labarum,'" *Byzantion* 12 (1937) 277-281.

Grégoire, Henri, "Eusèbe n'est pas l'auteur de la 'Vita Constantini' dans sa forme actuelle et Constantin n'est pas 'converti' en 312," *Byzantion* 13 (1938) 561-583.

Grégoire, Henri, "About Licinius' Fiscal and Religious Policy," *Byzantion* 13 (1938) 551-560.

Grégoire, Henri, "La vision de Constantin 'liquidé,'" *Byzantion* 14 (1939) 341-351.

Grégoire, Henri, "A propos du Martyre de S. Théodote d'Ancyre," *N. Clio* 4 (1952) 420.

Grégoire, Henri, "L'authenticité et l'historicité de la 'Vita Constantini' attribuée à Eusèbe de Césarée," *Bulletin de la classe des lettres et des sciences morales et politiques* 39 (1953) 462-479.

Grégoire, H., *Les persécutions dans l'empire romain* (Bruxelles, 1964).

Grégoire, Henri; P. Orgels, "La passion de S. Théodote etc.," *Byz. Zschr.* 44 (1951) 165-184.

Grossi-Gondi, F., "La battaglia di Costantino Magno a Saxa Rubra," *Civiltà Cattolica* 63 (1912) 385-403.

Grossi-Gondi, F., "La grande vittoria di Costantino," *Letture Costantiniane* (Rome, 1914).

Gwatkin, H.M., *Studies in Arianism* (Cambridge, 1882).

Gwatkin, H.M., "Constantine and His City," *Cambridge Medieval H.* (Cambridge U.P., 1957) vol. i, 1 ff.

Gwatkin, H.M., "Arianism," *ibid.* 118 ff.

Habicht, C., "Zur Geschichte des Kaisers Konstantin," *Hermes* 86 (1958) 360-378.

Halkin, F., "Le règne de Constantin d'après la Chronique inedite du Pseudo-Symeon," *Byzantion* 29-30 (1959-60) 7-27.

Halkin, F., "L'empereur Constantin converti par Euphratas," *Anal. Bolland.* 78 (1960) 5-17.

Halkin, F., "Constantin se violant la face?", *Anal. Bolland.* 85 (1967) 440.

Hartmann, W., "Konstantin der Grosse als Christ und Philosoph in seinen Briefen und Erlassen," *Beilage z. Programm d. Städt. Gymnasiums zu Fürstenwalde* (1902) 6 ff.

Hatt, Jean-Jacques, "La vision de Constantin au sanctuaire de Grand et l'origine celtique du labarum," *Latomus* 9 (1950) 427-436.

Heydenreich, E., "Constantin der Grosse in den Sagen des Mittelalters," *Deutsche Zeitschrift f. Gesch. Wissenschaft* 9 (1893) 1-27.

Höhn, Karl, *Konstantin der Grosse* (Leipzig, 1940).

Holsapple, L.B., *Constantine the Great* (New York, 1942).

Homo, Leon, *Les empereurs romains et le christianisme* (Paris, 1931).

Homo, Leon, *De la Rome païenne à la Rome chrétienne* (Paris, 1950).

Hülle, Hermann, *Die Toleranzerlasse römischer Kaiser für das Christentum bis zum Jahre 313* (Berlin, 1895).

Hunziker, Otto, "Zur Regierung und Christenverfolgung des Kaisers Diocletianus und seiner Nachfolger 303-313," *Untersuchungen zur römischen Kaisergeschichte* (Leipzig, 1868), v. ii, 113-286.

Huttmann, M.A., *The Establishment of Christianity and the Proscription of Paganism* (Columbia Univ., New York, 1914).

Huvelin, H., *Constantin, Nicée, Les hérésies* (Paris, 1965).

Istinsky, H.U., *Bischofstuhl und Kaiserthron* (München, 1955).

Ivanka, E. von, "Le christianisme de Constantin vu sous un nouveau jour," (in Hungarian), *Theologia* 6 (1939) 312-321.

Jeep, L., "Zur Geschichte Konstantins des Grossen," *Histor. und Philos. Aufsätze Ernst Curtius gewidmet* (Berlin, 1884) 79-95.

Jenko, H., *Heidentum und Christentum des Kaisers Konstantin des Grossen* (Sereth, 1907).

Jenko, H., *Kaiser Konstantin der Grosse als Gesetzgeber* (Sereth, 1909).

Jones, A.H.M., "Notes on the Genuineness of the Constantinian Documents in Eusebius' Life of Constantine," *J. of Eccl. Hist.* 5 (1954) 196-200.

Jones, A.H.M., *The Later Roman Empire 284-602* (Oxford, 1964).

Jones, A.H.M., *Constantine and the Conversion of Europe* (London, 1968).

Jones, H. Stuart, "Urbis Romae episcopi," *J. of Theological Studies* 26 (1925) 406-407.

Kähler, H., "Konstantin 313," *Jb. des deutschen archäologischen Instituts* 67 (1952) 1-30.

Kaniuth, A., *Die Beisetzung Konstantins des Grossen* (Breslau, 1941).

Karayanpulos, H., "Konstantin der Grosse und der Kaiserkult," *Historia* 5 (1956) 341-357.

Karpp, H., "Konstantins Gesetze gegen die private Haruspizin aus den Jahren 319 bis 321," *Zsch. N.T. Wiss.* 41 (1942) 145-151.

Karpp, H., "Konstantin der Grosse und die Kirche," *Theologische Rundschau* 19 (1951) 1-21.

Keim, Th., "Die römischen Toleranzedikte für das Christentum (311-313) und ihr geschichtlicher Wert," *Theol. Jahrbücher* 11 (1852) 207-259.

Keim, Th., *Der Ubertritt Constantins des Grossen zum Christentum* (Zürich, 1862).

Kettler, F.H., "Der melitianische Streit in Agypten," *Zsch. N.T. Wiss.* 35 (1936) 155-193.

Kidd, B.J., *A History of the Church to A.D. 461* (Oxford U.P., 1922) vol. 2.

Kluge, E., "Beiträge zur Chronologie der Geschichte Konstantins des Grossen," *Hist. Jb.* 42 (1922) 89-102.

Knipfing, J.R., "Das angebliche 'Mailänder Edikt' v. J. 313 im Lichte der neueren Forschung", *Zsch. für Kircheng.* 40 (1922) 206-218.

Knipfing, J.R., "Religious Tolerance during the Early Part of the Reign of Constantine the Great (306-313)," *The Catholic Historical Review* 4 (1925) 483-503.

Knöpfler, A., "Konstantins Kreuzevision," *Hist. polit. Blätter* 141 (1908) 182-199.

Koch, Hugo, *Konstantin der Grosse und das Christentum* (München, 1913).

Koch, Hugo, "Constantin le Grand," *Byzantion* 25-27 (1955-57) 457-472.

Koep, L., "Die Konsekrationsmünzen Kaiser Konstantins und ihre religions-politische Bedeutung," *Jb. f. Antike u. Christentum* I (1958) 94-104.

Kraft, H., "In welchem Zeichen siegte Konstantin?", *Theologische Literaturz.* 77 (1952) 118-120.

Kraft, H., "OMOOUCIOC," *Zsch. f. Kirchengesch.* 66 (1954-55) 1-24.

Kraft, H., *Kaiser Konstantins religiöse Entwicklung* (Tübingen, 1955).

Kraft, H., "Kaiser Konstantin und das Bischofsamt," *Saeculum* 8 (1957) 32-42.

Kraft, H., "Zur Taufe Kaiser Konstantins," *Studia Patristica* 1 (1957) 642-648.

Kraft, K., "Das Silbermedallion Constantins des Grossen mit d. Christus-monogramm auf dem Helm," *Jb. f. Numismatik und Geldgeschichte* 5 and 6 (1954-55), 151-178.

Kurfess, A., "Kaiser Konstantin und die Sibylle," *Theol. Quartalsch.* 118 (1936) 11-26.

Labriolle, P.; G. Bardy; J.R. Palanque, *De la paix Constantinienne à la mort de Théodose* (Paris, 1936).

Laqueur, Richard, "Die beiden Fassungen des sog. Toleranzedikts von Mailand," *Epitymbion Heinrich Swoboda dargebracht* (Reichenberg, 1927)

132-141.

Lathoud, D., "La consecration et la dédicace de Constantinople," *Echos d'Orient* 23 (1924) 289-314; 24 (1925) 180-201.

Lawlor, H.J., "The Chronology of Eusebius' Martyrs of Palestine," *Hermathena* 15 (1908) 177-201.

Lebreton, H.; H. Zeiller, *De la fin de 2e siècle à la paix constantinienne* (Paris, 1935).

Levi, M.A., "La campagna di Costantino nell' Italia Settentrionale," *Bollettino Storico bibliografico subalpino* 36 (1934) 1-10.

Lietzmann, H., "Der Glaube Konstantins des Grossen," *Sb. Preuss. Akad. Wiss. Phil.-hist. Klasse* (1937) 263-275.

Loeschke, G., *Konstantins Religionspolitik im Lichte der neueren Forschung* (Leipzig, 1885).

L'Orange, H.P., "Sol Invictus Imperator," *Symbolae Osloenses* 14 (1935) 86-114.

L'Orange, H.P., *Der spätantike Bilderschmuck des Konstantinbogens* (Berlin, 1939).

MacMullen, R., "Constantine and the Miraculous," *Greek and Roman and Byzantine Studies* 9 (1968) 81-96.

MacMullen, R., *Constantine* (London, 1970).

Maddalena, A., "Sulle fonti per la storia di Diocleziano e di Costantino," *Atti del r. Istituto Veneto di scienze, lettere e arti*, 95 (1935-36) 247-275.

Maes, C., *Il primo trofeo della croce da Costantino il Grande nel foro romano* (Rome, 1901).

Manso, J.C.F., *Leben Constantins d. Gr. nebst einigen Abhandlungen geschichtlichen Inhalts* (Breslau, 1817).

Marini, Nicolo, "Costantino Magno e l'unione della chiesa," *Bessarione* 29 (1913) 217-247; 393-419.

Marrou, H.I., "Autour du monogramme constantinien," *Mélanges E. Gilson* (Toronto, 1959) 403-414.

Martroye, F., "A propos de l'édit de Milan," *Bulletin d'ancienne literature et d'archéologie chrét.* 4 (1914) 47-52.

Martroye, F., ("Mesures prises par Constantin contre la superstition") *Bulletin de la société nation. des antiquaires de France* 5 (1915) 280-292.

Martroye, F., "La répression de la magie et le culte des gentils au IV siècle," *Rev. hist. de droit franç. et étranger* 9 (1930) 669-701.

Martroye, F., ("Le titre de pontifex maximus et empereurs chrétiens") *Bulletin de la soc. nation. des antiqu. de France* 18 (1928) 192-197.

Maurice, J., "Critique des Textes d'Eusèbe et de Lactance relatifs à l'Edit de Milan," *Bulletin de la soc. nation. des antiqu. de France* 3 (1913) 349-354.

Maurice, J., "Note sur le préambule placé par Eusèbe en tête de l'Edit de Milan", *Bulletin d'ancienne lit et d'arch. chrét.* 4 (1914) 45-47.

Maurice, J., "La politique religieuse de Constantin le Grand," *Comptes rendus Acad. des Inscriptions et Belles Lettres* (1919) 282-290.

Maurice, J., *Constantin le Grand* (Paris, 1924).

Meda, F., "Costantino e l'editto di Milano," *Rassegna Nazionale* 35 (1913) 473 ff.

Mickley, Paul, *Die Konstantin-Kirchen im heiligen Lande* (Leipzig, 1923).

Momigliano, A., *The Conflict between Paganism and Christianity in the Fourth Century* (Oxford, 1963).

Mommsen, Th., "Zweisprächige Inschrift aus Arykanda," *Archaeol.-epigr. Mitteilungen aus Oesterreich-Ungarn* 16 (1893) 93-102; 108.

Monaci, A., "La battaglia ad 'Saxa Rubra' e il bassorilievo Constiniano," *Atti Pont. Accad. Rom. di Archeologia* (1903) 105-134.

Monaci, A., "La campagna di Costantino in Italia nel 312," *Nuovo Bullettino di Archeologia Christiana* 19 (1913) 43-69.

Monaci, A., *La visione e il labaro di Costantino* (Rome, 1913).

Moreau, J., "Pont Milvius ou Saxa Rubra," *N. Clio* 4 (1952) 369-373.

Moreau, J., "Zur Religionspolitik Konstantins des Grossen," *Ann. Univ. Sarav.* 1 (1952) 160-168.

Moreau, J., "Sur la vision de Constantin (312)," *Revue des Etudes Anciennes* 55 (1953) 307-333.

Moreau, J., "Les 'Litterae Licinii'," *Ann. Univ. Sarav.* 2 (1953) 100-105.

Moreau, J., "Notes d'histoire romaine," *Ann. Univ. Sarav.* 2 (1953) 89-105.

Moreau, J., "Verité historique et propagande politique chez Lactance et dans la Vita Constantini," *Ann. Univ. Sarav.* 4 (1955) 89-97.

Moreau, J., "Zum Problem der 'Vita Constantini'," *Historia* 5 (1955) 234-245.

Moreau, J., *Scripta minora*, ed. by Walter Schmitthenner (Heidelberg, 1964).

Mueller, Alfons, "Lactantius' De Mortibus persecutorum 'oder' Die Beurteilung der Christenverfolgungen im Lichte des Mailänder Toleranzreskripts vom J. 313," *Konstantin d. G. und seine Zeit*, (edit. F.J. Dölger) (Freiburg, 1913) 66-88.

Müller, K., "Zu dem Erlass Konstantins an 'Aelafius' in den Anfängen des donatistischen Streits," *Zsch. neutest. Wiss.* 24 (1925) 287-290.

Müller, K., "Konstantins des Grossen Katechumenat," *Zsch. neutest. Wiss.* 24 (1925) 285-286.

Müller, K., "Konstantin der Grosse und die christliche Kirche," *Hist. Zsch.* 140 (1929) 261-278.

Musenga, F., *Iconografia, o sia descrizione in figura dell' apparizion della croce a Costantino il Grande etc.* (Naples, 1766).

Nesselhauf, H., "Das Toleranzgesetz des Licinius," *Hist. Zsch.* 74 (1954) 44-61.

Nogara, B., *L'editto di Milano e la vita religiosa, politica e sociale del quarto secolo dell'impero* (Monza, 1913).

Nordberg, H., "Athanasius and the Emperor," *Societas Scientiarum Fennica, Comment. Human Litter.* (Helsinki, 1963).

Opitz, H.G., "Die Zeitfolge des arianischen Streites von den Anfängen bis z. J. 328," *Zsch. f. die neutest. Wiss.* 33 (1934) 131-159.

Orgels, P., "La première vision de Constantin (310) et le temple d'Apollon à Nîmes," *Bullet. de l'Acad. roy. de Belg.* 26 (1948) 176-208.

Orgels, P., "A propos des erreurs historiques de la Vita Constantini," *Annuaire de l'Inst. Philol. Hist. Orient. Univ. Libre Bruxelles* 12 (1952), *Mélanges H. Grégoire* 4 (1953) 576-611.

Ortiz de Urbina, I., "La politica di Costantino nella controversia Ariana," *Atti del V Congresso Internazionale di Studi Bizantini* i (Rome, 1939) 284-298.

Palanque, J.-R., "Sur la politique religieuse de Constantin," *Rev. des Etud. Anc.* (1934) 233-235.

Palanque, J.-R., "A propos du prétendu édit de Milan," *Byzantion* 10 (1935) 607-616.

Palanque, J.-R., *The Church in the Roman Empire* (London, 1949).

Parkes, J., "Jews and Christians in the Constantinian Empire," *Studies in Church History* I, edit. by C.W. Dugmore and Ch. Duggan (London, 1964) 69-79.

Pears, Sir Edwin, "The Campaign against Paganism," *English Historical Review* 24 (1909) 1-17.

Peeters, P., "Comment saint Athanase s'enfuit de Tyr en 335," *Bull. de la Classe des Lettres et des Sciences, Acad. Roy. Belg.* 30 (1944) 131-177.

Peeters, P., "L'épilogue du Synode de Tyr en 335," *Anal. Bolland.* 63 (1945) 131-144.

Perugi, G.L., "Storia di una controversia," *Roma e l'Oriente* 6 (1913) 7-12.

Perugi, G.L., "La fonte giuridica dell' Editto di Milano," *Roma e l'Oriente* 6 (1913) 13-40.

Petit, Paul, "Libanius et la Vita Constantini," *Historia* 1 (1950) 562-582.

Pfättisch, J.M., *Die Rede Konstantins des Grossen an die Versammlung der Heiligen auf ihre Echtheit untersucht, Strassburger Theol. Studien* 9 (1908).

Pichon, R., "La politique de Constantin d'après le Panegyrici Latini," *Comptes rendus Acad. Inscr. et Belles Lettres* (1906) 289-297.

Piganiol, A., *L'Empereur Constantin* (Paris, 1932).

Piganiol, A., "Dates Constantiniennes," *Revue d'Histoire et de Philosophie religieuses* 12 (1932) 360-372.

Piganiol, A., *L'Empire Chrétien 325-395* (Paris, 1947).

Piganiol, A., "L'état actuel de la question constantinienne," *Historia* 1 (1950) 82-96.

Pincherle, A., "La politica ecclesiastica di Massenzio," *Studi italiani di filologia Class.* 7 (1929) 131-143.

Pincherle, A., "Cristianesimo et impero romano," *Riv. Stor. Ital.* (1933) 454-470.

Pistelli, A., *I documenti Constantiniani negli scrittori ecclesiastici* (Florence, 1914).

Pitt-Rivers, G., *The Riddle of the Labarum and the Origin of Christian Symbols* (London, 1966).

Preger, Th., "Konstantinos Helios," *Hermes* 36 (1901) 457-469.

Riccioletti, G., *La "era dei martiri". Il cristianesimo da Diocleziano a Costantino* (Rome, 1953).

Rinieri, I., "La battaglia di Ponte Milvio," *La Scuola Cattolica* 41 (1913) 16-25.

Romane, A., *Essai sur Constantin et ses rapports avec l'église chrétienne* (Strassbourg, 1867).

Rossi, G.B. de, "Una questione sull' Arco trionfale dedicato a Costantino," *Nuovo Bullettino di Archeol. Crist.* 19 (1913) 7-19.

Rossi, G.B. de, "L'inscrizione dell' Arco trionfale di Costantino," *Nuovo Bullettino di Archeol. Crist.* 19 (1913) 21-28.

Rossi, S., "Il concetto di 'storia' e la prassi storiografica di Lattanzio e del 'de mortibus'," *Giorn. Ital. di filol.* 14 (1961) 193-213.

Rossignol, J.P., *Virgile et Constantin le Grand* (Paris, 1845).

Ste Croix, G.E.M. de, "Aspects of the 'Great' Persecution," *Harvard Theol. Review* 42 (1954) 75-113.

Salvatorelli, L., *Costantino il Grande* (Rome, 1928).

Salvatorelli, L., "La politica religiosa e la religiosità di Costantino," *Ricerche relig.* 4 (1928) 289-328.

Santucci, Carlo, "L'editto di Milano nei riguardi del diritto," *Nuovo Bullettino di Archeol. crist.* 19 (1913) 71-75.

Sarabia, R., *Constantino Magno, el primer caudillo cristiano* (Madrid, 1951).

Savio, F., "La guerra di Costantino contro Massenzio e le apparizioni miraculose della Croce de Salvatore," *La Civiltà Cattolica* 64 (1913) 11-32.

Savio, F., "Le spiegazioni naturalistiche dell' apparizione della Croce a Costantino," *La Civiltà Cattolica* 64 (1913) 3-27.

Schaskolky, P., "La leggenda di Costantino il Grande e di Papa Silvestro," *Roma e l'Oriente* 6 (1913) 12-25.

Schmidinger, H., "Konstantin und die Konstantinische Aera," *Freiburger Zsch. f. Philos. und Theologie* 16 (1969) 3-21.

Schneemelcher, W., "Athanasius von Alexandrien als Theologe und als Kirchenpolitiker," *Zsch. f. N.T. Wiss.* 43 (1950-51) 242-256.

Schnyder, G., "L'editto di Milano, ed i recenti studi critici che lo riguardono," *Dissertazioni della Pontifica Accad. Rom. di Archeol.* (1903) 149-179.

Schnyder, W., *Die Anerkennung der christlichen Kirche von seiten des römischen Staates unter Konstantin d. Grossen* (Luzern, 1913).

Schoenebeck, H. von, *Beiträge zur Religionspolitik des Maxentius und Con-*

199

stantin (Leipzig, 1939).

Schrörs, H., "Die Bekehrung Konstantins des Grossen in der Überlieferung," *Zsch. f. katholische Theologie* 40 (1916) 238-257.

Schrörs, H., "Zur Kreuzerscheinung Konstantins des Grossen," *Zsch. f. katholische Theologie* 40 (1916) 485-523.

Schultze, V., "Untersuchungen zur Geschichte Konstantins des Grossen," *Zsch. f. Kircheng.* 7 (1885) 343-352; 8 (1886) 517-542.

Schultze, V., "Quellenuntersuchungen zur Vita Constantini des Eusebius," *Zsch. f. Kircheng.* 14 (1894) 503-555.

Schwartz, E., *Kaiser Konstantin und die Christliche Kirche* (Berlin, 1936).

Seeberg, E., *Die Synode von Antiochien v. J. 324/5* (Neue Studien zur Geschichte der Theologie der Kirche 16) (Berlin, 1913).

Seeck, Otto, "Die Zeitfolge der Gesetze Constantins," *Zsch. Sav. Stift. f. Rechtsgesch.* 10 (1889) 177-251.

Seeck, Otto, "Quellen und Urkunden über die Anfänge des Donatismus," *Zsch. f. Kirchengesch.* 10 (1889) 505-568.

Seeck, Otto, "Die Verwandtenmorde Konstantins des Grossen," *Zsch. f. Wiss. Theologie* 33 (1890) 63-77.

Seeck, Otto, "Das sogenannte Edikt von Mailand," *Zsch. f. Kirchengesch.* 12 (1891) 381-386.

Seeck, Otto, "Untersuchungen zu Geschichte des Nicäischen Konzils," *Zsch. f. Kirchengesch.* 17 (1896) 1-71; 319-362.

Seeck, Otto, "Die Urkunden der Vita Constantini," *Zsch. f. Kirchengesch.* 18 (1897) 321-345.

Seeck, Otto, "Urkundenfälschungen des 4. Jahrhunderts," *Zsch. f. Kirchengesch.* 30 (1909) 181-227; 399-433.

Sesan, V., "Die Religionspolitik der christlich-röm. Kaiser von Konstantin d. Gr. bis Theodosius d. Gr. (313-380)," *Kirche und Staat im römisch-byzantinischen Reiche seit Konstantin d. Grossen bis zum Falle Konstantinopels I* (Czernowitz, 1911).

Seston, W., "La religion de Maximin Daia," *Byzantion* 8 (1933) 49-56.

Seston, W., "La vision païenne de 310 et les origines du chrisme constantinien," *Ann. de l'Inst. de Philol. et d'Hist. Orient. de Univ. libre de Bruxelles* 4 (1936) 373-396.

Seston, W., "L'opinion païenne et la conversion de Constantin," *Rev. Hist. Phil. Rélig.* 16 (1936) 250-264.

Seston, W., "Recherches sur la chronologie du règne de Constantin le Grand," *Rev. Etud. Anc.* 39 (1937) 197-218.

Seston, W., "Constantine as a bishop," *J. of Roman Studies* 37 (1947) 127-131.

Shepherd, M.H., "Before and after Constantine," *The Impact of the Church upon its Culture. Reappraisals of the History of Christianity.* Edit. J.C. Bauer, *Essays in Divinity* 2 (Chicago, 1968) 17-38.

Skard, E., "Vexillum virtutis," *Symb. Oslo.* 25 (1947) 26-30.

Smith, J.H., *Constantine the Great* (London, 1971).

Solari, A., "L'unione religiosa umbro-etrusca in un rescritto di Costantino," *Studi Etruschi* 14 (1940) 161-162.

Spanneut, M., *Recherches sur les éscrits d'Eustathe d'Antioche* (Lille, 1948).

Staehelin, F., "Constantin der Grosse und das Christentum," *Zsch. f. Schweiz. Gesch.* 17 (1937) 385-417.

Staehelin, F., "Nachlese zu Constantin," *Zsch. f. Schweiz. Gesch.* (1939) 396-403.

Stein, A., "Konstantin der Grosse gelangte 324 zur Allenherrschaft," *Zsch. NT Wiss.* 30 (1931) 177-185.

Stephanides, B., "Die Visionen Konstantins des Grossen," *Zschr. f. Kirchengesch.* 59 (1940) 463-464.

Stockmeier, P., "Konstantinische Wende und Kirchengeschichtliche Kontinuität," *Hist. Jbuch* 82 (1963) 1-21.

Straub, J., *Vom Herrschersideal in der Spätantike* (Stuttgart, 1939).

Straub, J., "Konstantins christliche Sendungsbewusstsein," *Das neue Bild der Antike* 2 (1942) 374-394.

Straub, J., "Konstantins Verzicht auf dem Gang zum Kapitol," *Historia* 4 (1955) 296-313.

Straub, J., "Kaiser Konstantin als EPISKOPOS TON EKTOS," *Studia Patristica* 1 (1957) 678-695.

Straub, J., "Constantine as KOINOS EPISKOPOS," *Dunbarton Oaks Papers* 21 (1967) 37-55.

Stroheker, K.F., "Das konstantinische Jahrhundert im Lichte der Neuerscheinungen 1940-1951," *Saeculum* 3 (1952) 654-680.

Sulzberger, M., "Le symbole de la croix et les monogrammes de Jésus chez les premiers chrétiens," *Byzantion* 21 (1925) 337-448.

Telfer, W., "Arius Takes Refuge at Nicomedia," *J. of Theological Studies* 38 (1936) 60-63.

Telfer, W., "When did the Arian Controversy Begin?" *J. of Theological Studies* 47 (1946) 129-142.

Telfer, W., "The Author's Purpose in the Vita Constantini," *Studia Patristica* 1 (1957) 157-167.

Tengström, E., *Donatisten und Katholiken* (Göteborg, 1964).

Thomas, G.S.R., "Maximin Daia's Policy and the Edicts of Toleration," *L'Antiquité Classique* 37 (1968) 172-185.

Turmel, J., "La Vision de Constantine," *Revue du Clergé Français* 48 (1906) 518-526.

Turner, C.H., "Notes on the Antidonatist Dossier and on Optatus' Books I-II," *J. of Theological Studies* 27 (1926) 283-296.

Violet, Bruno, *Die palestinischen Märtyrer* (Leipzig, 1896).

Vittinghoff, "Eusebius als Verfasser der 'Vita Constantini," *Rheinisches*

Museum für Philologie 96 (1953) 330-373.

Völkl, L., "Die Konstantinischen Kirchenbauten nach Eusebius," *Riv. di Archeol. Christ.* 29 (1953) 49-66; 187-206.

Völkl. L., *Der Kaiser Konstantin* (München, 1957 and 1958).

Völkl, L., *Der Kaiser Konstantin. Annalen einer Zeitenwende* (München, 1960).

Völkl, L., *Die Kirchenstiftungen des Kaisers Konstantin im Lichte des römischen Sakralrechts* (Cologne, 1964).

Vogt, J., "Die Bedeutung des Jahres 312 f. d. Religionspolitik Konstantins des Grossen," *Zschr. f. Kirchengesch.* 61 (1942) 171-190.

Vogt, J., "Streitfragen um Konstantin den Grossen," *Mitteilungen des Deutschen Archeol. Inst.* (1943) 190-203.

Vogt, J., "Zur Frage des christlichen Einflusses auf die Gesetzgebung Konstantins d. G.," *Festschrift L. Wenger* 2 (1945) 118-148.

Vogt, J., *Konstantin d. G. und sein Jahrhundert* (München, 1949 and 1960).

Vogt, J., "Berichte über Kreuzerscheinungen aus dem 4 Jh. n. Chr.," *Ann. Inst. Philol. & Hist. Orient. & Slaves* 9 (1949) 593-606.

Vogt, J., "Der Erbauer der Apostelkirche in Konstantinopel," *Hermes* 81 (1953) 111-117.

Vogt, J., "Die 'Vita Constantini' des Eusebius über den Konflikt zw. Constantin u. Licinius," *Historia* 2 (1953/54) 463-471.

Vogt, J., "Kaiser Julian über seinen Oheim Konstantin den Grossen," *Historia* 4 (1955) 339-352.

Vogt, J., "Die Bekehrung Konstantins," *Relazioni X Congr. Intern. Scienze Storiche* 6 (1955) 733-779.

Vogt, J., *Konstantin der Grosse und das Christentum* (Zürich, 1960).

Vogt, J., "Pagans and Christians in the Family of Constantine," *The Conflict between Paganism & Christianity in the Fourth Century*, edit. Arnaldo Momigliano (Oxford, 1963) 38-54.

Winkelmann, F., *Die Vita Constantini des Eusebius etc.* (Halle, 1959).

Winkelmann, F., "Konstantins Religionspolitik und ihre Motive im Urteil d. literarischen Quellen des iv. und v. Jahrhunderts," *Acta Antiqua Acad. Scient. Hungariae* 9 (1961) 239-256.

Winkelmann, F., *Die Textbezeugung der Vita Constantini des Eusebius von Caesarea - Texte u. Untersuchungen* 84 (Berlin, 1962).

Winkelmann, F., "Zur Geschichte des Authentizitätsproblems der Vita Constantini," *Klio* 40 (1962) 187-243.

Winkelmann, F., "Die Beurteilung des Eusebius von Caesarea und seiner Vita Constantini im griechischen Osten," *Byzantinische Beiträge* (Berlin, 1964) 91-119.

Wittig, Joseph, "Das Toleranzreskript von Mailand 313," *Constantin d. G. und seine Zeit*, edit. F.J. Dölger (Freiburg. 1913) 40-65.

Yuge, T., "The So-called Milan Edict Discussed," (in Japanese) *J. of Classical*

Studies (Japan) 2 (1954) 89-95.

Zahn, Th., "Konstantin d. Gr. u. die Kirche," *Skizzen aus dem Leben der alten Kirche* (Erlangen-Leipzig, 1894) 214-266.

Zeiller, J., "L'empereur Constantin et ses plus recents historiens," *Le Correspondant* (1933) 79-92.

Zeiller, J., "Quelques remarques sur la vision de Constantine," *Byzantion* 14 (1939) 329-339.

condemned by the Council of Nicaea, 131;

208

Felix, Bishop of Aptunga, 60; 68-72; 74-75; 96;
  Acts of the Vindication of, 68-74.
Fortis, Donatist Bishop, 86-89.
Forty Martyrs of Sebaste, 103.

Galerius, Emperor, 32;
  Edict of toleration of, 39; 49; 55; 105.
Gallienus, Emperor, 39;
  constitutions of, 45.
Gaudentius, Imperial Commissar, 158; 159.
George, Priest of Arethusa, 146.
Gladiatorial Games, 174-175.
Goths, 101.
(Great) Persecution, 39; 59-60; 82; 83-84; 111-112; 113; 124.

Hadrianople, 78.
Heavenly Sign of Constantine, 13; 17; 27-28; 35;
  see also, Cross.
Helena, Mother of Constantine, 178.
Heresies, 135-137; 179.
Heretics, 68;
  edict of Constantine on, 135-137.
Homoousios, 130;
  see also, Consubstantial.
Hosius, Bishop of Cordova, 39; 123; 125.

Ingentius, 68; 70-75; 96.
Ischyras, 149; 163.

Jerusalem, Council of, 160; 163.
Jews, 133-135; 180-181.
John Arcaph, 149; 151-152; 160; 162;
  letter of Constantine to, 151-152.
Julian the Apostate, 170-171; 181.
Jupiter, Capitoline, 30-31.

labarum, 14; 27-29; 35; 104; 114; 183.
Lapsed, 124.
Lactantius, 17; 19-24; 30; 45-46; 51; 55; 57.
Libanius, 170-171; 181.
Libya, 118; 155.
Licinius, Emperor, 42; 46-47; 49-53; 55; 57; 73; 75; 78; 101-105; 111; 119;
  170; 182;

210

and Christianity, 102-103;
ecumenical prayer of, 57;
Edict of Milan and, *see also*, Edict of Milan, 42-51;
persecuting the Church, 102-103; 139;
wars between Constantine and, 78; 101-105; 139;
wars between Maximinus Daia and, 47; 55-57.
Lucian of Antioch, 117-118.
Lucilla, 60; 83; 86; 92; 93; 94; 95.

Macarius, Bishop of Jerusalem, 178.
Macarius, Priest of Athanasius, 149; 163.
Majorinus, Donatist Bishop of Carthage, 59.
Marcellus, Bishop of Ancyra, 145.
Marcionites, 136.
Marcus, Associate of Pope Miltiades, 61.
'Mareotic Commission,' 162.
Marinus, Bishop of Arles, 62; 66.
Maternus, Bishop of Autun, 62; 66.
Maxentius, Emperor, 9-18; 22-24; 26-27; 29-30; 32-36; 41-42; 46; 52; 60;
104; 171; 182;
Constantine's campaign against, 9-26.
Maximianus, Emperor, 53; 56; 84.
Maximinus Daia, Emperor, 18; 47; 49; 52-57;
Constantine and, 51-53;
Licinius and, 47; 55-57;
letter to Sabinus, 53-55;
edict of toleration by, 56.
Melitians, 147-150.
Melitius, Bishop of Lycopolis, 123-124; 131; 149;
Schism of, 123-124; 131.
Mensurius, Bishop of Carthage, 60.
Milan, 42; 44-51; 53;
see also, Edict of.
Miltiades, *see*, Pope Miltiades.
Milvian Bridge, Battle of the, 9-12; 16; 18; 21; 26; 28; 38; 171.
Moesia, 101.
Montanists, 137.

Nicaea, 125-127; 131; 138; 140-141; 144; 146; 148; 159;
Council of, 125-135; 140; 147; 148; 181; 186;
Reconvened Council of, *or* Nicaea II, 144; 148; 152;
Speech of Constantine to, 126-127;
Creed of the Council of, 129; 131; 141; 143-145; 152; 159;

Recticius, Bishop of Cologne, 62.
Rome, 9-12; 14-18; 27; 30-34; 36; 47; 64-66; 64-66; 78; 102;
    Council of, 62; 64.

Sabellian Heresy, 146.
Sabinus, Donatist Bishop, 88-89.
Sabinus, Praetorian Prefect, 53; 55;
    letter of Maximinus Daia to, 53-55.
Sapor, King of Persia, letter of Constantine to, 183-185.
Sardica, 100.
Schismatics, 61; 77; 96-99; 135; 186.
Secundus, Bishop of Ptolemais, 131.
Secundus, Bishop of Tigisis, 60; 83.
Senecio, 78.
Severus, Emperor, 17; 32.
Sibylla, Erythraean, 155.
Sign of Salvation, 12; 14; 15; 17; 34;
    see also, Cross; Heavenly Sign of Constantine; Statue of Constantine;
    labarum.
Silvanus, Donatist Bishop of Cirta, Acts of the Proceedings against, 83-96.
Silverster, 66-68; 167.
Sixtus V, see, Pope Sixtus V.
Slaves, 174; 175-176.
Socrates, 170.
Sozomen, 170.
Statue of Constantine, 12; 17; 34-35.
Sunday, Observance of, 179.
Sylverster, see, Pope Sylvester and Silvester.
Syncletius, Imperial Commissar, 158; 159.
Synod of Antioch, 146;
    letter of Constantine to, 146;
    see also, Antioch.
Synod of Tyre, 160; 161; 162; 163; 164;
    see also, Council of Tyre.

Theodoretus, 170.
Theodotus, Bishop of Laodicaea, 141; 146;
    letter of Constantine to, 141.
Theognius, Bishop of Nicaea, 131; 137; 140-141; 144; 146; 163; 165.
Theonas, Bishop of Marmarice, 131.
Thessalonica, 104.
Thrace, 78; 101.
traditor, traditores, 59-60; 66; 68; 72; 74; 79; 82-83; 86; 89-94.

Trèves, 31-33; 36; 79; 165.
tricennalia, 32; 160.
Tyre, Council of, 145; 160-165;
   see also, Council of.

Valentinians, 136.
Valerian, Emperor, 39; 184.
Verinus, Deputy-Prefect of Africa, letter of Constantine to, 96.
Verus, Deputy-Prefect of Africa, 68; 75.
vicennalia, 32.
'Vision of Apollo,' 20-23.
'Vision of Licinius,' 21; 25.
'Vision,' pagan, *see*, 'Vision of Apollo.'
Vision of St. Paul, the Apostle, 25-26; 168.
Visions of Constantine, 13-30; 35; 171; 182.
Visions of St. Joan of Arc, 25-26.

Zenophilus, Consular of Numidia, 83-95.
Zosimus, 170-171; 181.

Maximinus Daia warned, 52.
Eusebius, *H. E.* IX, ixA, 1-9:
letter of Maximinus Daia to Sabinus, 53-54.
Eusebius, *H. E.* IX, x, 7-11:
edict of Maximinus Daia on the Christians, 56.
Eusebius, *H. E.* X, v, 1-14:
Edict of Milan, 42-44.
Eusebius, *H. E.* X, v, 15-17:
letter of Constantine to Anullinus, 38-39.
Eusebius, *H. E.* X, v, 18-20:
letter of Constantine to Pope Miltiades, 61-62.
Eusebius, *H. E.* X, v, 21-24:
letter of Constantine to Chrestus, 63-64.
Eusebius, *H. E.* X, vi, 1-5:
letter of Constantine to Caecilian, 39-40.
Eusebius, *H. E.* X, vii:
letter of Constantine to Anullinus, 40-41.
Eusebius, *Vita Constantini* I, 26-40:
Constantine's campaign against Maxentius, 12-17.
Eusebius, *Vita Constantini* I, 40:
the inscription of the Statue of Constantine, 17.
Eusebius, *Vita Constantini* II, 5:
Licinius on Constantine and Christianity, 104.
Eusebius, *Vita Constantini* II, 24-42:
edict of Constantine on the Eastern Provinces, 106-111.
Eusebius, *Vita Constantini* II, 46:
letter of Constantine to Eusebius of Caesarea, 116.
Eusebius, *Vita Constantini* II, 48-60:
edict of Constantine on the People of the Eastern Provinces, 112-115.
Eusebius, *Vita Constantini* II, 64-72:
letter of Constantine to Bishop Alexander and Arius, 119-123.
Eusebius, *Vita Constantini* III, 12:
Constantine's address to the Council of Nicaea, 126-127.
Eusebius, *Vita Constantini* III, 17-20:
letter of Constantine to the whole Church, 133-135.
Eusebius, *Vita Constantini* III, 64-65:
edict of Constantine on heretics, 138-140.
Eusebius, *Vita Constantini* IV, 9-13:
letter of Constantine to King Sapor, 183-185.
Eusebius, *Vita Constantini* IV, 42:
letter of Constantine convoking the Council of Tyre, 161.

Gelasius Cyz., *H. E.* II, 37:

216

letter of Constantine to the whole Church, 133-135.
Gelasius Cyz., *H. E.* III, 14:
letter of Constantine to Athanasius, 14ͻ.
Gelasius Cyz., *H. E.* III, 15, 1:
letter of Constantine to Bishop Alexander of Alexandria, 143.
Gelasius Cyz., *H. E.* III, 19:
letter of Constantine to Arius and Arians, 152-158.
Gelasius Cyz., *H. E.* III, *App.* i:
letter of Constantine to the Catholic Church of Nicomedia, 138-140.
Gelasius Cyz., *H.E.* III, *App.* ii:
letter of Constantine to Bishop Theodotus, 141.

Lactantius, *De mortibus persecutorum* 44:
Constantine's campaign against Maxentius, 17-18.
Lactantius, *De mortibus persecutorum* 46, 6:
Licinius' ecumenical prayer, 57.
Lactantius, *De mortibus persecutorum* 48:
Edict of Milan, 42-44.

Optatus, I, 22:
Donatist petition to Constantine, 59.
Optatus, *App.* I:
Acts of Silvanus, 83-95.
Optatus, *App.* II:
Vindication of Felix of Aptunga, 68-74.
Optatus, *App.* III:
letter of Constantine to Aelafius (or Ablabius, or Aelius Paulinus), 64-66.
Optatus, *App.* IV:
letter of the Council of Arles to Pope Silvester, 66-68.
Optatus, *App.* V:
letter of Constantine to the Council of Arles, 75-77.
Optatus, *App.* VI:
letter of Constantine to the Donatist Bishops, 78-79.
Optatus, *App.* VII:
letter of Constantine to Domitius Celsus, 80-81.
Optatus, *App.* VIII:
letter of Petronius Annianus and Julianus to Domitius Celsus, 80.
Optatus, *App.* IX:
letter of Constantine to the Catholic Bishops and laity of Africa, 97-98.
Optatus, *App.* X:
letter of Constantine to the Bishops of Numidia, 98-100.

Socrates, *H. E.* I, 8:

letter of Eusebius of Caesarea to his Church, 128-130.
Socrates, *H. E.* I, 9, 17-25:
letter of Constantine to the Catholic Church of Alexandria, 131-132.
Socrates, *H. E.* I, 9, 30-31:
edict of Constantine against the Arians, 158-159.
Socrates, *H. E.* I, 9, 32:
letter of Constantine to the whole Church, 133-135.
Socrates, *H. E.* I, 25:
letter of Constantine to Arius, 142.
Socrates, *H. E.* I, 26:
letter of Arius and Euzoius to Constantine, 142.
Socrates, *H. E.* I, 27, 4:
letter of Constantine to Athanasius, 148.
Socrates, *H. E.* I, 34:
Constantine's letter to the Council of Tyre, 164-165.

Sozomen, *H. E.* I, 19:
Constantine's address to the Council of Nicaea, 126.
Sozomen, *H. E.* II, 27:
letter of Arius and Euzoius to Constantine, 142.
Sozomen, *H. E.* II, 22, 5:
letter of Constantine to Athanasius, 148.
Sozomen, *H. E.* II, 28:
letter of Constantine to the Council of Tyre, 164-165.

Syriac Text, *Codex Syriacus* 38:
Constantine's letter calling all bishops to Nicaea, 125.

Theodoretus, *H. E.* I, 3:
Bishop Alexander of Alexandria to Bishop Alexander of Byzantium, 119.
Theodoretus, *H. E.* I, 9:
letter of Constantine to the whole Church, 133-135.
Theodoretus, *H. E.* I, 11:
letter of Eusebius of Caesarea to his Church, 128-130.
Theodoretus, *H. E.* I, 27:
letter of Constantine convoking the Council of Tyre, 161.